ELEMENTS OF CHEMISTRY:

THEORETICAL AND PRACTICAL.

BY

WILLIAM ALLEN MILLER, M.D., LL.D.,

TREASURER AND VICE-PRESIDENT OF THE ROYAL SOCIETY;
VICE-PRESIDENT OF THE CHEMICAL SOCIETY;
PROFESSOR OF CHEMISTRY IN KING'S COLLEGE, LONDON;
HON. FELLOW OF KING'S COLLEGE, LONDON.

CHEMICAL PHYSICS.

PART II.

ELECTRICITY AND MAGNETISM.

FROM THE THIRD LONDON EDITION.

NEW YORK:
JOHN WILEY, 535 BROADWAY.
1864.

ELECTRICITY AND MAGNETISM.

CHAPTER VI.

MAGNETISM AND ELECTRICITY.

I. *Magnetism.*—II. *Static Electricity.*—III. *Dynamic or Voltaic Electricity.*—IV. *Electro-Magnetism.*—V. *Magneto-Electricity.*—VI. *Thermo-Electricity.*—VII. *Animal Electricity.*—VIII. *Diamagnetism.*

(214) The forces of magnetism and electricity are now found to be so intimately related, that it is hardly possible to study the operations of either separately.

The power of the loadstone to attract small pieces of iron was recognised as a remarkable natural phenomenon for centuries before the Christian era; and the 'pointing' of the magnetic needle north and south, was early applied to the purposes of navigation by the Chinese; but it was not employed for that purpose by European nations till the latter end of the fifteenth century. The property of temporarily attracting light objects which amber acquires when rubbed, was also familiar to the Grecian philosophers; but it was not till about 260 years ago that Gilbert laid the foundation of electrical science, and that Otto de Guericke and Hauksbee contrived the first electrical machines. Nautical men, likewise, had often observed that after a ship had experienced a stroke of lightning, the compass was deranged or its poles were reversed; but it was not until the year 1819 that the true connexion between electricity and magnetism was pointed out by Oersted, when he published his memorable discovery, that a magnetic needle if suspended freely at its centre, would place itself at right angles to a wire which was transmitting an electric current. After the publication of Oersted's discovery, the means of obtaining powerful temporary magnets by transmitting electrical currents through wires coiled around masses of soft iron, or in other words, the methods of preparing electro-magnets, were speedily devised; and thus the dependence of magnetism on electricity in motion was shown; whilst in 1831 the completion of this chain of discovery was effected by Faraday, who announced that a current of electricity might be obtained in a closed conducting wire from the magnet, by moving it across the line of the conductor.

In its chemical bearings, particular importance attaches to Volta's invention of the voltaic pile or battery, which, in the hands of Davy, led to the discovery of the metallic bases of the alkalies and of the earths, and effected a complete change in the aspect of chemical science. In later years, the applications of the voltaic battery to the chemical arts of gilding, silvering, zincing, &c., have rendered it an instrument of great importance in the industrial arts.

§ I. Magnetism.

(215) It will not be necessary to enter fully into the subject of magnetism, but a few remarks upon the more important peculiarities of this force will materially aid in fixing upon the mind clear ideas of polarity and polar action.

Electricity is, like magnetism, a polar force, and the phenomena of chemical attraction also fall into the class of polar actions.

The most obvious character of magnetism is seen in the power of attracting masses of iron, which is displayed to a greater or less extent by magnetized bodies. This power of attracting iron was first observed by the ancients in an iron ore obtained from Magnesia in Asia Minor; hence the property was termed *magnetism*, and when in more recent times its directive property was observed, the mineral itself was named the *lead-stone* or loadstone. A steel bar if rubbed in one direction with the loadstone acquires similar properties; when poised horizontally, as may be done by supporting it upon a point, such a bar will take up a fixed position with regard to the poles of the earth; in this country it will point nearly north and south. The end of a magnetic bar which points towards the north is distinguished by a mark, and is hence often termed the *marked end* of the magnet. This peculiarity in the magnet of taking a fixed direction, renders it invaluable to the navigator. A magnetized needle attached to a card marked with the cardinal points, and properly poised, constitutes the *mariner's compass*.

If a sheet of paper be laid over a magnetized steel bar, and iron filings be evenly sifted upon the paper, it will be found, on gently tapping the paper, that the particles of iron accumulate in two groups, one around each extremity of the bar as a centre, and that from these points the filings arrange themselves in curved lines, somewhat resembling those shown in fig. 153, extending from one end of the bar to the other. This experiment shows that the attractive forces are concentrated near the two extremities of such a bar. A soft iron wire freely suspended at its centre in a horizontal direction, will be attracted indifferently at both ends by either end of the magnetic bar; but if a second magnetic bar be poised in the same way as the iron wire, it will be found that one end of this bar will be attracted when the magnet is brought near it in one direction, whilst the same end will be repelled if the opposite end of the magnet be presented to it. Further examination shows, that this repulsion takes place when the ends presented to each other are those which would naturally point in the same direction; two north ends repel each other, and similar repulsion ensues when two south ends are presented to each other; whereas, if the extremities presented naturally point in opposite directions, attraction ensues between them; the north end of one bar attracts the south end of the other. Thus it appears that there are two kinds of magnetism endowed with qualities analogous, but opposite, to each other. The two magnetic forces are always developed simultaneously, are always equal in amount, but are opposite in their tendencies; and thus are capable of exactly neutralizing each other. They accumulate at opposite ends of the bar. These ends are termed the *poles* of the magnet. Forces which exhibit these combinations of two equal powers, which act in opposite directions, are termed *polar forces.*

Fig. 153.

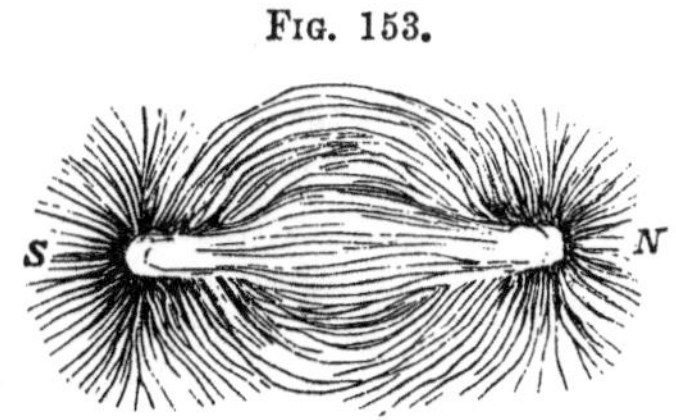

(216) *Magnetic Induction.*—Magnetism acts through considerable intervals of non-magnetic matter upon bodies such as iron, which are susceptible of magnetism, and it produces a temporary development of magnetism in such magnetizable substances. A piece of soft iron brought near to a magnet immediately assumes the magnetic state. This influence of the magnet operating at a distance is termed *magnetic induction*, and it is in consequence of this action that the iron is attracted. If the north end, N, of a magnet, L (fig. 154), be presented to a piece of soft iron, the latter becomes a magnet with its poles similarly arranged; that is to say, the soft iron acquires in the extremity S, presented to the permanent magnet, magnetism of the opposite kind to that of the end, N, of the magnet, L, which it is made to approach. The soft iron will now attract other pieces of iron, *s n*, *s n*, and they in turn will act upon others by a continuation of the inductive force. On gradually removing the permanent magnet, the effects diminish as the distance increases, and at length disappear altogether. This diminution in the effect takes place much more rapidly than in the ratio of the squares of the distance from the magnetic pole, but the exact law has not as yet been ascertained. The polar character of magnetic induction may be seen by suspending two pieces of soft iron wire over one of the poles of a magnet S, (fig. 155); the lower end of the wires, *n n*, repel each other, but are both drawn towards the magnet, and the upper ex-

Fig. 154.

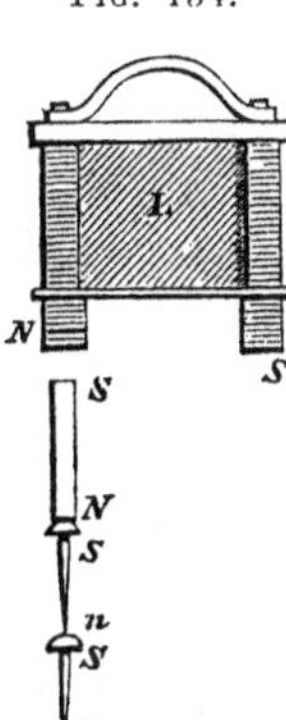

tremities, *s*, *s*, also repel each other. It is this mutual repulsion of the corresponding ends of the pieces of iron which causes the iron filings (fig. 153) to distribute themselves in curves around the magnet; for in this experiment each particle of iron becomes for the time a magnet with opposite poles. It is likewise in consequence of this polarity that a number of pieces of fine iron wire under induction form a continuous chain. A bar of soft iron placed on a magnet of equal dimensions neutralizes its action for the time; by connecting the two extremities of the magnet, it diverts the induction from surrounding bodies, and concentrates it upon itself. On the other hand, the induction is much strengthened if the magnetic circle be completed, as in fig. 156, by uniting the piece of iron suspended from either pole by the connecting piece, *a b*. This induction is maintained across the greater number of bodies, such as atmospheric air, glass, wood, and the metals. It is, however, modified by the interposition of iron, cobalt, and nickel, which are themselves powerfully susceptible of magnetism.

FIG. 155.

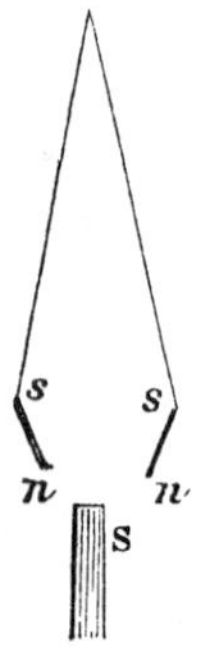

FIG. 156.

Magnetic induction differs essentially from electric induction (228) in this particular—viz., that it is not possible to insulate either kind of magnetism from the other. For instance, if one end of the two united pieces of iron, *s n*, *s n* (fig. 156), exhibit the properties of a north magnetic pole, the other end will exhibit those of a south magnetic pole; but if the two pieces of iron, whilst still under the influence of induction, be separated from each other, and then the magnet be withdrawn, both pieces of iron will have lost their magnetism. Again, if a magnet be broken in the middle, it will not be separated into one piece with a north and another with a south pole; each fragment will still possess two poles, turned in the same direction as those of the original bar (fig. 157); and each fragment may again be subdivided into an indefinite number of smaller fragments, each of which will still possess a north and a south pole.

FIG. 157.

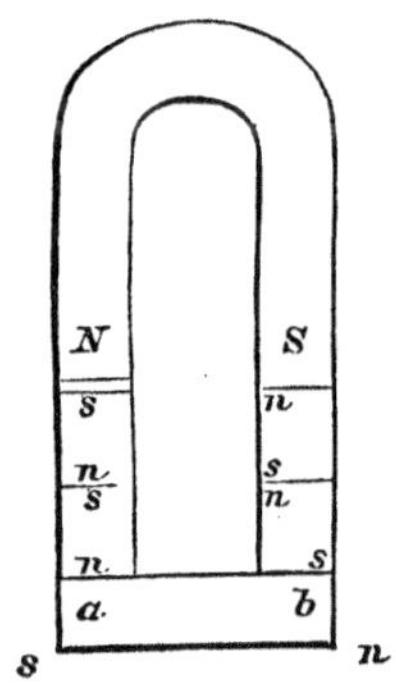

These phenomena may be explained by supposing that a magnet consists of a collection of particles, each of which is magnetic and endued with both kinds of magnetism. In the unmagnetized condition of the bar, these forces are mutually combined, and exactly neutralize each other; but when the mass becomes magnetized, the two forces are separated from each other, though without quitting the particle with which they were originally associated. The two halves of each particle assume an opposite magnetic condition. All the north poles are disposed in one direction; whilst all the south poles are disposed in the opposite direction. Each particle thus acquires a polar condition, and adds its inductive force to that of all the others; as a necessary consequence of such an arrangement, the opposite powers become accumulated at the opposite extremities of the bar. If in fig. 158 the small circles be taken to represent the ultimate magnetic particles, the portions in shadow would indicate the distribution of south magnetism, whilst the unshaded half of the particles would show the distribution of magnetism of the opposite kind. This hypothesis is supported by the fact that a magnet whilst producing induction loses none of its force, but on the contrary suffers temporary increase of power owing to the reaction of the induced magnetism of the soft iron upon it.

Fig. 158.

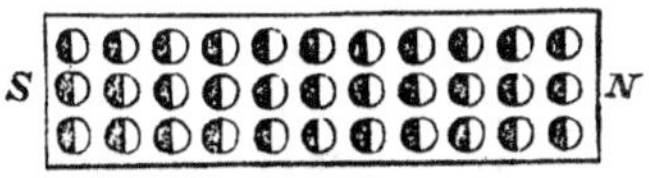

(217) *Preparation of Magnets.*—Pure soft iron loses its magnetism as soon as it is withdrawn from the inductive influence; but the presence of certain foreign bodies in combination with the iron, particularly of oxygen, as in the natural loadstone, and of carbon, as in steel, enables the body to retain the magnetic power permanently. Hardened steel is always the material employed in the preparation of permanent magnets; it is not susceptible of so intense a degree of magnetization as soft iron, but when induction has once been produced within it, the effect is retained for an indefinite length of time. The development of this power in steel is much facilitated by friction; and the amount of force developed by this means is greatly dependent upon the direction in which the friction is performed. A simple method of magnetizing a bar consists in placing the bar on its side and bringing down upon one of its extremities either of the ends of a bar magnet. If the north end be brought down on the steel bar, it must be drawn slowly along towards that extremity of the bar which it is intended shall possess south magnetic force; this operation must be repeated three or four times in the same direction. A more effectual plan is to bring down upon the centre of the bar the two ends of a powerful horseshoe magnet, as represented in fig. 159; the south pole being directed towards the end of the bar that is intended to possess the northern polarity, and *vice versa.* It is then moved along the surface from the centre, alternately towards either extremity, taking care not to carry the horseshoe beyond the extremities of the bar, and to withdraw the horseshoe from the bar when at its centre *c*. The bar is then turned over and the process repeated on the opposite side, but in the same direction, for an equal number of times. When two bars are to be magnetized, they may be placed parallel to each other, the extremities being connected by pieces of soft iron. Both the

Fig. 159.

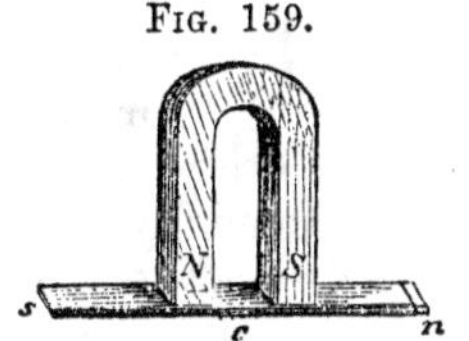

poles of the horseshoe are brought down upon the centre of one of the steel bars, and it is carried round the parallelogram always in the same direction, taking care, as before, to withdraw it when over the centre of one of the bars. In the last arrangement, the induction of one bar acts upon and exalts the intensity of the magnetism excited in the other. For this reason, the opposite poles of magnets, when not in use, should be connected by pieces of soft iron, so that the continued induction shall maintain the force of each.

In the act of magnetization, the horseshoe loses nothing of its power; but the north and south magnetism, which are supposed to exist in every particle of steel and iron, and which in the unmagnetized condition are so combined as exactly to neutralize each other, appear from the effect of the induction to which they have been subjected, to be permanently disturbed in their equilibrium in the newly-magnetized bars. The more intense the power of the horseshoe, the greater is this disturbance, and the more powerful are the magnets which are produced.

By uniting together several bar magnets, taking care that the corresponding poles of each are in the same direction, *magnetic batteries* of great power may be obtained. The magnets should be all as nearly as possible of the same strength; because if one of the bars be weaker than the others, it materially diminishes the power of the whole, and acts in the same manner as a bar of soft iron would do, though to a more limited extent. As a matter of convenience, the bar magnet is often bent into the form of a horseshoe, so that the inductive and attractive power of both poles may be simultaneously exerted on the same piece of iron; the effect is in this manner much increased, and the weight sustained by the two poles united is much greater than the sum of the two weights which would be supported by each pole separately. For this reason, the soft iron armatures N, S, of a loadstone (fig. 154) add greatly to its power, and by facilitating the application of the *keeper*, or piece of soft iron which connects the two poles when not in use, prevent the loss of the magnetic power.

(218) *Influence of Molecular Motions on Magnetism.*—It has been mentioned that the friction of a steel bar, whilst under induction, facilitates its magnetization. The same effect is occasioned by percussion of the bar, or by any other mode of producing vibration in it whilst it is under magnetic induction. On the other hand, if a bar has been fully magnetized, its force is reduced by the application of a sudden blow; even the simple act of scratching the surface with sand-paper, or with a file, may seriously impair the power of a good magnet.

The influence of heat on magnetism is remarkable. If a steel bar be ignited and placed under induction, and whilst still in this condition it be suddenly quenched, it will be found to be powerfully magnetic. Again, if a steel magnet be ignited, and allowed to cool slowly, all its acquired magnetism will have disappeared. Elevation of temperature, therefore, evidently favours the transfer of magnetic polarity within its particles. Further, if the temperature of a piece of iron be raised to redness (about 1000° F.), it will become indifferent to the presence of a magnetic needle, though on again cooling it will be as active as before. A similar effect is produced upon cobalt at the temperature of melting copper.* Nickel, at a much lower temperature, loses its action upon the magnet, as at 600° it exerts scarcely any attractive effect on the needle. So great is the influence of temperature upon a magnetic bar, that at the boiling-point of water, the diminution of its power is perceptible by the rudest tests. If the temperature do not exceed 212°, the magnet regains its force on cooling. On the other hand, by cooling a magnet artificially, its power is for the time exalted.

(219) *Measurement of Magnetic Intensity of a Bar.*—The simplest method of ascertaining the intensity of the power of a magnet, consists in attaching to its armature a scale-pan, and ascertaining the amount of weight which it will support; but it is obvious that this plan is not susceptible of any high degree of accuracy; it is, moreover, in many cases, quite inapplicable. A still easier, and more generally useful, because far more accurate, method, consists in suspending the magnet horizontally at its centre, by means of a few fibres of silk, and allowing it to take a fixed direction under the influence of a standard magnet; it is then displaced from its position of equilibrium, and the number of oscillations which it describes in a given time is counted. The relative intensity of the power of two or more bars, which may thus be compared, is proportionate to the square of the number of vibrations performed in equal intervals of time. For estimating low degrees of power, the torsion of a glass thread, as employed in Coulomb's electrometer (226), may be used. The mutual action of two magnets is inversely as the square of the distance between them.

(220) *Magnetism of the Earth—The Dip.*—The remarkable fact of the pointing of the needle towards the north pole of the earth has been explained upon the hypothesis that the globe of the earth itself is a magnet, the poles of which are situated nearly in the line of the axis of rotation; the magnetism of the earth's north pole being of the same kind as that of the unmarked end of the magnet. If a small magnetized needle, *s n*, be freely suspended horizontally by a thread over the equator of a sphere (fig. 160) nine or ten inches in diameter, passing through the centre of which a small magnetic bar, N S, at right angles to the

FIG. 160.

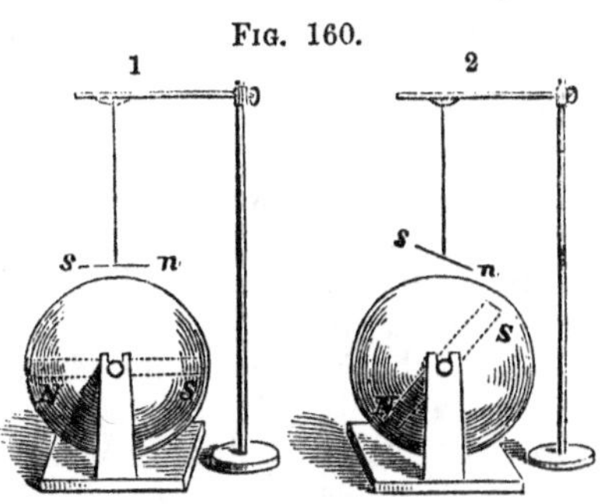

* Faraday has, however, shown that in the case of cobalt its magnetic power increases as the temperature rises until it reaches about 300°, beyond which it slowly diminishes, and at length becomes nearly evanescent. (*Phil. Trans.* 1856, 179).

points of suspension of the globe, is placed, the needle will, when the magnetic bar is horizontal, as in No. 1, assume a direction parallel to the magnetic bar, and will point towards N and S, preserving its horizontal position; for it is equally attracted by the north and south polarities of the bar; but if one of the ends of the magnetic bar be made gradually to approach the needle, as at 2, that end of the needle which previously pointed towards this pole will begin to incline downwards, or to *dip*, until, when the end S of the bar is exactly under the point *n* of the needle, the direction of the needle will become vertical. On bringing the opposite end of the bar towards the needle, like results may be obtained with the other end of the needle. Similar phenomena are also exhibited when a magnetic needle, poised horizontally at the equator of the earth, is carried towards either of its poles. A needle, therefore, which when unmagnetized is so poised as to assume a horizontal position, in the latitude of London, appears to become heavier at its marked end by the process of magnetization. An instrument by means of which the angular amount of this *inclination* can be accurately observed, is called a *dipping-needle.*

(221) *Declination or Variation.*—In each hemisphere there is a single point at which the dipping-needle stands vertically, *i.e.*, where the dip is 90°. In the northern hemisphere this point is situated in about 96° 40′ W. lon. and 70° 14′ N. lat.; the point where it would be vertical in the southern hemisphere being nearly in 73° S. lat. and 130° E. lon. *The line of no dip* does not correspond to the earth's equator; it forms an irregular curve inclined to it at about 12°, and crossing it in four places. This arises from the fact that the magnetic system of the earth is much more complicated than is represented in the foregoing paragraph. Instead of being single, it appears to be *double*, as was first pointed out by Halley, and in neither of these two systems does the magnetic axis coincide with the axis of rotation of the earth. Consequently in most places the needle does not point to the true geographical north. At the present time the needle in London points rather more than 21° west of north. This deviation from the true north is termed the *variation* or *declination* of the needle.

In the northern hemisphere there are four lines of no declination; two of which may be considered to pass through the point of 90° of dip, and two others which do not pass through this point. These four lines of no declination have reference to a double magnetic system of which the two points of maximum force in the Northern hemisphere are resultants; and these points were called by Halley *magnetic poles.* They do not correspond to either of the points of 90° of dip, which have also been called magnetic poles.

It is remarkable that the declination of the magnetic needle is not constant at the same spot. In the year 1657, the needle pointed due north at London. It then gradually assumed a declination to the west, which continued to increase until about the year 1840, at which time the variation to the west, in London, was nearly 25°; since this period it has been gradually returning towards the east, and in May, 1863, it was 21° 25′ W. at Kew. The rate of its motion differs in different parts of its progress, becoming slower as it approaches the point of retrogression; at present it is about 6′ annually. Independently of these gradual and progressive changes, the variation is subject to diurnal movements of very small amount; north of the magnetic equator in England and the middle latitudes the north end of the needle moves slowly eastward in the forenoon, attaining its maximum between the hours of seven and ten A.M., and returns to its mean position at about ten in the evening. Connected with these alterations are corresponding variations in the dip, which during the last fifty years has been observed in London to diminish annually about 2′·6. From observations made at the Kew Observatory, the dip in May, 1863, was 68° 15′.

(222) *Variation in the Intensity of the Earth's magnetism.*—The *intensity* of the earth's magnetism is also found to vary at different points of the surface, but the law of its increase has not been clearly determined; the line of minimum intensity, or *magnetic equator*, as it is sometimes called, is in the vicinity of the geographical equator, but does not coincide either with this or with the line of no dip; it forms an irregular curve cutting both of these lines. The points of greatest intensity, moreover, do not coincide with those at which the dipping-needle is vertical. The highest degree of intensity that has been actually measured is 2·052, the lowest 0·706.* Both the maximum and minimum here mentioned are in the southern hemisphere. If it be supposed that the globe be divided by a plane passing through the meridians of 100° and 260°, the western hemisphere, comprising America and the Pacific Ocean, presents a higher intensity than the eastern; but the charge of the northern and of the southern hemisphere is equal. In the northern hemisphere there are two points of maximum intensity, the most powerful being in North America, and determined by Lefroy, in 1843–44, to be situated in 52° 19′ N. lat. 92° W. lon., the intensity being 1·88. The weaker maximum was found by Hansteen in 1828–29 in Siberia, in 120° E. lon. with an intensity of 1·76. Sir James Ross, in 1840–43, found the principal maximum in the southern hemisphere in about the meridian of 134° E., and a few degrees North of the Antarctic circle, whilst the weaker maximum in the southern hemisphere, according to Sabine, is about 130° W. The intensity of the magnetic force at London is now 1·372.

The intensity of the earth's magnetism, like the variation and the dip, is found to suffer periodical changes. Besides these regular variations of the magnetism of the earth, other irregular

* The unit of intensity used in the text is that proposed by Humboldt, derived from the value of a particular magnet which he employed; but in the later magnetic observations the unit of intensity employed has been that recommended by the Royal Society, viz.: a second of time, a foot of space, and a grain of mass. The magnetic intensity upon this scale at London is at present 10·31.

variations have been observed. These have been termed *magnetic storms:* they are indicated by sudden and considerable disturbances of the magnetic instruments, of short duration, which are produced by some widely acting causes, as these disturbances have been noticed simultaneously at very distant parts of the earth's surface. In extreme cases, the diminution of the magnetic intensity during the 'storms' has amounted to a large proportion of its total force. Sabine considers that these magnetic storms are connected with changes in the solar atmosphere, which are indicated by variations in the number and form of the spots upon the sun's disk; their epochs of maximum recurring at decennial intervals, with epochs of minimum intensity occurring midway between each maximum. These intervals coincide with the decennial epochs of maximum and minimum of the solar spots observed by Schwabe.*

Since, then, the earth may be looked upon as an immense magnet of small intensity, it is natural to expect that, under favourable circumstances, magnetic induction should arise from its influence. Such effects are indeed continually observed. If a soft iron bar be placed in the line of the dip, it acquires temporary magnetic properties, the lower extremity acting as the marked pole of a magnet upon a magnetized needle, while the upper extremity acts as the unmarked pole. By reversing the position of the bar, the end which is now the lower will still possess the magnetism of the marked pole. A bar of steel, such as the poker or tongs, which is kept in a vertical position (a line in this latitude not far removed from that of the dip), is from this cause frequently found to be permanently, though weakly, magnetic. It is to the same cause operating through the lapse of ages, in the same direction, upon the loadstone, that its polarity is to be ascribed.

If a steel bar be made to vibrate while placed in the line of the dip, as by giving it a smart blow, it is magnetized still more powerfully, and this effect may be still further increased by the inductive influence of other masses of iron placed in contact with it. Thus by allowing a steel bar, supported in the line of the dip, to rest upon an anvil, and striking it strongly with a hammer, it becomes decidedly magnetized. All permanent magnetism may, however, again be removed from it by placing it *across* the line of dip, and striking it two or three blows as before.

Iron, nickel, and cobalt are the only substances which are powerfully magnetizable; but a susceptibility to magnetism in a much feebler degree has, by the researches of Faraday and others (323), been proved to exist in a variety of other bodies. Before describing the method in which these experiments were

* A singular corroboration of this theory is afforded by an observation of Mr. Carrington, who was watching a large spot on the sun on 1st September, 1859: suddenly, at 11 h· 20′ A.M., a bright spot was seen in the middle of the dark one; this appearance lasted for about ten minutes, and a corresponding disturbance in time and duration was indicated by the self-registering magnetometers at Kew.

conducted, it will be necessary to examine the leading phenomena of electricity; and these will now be considered.

§ II. Static Electricity.

(223) The force of electricity is one of those subtle and all-pervading influences which are intimately connected with the operations of chemical attraction. Indeed some of our most eminent philosophers have been disposed to regard electricity and chemical attraction in the light of different manifestations of the same agent.

For upwards of 2000 years it has been known that when amber is rubbed upon bodies such as fur, or wool, or silk, it acquires for a short time the property first of attracting light objects, such as fragments of paper or particles of bran, and afterwards of repelling them. Until about 260 years ago, amber was the only known substance by which such effects were produced. About that time Gilbert discovered that a number of other bodies, such as glass, sealing-wax, and sulphur, might be made to excite similar motions. The power thus called into action has been called *electricity*, from ἤλεκτρον (amber), the body in which it was first observed. Independently of its origin in friction, it has been found that electricity is liberated by chemical action, by certain vital operations, by heat, by magnetism, by compression, and in fact by almost every motion that occurs upon the face of the globe. Electricity neither increases nor diminishes the weight of bodies under its influence, and neither enlarges nor reduces their bulk. It may be excited in all substances, may be communicated from one electrified or *excited* body to another previously in a *neutral* or unelectrified condition, and it may be stored up for the purposes of experiment.

(224) *Two kinds of Electricity.*—A very simple contrivance will suffice for examining the fundamental phenomena of electricity as developed by friction:—

Fig. 161.

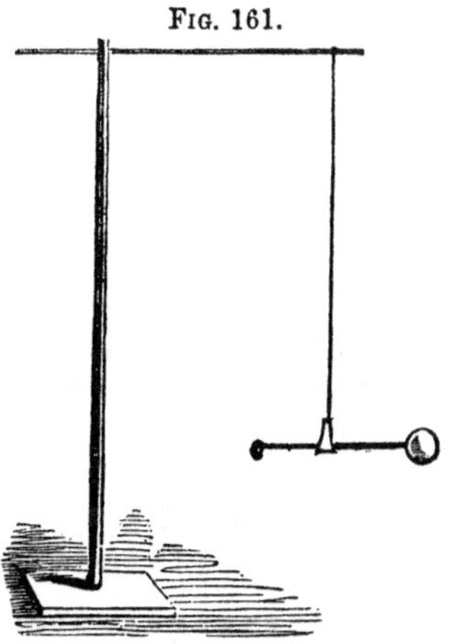

Soften a little sealing-wax in the flame of a candle, and draw it out into a thread 8 or 10 inches long, and of the thickness of a stout knitting pin. Attach to one end of it a disk of paper about an inch square, as represented in fig. 161; suspend this rod and disk by means of a paper stirrup and a few fibres of unspun silk from a glass rod fixed horizontally to some convenient support. Now rub a stick of sealing-wax with a bit of dry flannel, and bring it near the paper disk: the disk will at first be strongly attracted, and will then be as strongly driven away. Whilst it is in this condition of repulsion by the wax, bring towards it a warm glass tube that has been rubbed with a dry silk handkerchief; the disk will be immediately attracted, and in an instant afterwards it will again be repelled, but it will now be found to be attracted by the wax. It is therefore evident, that by the friction of the glass and of the wax, two similar but opposite powers are developed. A body which has been electrified or *charged* with electricity from the wax is repelled by the wax; but it is attracted by the excited glass, and *vice versa.* In order to distinguish these two opposite powers from each other, that power which is obtained from the glass has been termed *vitreous* or *positive* electricity: that from the wax *resinous* or *negative* electricity.

Let us suppose that the paper disk has been charged by means of the glass tube, so that it is repelled on attempting to bring the glass near it; this state will be retained by the disk for many minutes. This contrivance forms, in fact, an *electroscope,* for it furnishes a means of ascertaining whether a body be electrified or not, and even of indicating the kind of electricity. Suppose that a body suspected to be electrified is brought near the disk, which is in a state repulsive of the glass tube; if repulsion occur between the disk and the body which is being tested for electricity, it is at once obvious that the substance is electrified; and moreover, that it is vitreously electrified, since it produces an effect similar to that which would be exhibited by an excited glass tube.

Fig. 162.

The phenomena of attraction and repulsion may be further exemplified by the following experiments:—Suspend two straws, separately, by a fibre of silk, each to a glass rod (fig. 162); bring an excited stick of sealing-wax towards each; each will be first attracted and then repelled; whilst thus repulsive to the wax, bring the one near to the other; they will recede from each other as they did from the wax. If both straws be excited by glass, they will in like manner repel each other; but if one be excited by the glass and the other by the wax they will attract each other. Hence we learn, that bodies similarly electrified repel, those differently electrified attract each other.

Proceeding a step further, it will be found that whenever two bodies are rubbed together, both kinds of electricity are liberated, but so long as the two bodies remain in contact, no sign of the presence of either electricity appears; on separating them, both are found to be electrified—the one vitreously, the other resinously: for example, stretch a piece of dry silk over a brass plate, and rub it upon a glass plate; so long as the two bodies are in contact, the quantities of each kind of electricity set free are precisely sufficient to neutralize each other, and the combined plates will not affect the electroscope, but as soon as the glass plate and the silk are separated, the glass will repel the disk (fig. 161), while the silk will attract it.

(225) *Insulators and Conductors.*—Bodies that have been thus electrically excited, return to their neutral condition when touched by other substances, but with degrees of rapidity depending on the kind of body which touches them. A rod of sealing-wax or of shell-lac, for example, may be held in contact with any electrified body without sensibly lessening the charge; but the momentary touch of a metallic wire, or of the hand, is sufficient to remove all indications of electric excitement: it is therefore clear that there are some bodies which, like the wire or the hand, readily allow the passage of electricity, and these are termed *conductors;* whilst there are others which, like shell-lac, do not easily allow its passage, and these are called *insulators.* There is, however, no absolute line of distinction between these two classes of bodies; there is no such thing as either perfect insulation, or perfect conduction, for the two classes of bodies pass gradually one into the other.

In the following table each substance enumerated is superior in insulating power to all those which follow it. The nearer the substance is to the bottom of the table, the better, on the contrary, is its conducting power:—

Insulators.

Dry gases and Dry Steam.
Shell-Lac.
Sulphur.
Amber.
Resins.
Gutta Percha and Caoutchouc.
Diamond, and some other precious stones.
Silk.
Dry Fur.
Glass.
Ice.
Spermaceti.
Turpentine and Volatile Oils.
Fixed Oils.
String and Vegetable Fibres.
Moist Animal Substances.
Water.
Saline Solutions.
Flame.
Melted Salts.
Plumbago.
Charcoal.
All the Metals.

Conductors.

Any object is spoken of as being electrically *insulated* when it is supported by means of some badly conducting substance which prevents the free escape of the electricity. The presence of moisture deposited from the air upon the surface even of the best insulator converts it for the time into a conductor, and is one of the most annoying impediments to the success of electrical experiments, as the power is carried off as fast as it is accumulated. Glass is especially liable to this inconvenience, but by varnishing it when practicable, and keeping it thoroughly warm, the difficulty is diminished. By due precautions, instruments may be constructed which, in dry air, will preserve a charge for several hours.

The most perfect insulators still allow electric power to traverse them, although by a process different from conduction, and hence they are termed *Dielectrics* (230). Thus, if one side of a plate of glass be electrified by rubbing it with a piece of silk, the opposite face also acquires the power of attracting particles of bran or other light objects.

(226) *Electroscopes.*—Various instruments have been devised for detecting feeble charges of electricity. One of the most convenient of these is the *gold-leaf electroscope* (fig. 163), which is sensible to extremely small charges. It consists of a pair of gold leaves suspended from the lower extremity of a metallic wire which terminates above in a brass plate. The wire is insulated by passing it through a varnished glass tube packed with silk, and the whole is surrounded and supported by a glass case. The approach of an excited body instantly causes the divergence of the leaves. If a glass tube be rubbed with a dry handkerchief and touched with a small disk of paper insulated by attaching it to a rod of sealing-wax, as directed in preparing the electroscope (fig. 161), a small vitreous charge will be received by the paper, and if carried by it to the cap of the electroscope, the leaves will diverge permanently with vitreous electricity. The approach of the glass rod would cause the leaves to diverge further, whilst that of a stick of excited wax would cause them to collapse.

Fig. 163.

An instrument (fig. 164) called a *torsion electrometer* was devised by Coulomb for accurately measuring minute differences in the amount of electrical force. The force which he opposed to that of electricity was the resistance to twisting which is offered by an elastic thread. A fibre of silk, a fine silver wire, or a thread of glass, has been used for the purpose of measuring the angle of torsion, this angle in perfectly elastic bodies being exactly proportioned to the force applied.

Fig. 164.

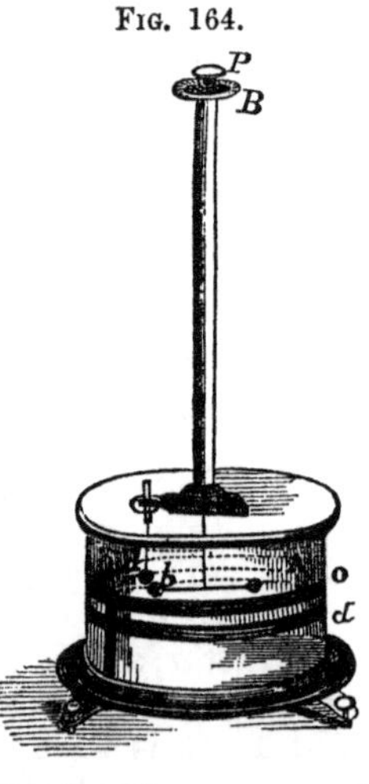

By means of a long glass thread fastened above to a pin, P (carrying an index which traverses the graduated plate B), a needle of shell-lac is suspended freely in the glass case A. This needle is terminated at one end by a gilt ball *b*, at the other by a paper disk which serves to check its oscillations. In the glass cover of the instrument is a small aperture through which another gilt ball, *a* (the *carrier*), also suspended by shell-lac, can be introduced and withdrawn. In order to equalize the induction, two narrow strips of tinfoil, *c* and *d*, connected with the earth, and having a narrow interval between them, are pasted upon the inside of the glass cylinder, one a little above and the other a little below the level of the balls; a graduated circle is pasted on the glass for reading off the angular deviation of the needle. When the instrument is to be used, the carrier-ball is adjusted so that after it has been removed it can with certainty be replaced in the same position as at first; the ball upon the needle is adjusted by turning the pin until, without any twist upon the thread, it shall just touch the carrier, its centre being at the zero of the scale, and the position of the index on the upper graduated plate, B, is noted. The carrier-ball, *a*, is next made to touch the object the electricity of which is to be measured: it takes off a quantity proportioned to the amount accumulated on the spot. The ball *a* is immediately replaced in the instrument; it divides its charge with the ball *b* on the needle, and repulsion ensues. The thread which supports the needle is then twisted until the centre of the ball *b* is, by the force of torsion, brought back towards the carrier, *a*, to some determinate angle (say 30°) marked on the graduation of the glass case; suppose the number of degrees through which it has been necessary to twist the thread to be 160°; 160° + 30°, or 190°, will represent the repulsive force. To compare this amount with any other quantity, the balls must be discharged, and the experiment repeated under the new conditions, noting the number of degrees of torsion required to make the needle stand at 30° as before: the amount of the force is directly proportionate to the torsion angle in the two cases. Suppose in a second experiment that the thread sustain a twist of 180° before the ball *b* is brought back to the angle of 30°; the force will now be 180° + 30°, or 210°, and the relative electrical repulsions in the two experiments will be as 190 : 210.

Another very convenient electrometer was devised by Peltier, in which the directive force exerted by the earth upon a small magnet is substituted for the torsion of a wire. Fig. 165 represents Peltier's electroscope: *a b* is a metallic wire terminating above in a brass knob, and cemented by means of shell-lac into an insulating foot of ebonite, C. At *b* is a brass ring, from which proceed two brass arms, *d*, *d*. In the ring is supported a light metallic needle, *e*, which moves freely upon a pin like a compass-needle. This metallic needle carries a small magnetized steel wire, *m*. In order to use the instrument, it is placed so that the needle, *e*, when the steel wire, *m*, is exactly in the magnetic meridian, is just made to touch the arms, *d*, *d*. On communicating a charge of electricity to the

FIG. 165.

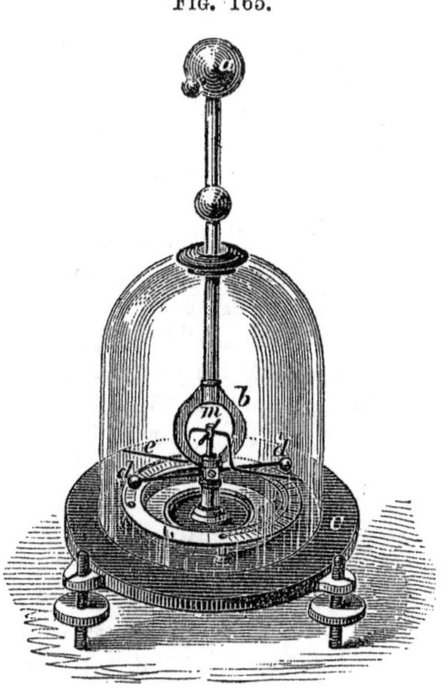

ball *a*, it spreads over the insulated wire and needle *e*; the needle is immediately repelled by the fixed arms *d*, *d*, and the amount of its angular deviation gives the means of estimating the force, which, however, is not directly proportionate to the number of degrees which represent the angle of deviation. These values must be ascertained by direct experiment.

It was long imagined that non-conductors only were capable of excitement by friction, and hence they were termed *electrics*; all bodies, however, exhibit this phenomenon, if proper care be taken to insulate them. If, for example, a piece of brass tube insulated by a glass handle be rubbed upon fur, it receives a charge, as may be shown by bringing it near the disk of the electroscope (fig. 161). Even two dissimilar metals, after being brought into contact with each other, may, with proper precautions, be made to show signs of electric excitement on being separated (257). The friction of glass against metal spread over silk is attended by a more powerful development of electricity than when silk alone is used; and an *amalgam* consisting of 1 part of tin, 2 of zinc, and 6 of mercury, rubbed to fine powder and mixed with a little lard, is found to be highly effectual in exalting the force which is developed. The same substance, however, does not always manifest the same electrical condition when rubbed: glass when rubbed upon silk becomes vitreously excited; but if rubbed on the fur of a cat it exhibits resinous electricity. The amount of friction necessary to produce electric excitement is exceedingly small; the mere drawing of a handkerchief across the top of the electroscope (fig. 163), or even across the clothes of a person insulated by standing on a cake of resin, or on a stool with glass legs, provided he touch the cap of the instrument, is sufficient to cause divergence of the leaves. The simple act of drawing off silk stockings, or a flannel waistcoat, or the combing of the hair in frosty weather, frequently occasions the snapping and crackling noise due to the electric spark; and the stroking of the fur of a cat at such a season is known to produce similar effects.

(227) *Electrical Hypotheses.*—These various phenomena have been accounted for by two principal hypotheses.

One of these, commonly known as the 'theory of one fluid,' is due to Franklin. Electricity, upon this view, is supposed to be a subtle imponderable fluid, of which all bodies possess a definite share in their natural or unexcited state. By friction, or otherwise, this normal state is disturbed. If the body rubbed receive more than its due share, it acquires vitreous electricity, or, in the terms of Franklin, becomes electrified positively, or +; whilst at the same time the quantity of electricity in the rubber which becomes resinously charged is supposed to be diminished, and thus the rubber acquires a negative or − state. Franklin supposed the particles of the electric fluid to be highly self-repulsive, and to be powerfully attractive of the particles of matter.

The other hypothesis, the 'theory of two fluids,' was originally proposed by Dufay. According to this view there are two electric fluids, the vitreous and the resinous, equal in amount but opposite in tendency; when associated together in equal quantity they neutralize each other perfectly: a portion of this compound fluid pervades all substances in their unexcited state. By friction the compound fluid is decomposed; the rubber acquires an excess of one fluid, say the resinous, and thus becomes resinously excited; the body rubbed takes up the corresponding excess of vitreous electricity, and becomes excited vitreously to an equal extent. Upon this view the particles of each fluid are self-rèpulsive, but powerfully attract those of the opposite kind.

The language of either theory may be employed in order to distinguish the two kinds of electricity: the term vitreous or positive may be used indifferently for one kind, and resinous or negative for the other kind, provided it be borne in mind that positive and negative are mere distinguishing terms: negative electricity being as real a force as the positive.

It is manifest that one or other of these hypotheses must be false, yet either will serve to connect the facts together. The supposition of an electric fluid is, notwithstanding, gradually being abandoned. The supposition of a gravitative fluid might, with nearly as much propriety, be insisted on to explain the phenomena of gravitation, or a cohesive fluid to account for those of cohesion.

Electricity is now regarded as a compound force, remarkable for the peculiar form of action and reaction which it exhibits. This kind of action and reaction follows the same law of equality and opposition in its manifestations as that which is exhibited more obviously in the phenomena of mechanics. Whenever vitreous electricity is manifested at one point, a corresponding amount of resinous electricity is invariably developed in its vicinity, reacting against it, and thus enabling its presence to be recognised, although this reacting force may not be immediately perceptible.

The phenomena of vitreous and resinous electricity may be rudely but not inaptly illustrated by those of elasticity exhibited by an ordinary spring, as shown at s, fig. 166. The spring in its unstretched state may represent the body in its unelectrified condition; it then displays nothing of the peculiar power that it possesses. The spring cannot be stretched from one extremity only; but if fixed at one end, as by hooking it to the pin, P, a weight, w, may be applied to the other end, and it will seem to be stretched by one force only. In reality, however, it is not so; for by substituting at V a weight equal in amount to that at w, instead of the fixed point P, the strain upon the

Fig. 166.

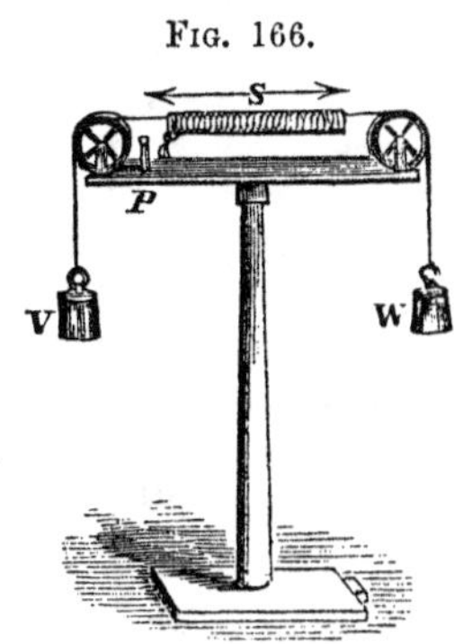

spring remains unaltered, but a reaction, equal in amount to the original action of the weight w, is instantly rendered evident.

So it is with electricity; cases not unfrequently occur where one kind only of electricity seems to be present, but a careful examination will always detect an equal amount of the opposite kind. This essential character of action and reaction in the electrical force will be more clearly manifested in the following remarks and experiments.

(228) *Electrical Induction.*—In the preceding cases the electricity has been excited by friction and communicated to other bodies by contact. An insulated charged body, however, exerts a remarkable action upon other bodies in its neighbourhood. Long before contact occurs, the mere approach of an excited glass tube towards the electroscope causes divergence of the leaves, and on removing the glass tube, if it have not been allowed to touch the cap of the instrument, all signs of disturbance cease.

The following mode of performing the experiment will afford a means of examining this action of an electrified substance upon objects at a distance:—

Place two cylinders of wood, or of metal, each supported on a varnished stem of glass, so as to touch each other end to end (fig. 167, 1); from the outer extremity of each suspend a couple of pith balls by a cotton thread, and bring the excited glass tube near one end of the arrangement as shown at 2. Electric disturbance will be shown by the repulsion of both pairs of balls. Separate the two cylinders without touching the conducting portion, and then remove the glass tube; the balls will still continue to diverge (3). But let the glass be again brought near; the balls on the cylinder originally *nearest* the glass will collapse, showing this cylinder to be *negatively* excited, while the same excited glass will cause the balls on the *further* cylinder to diverge from the presence of *positive* electricity. Again, remove the glass altogether, and bring the two cylinders into contact; a spark may generally be seen to pass between them, and both pairs of balls will immediately collapse and continue at rest. The entire amount of force existing upon the two cylinders taken together remains the same throughout the whole period of the experiment, but its distribution is altered, as is shown by the position of the signs + and —. The experiment may be explained in the following manner:—Suppose the two cylinders to be in the neutral state (No. 1); on bringing the excited glass tube near to them, a portion of the negative electricity appears to be drawn towards the end of the cylinder nearest to the glass, as in No. 2, whilst the corresponding quantity of disengaged positive electricity

Fig. 167.

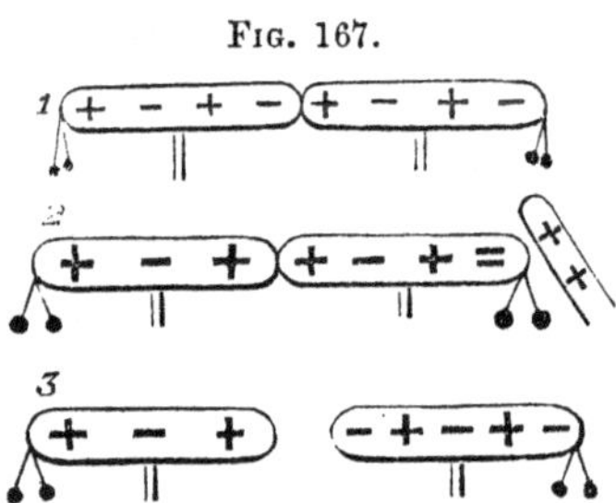

causes the balls on both cylinders to diverge: the moment the glass is removed, the negative electricity redistributes itself as in No. 1, and the balls collapse; but if the two cylinders be separated before the glass is removed, and if the excited glass be then withdrawn,* the results will be such as are represented in No. 3, in which the negative electricity on one of the cylinders is more than sufficient to neutralize the positive, and hence the balls diverge negatively; while on the other it is less than sufficient for the positive, consequently the balls diverge with positive electricity. On causing the two cylinders to approach each other when in this state, the two forces will neutralize each other, and if of sufficient power, the reunion will be attended with a slight spark.

This action at a distance of one electrified body upon others in its neighbourhood is termed *electrical induction.* It is a principle of very extensive application, and indeed it furnishes a key to the explanation of the greater number of electrical phenomena.

An instance of electrical induction is afforded in the action of the gold leaf electroscope. Let 1 (fig. 168) represent the instru-

FIG. 168.

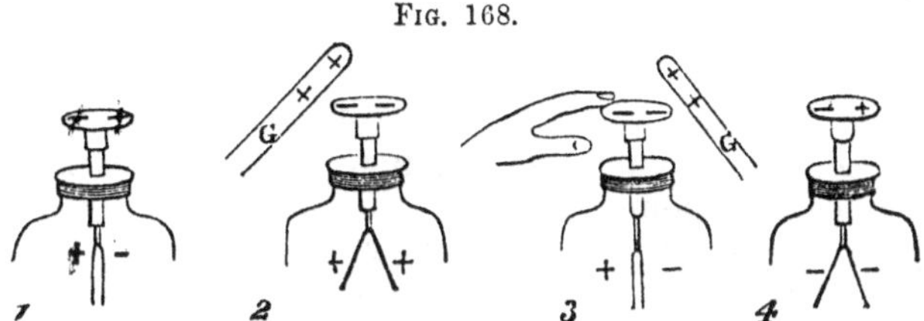

ment in a neutral state. As soon as an excited glass tube, G, is caused to approach the cap of the electroscope, the leaves will diverge, as at 2. Whilst the glass tube is still near the instrument, let the cap of the electroscope be touched with the hand, so as to uninsulate it for a moment, as at 3, by placing it in communication with the earth through the body, which acts the part of a conductor; the leaves will collapse, and the instrument will seem to be quiescent; now remove the finger from the cap, and then take away the glass tube, G; instantly the leaves diverge, and the electroscope is permanently charged, in consequence of a change in the distribution of the electricity, as represented at 4. Its charge, however, is not positive like that of the glass, but negative; for, if the glass be again brought near, the leaves will collapse, while a stick of excited wax will make them open out further. These effects arise from electrical induction, and the process which takes place is believed to be the following. The

* If the glass tube be withdrawn *gradually* to a certain distance, the balls upon the cylinder nearest the tube will gradually collapse, in proportion as the inductive power is weakened by distance; a portion of the negative electricity being liberated in quantity sufficient to neutralize the free positive charge, and, on completely withdrawing the excited tube, the excess of negative electricity is set free, and the balls now diverge negatively.

approach of the tube in the first instance causes the negative electricity to accumulate in the cap, as at 2, where it is retained by a species of attraction, in which condition it is said to be *disguised.* The leaves therefore diverge with a corresponding quantity of positive electricity thus set free; things being in this state, a touch is sufficient to neutralize the excess of positive electricity, as seen in 3, and the instrument appears to be quiescent. Remove the glass tube, however, and the negative electricity, that had been accumulated on the surface of the cap, spreads over the whole instrument (though in the diagram this is only represented as taking place upon the leaves), and the leaves diverge with negative electricity, as shown at 4.

In all these cases, the excited body itself neither loses nor gains electricity by the process just described. The mode in which this transfer of force from a distance is effected still remains to be considered.

(229) *Faraday's Theory of Induction.*—We owe to Faraday a theory of these effects, which has been thus concisely summed up by Snow Harris (*Rudimentary Electricity*, first ed., pp. 33, 34). Faraday 'conceives electrical induction to depend on a physical action between contiguous particles, which never takes place at a distance without operating through the molecules of intervening non-conducting matter. In these intermediate particles, a separation of the opposite electricities takes place, and they become disposed in an alternate series or succession of positive or negative points or poles: this he terms a *polarization* of the particles, and in this way the force is transferred to a distance.

FIG. 169.

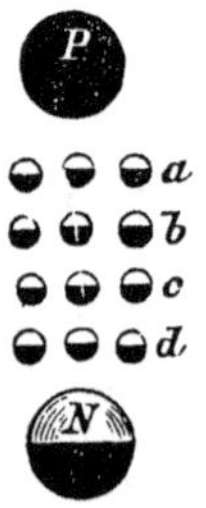

Thus, if in fig. 169, P represents a positively charged body, and *a*, *b*, *c*, *d*, intermediate particles of air, or other non-conducting matter, then the action of P is transferred to a distant body, N, by the separation and electrical polarization of these particles, indicated by the series of black and white hemispheres. Now, if the particles can maintain this state, then insulation obtains; but if the forces communicate or discharge one into the other, then we have an equalization or combination of the respective and opposite electricities throughout the whole series, including P and N.' . . .

'He assumes that *all particles* of matter are more or less conductors: that in their quiescent state they are not arranged in a polarized form, but become so by the influence of contiguous and charged particles. They then assume a forced state, and tend to return, by a powerful tension, to their original normal position; that being *more* or *less* conductors the particles charge either *bodily* or by *polarity;* that contiguous particles can communicate their forces more or less readily one to the other. When less readily, the polarized state rises higher, and *insulation* is the result: when more readily, *conduction* is the consequence.' . . . . 'Induction of the ordinary kind is the action of a charged body upon insulating matter, or matter the particles of which communicate the electrical forces to each other in an extremely minute degree; the charged body producing in it an equal amount of the opposite force, and this it does by polarizing the particles, (fig. 169).

(230) *Distribution of Electric Charge.*—Bodies susceptible of this polarization are termed *dielectrics;* and whether they be solid, liquid, or aëriform, the electric force is transmitted through them freely. A pane of glass interposed between the excited tube and the cap of the electroscope will in no sensible manner affect the divergence of the leaves, which will occur as usual; but the interposition of an uninsulated sheet of tin-plate, or even of a screen of wire gauze, will effectually stop all signs of electric excitement on the leaves.

Owing, however, to the molecular action by which induction is propagated, Faraday has shown that it may, under certain circumstances, be traced round the edges of such a screen, and it may be continued either in *curved* or in straight lines. Let S (fig. 170) represent a mass of shell-lac which has been excited by friction at its upper part; B, a brass plate resting on the shell-lac, but also in conducting communication with the ground. At *a*, a strong inductive action is perceived, which is weaker at *b*, weaker still at *c*, and very trifling at *d;* at *e* it increases, and at *f* is nearly as strong as at *b*, whilst at *g* it again decreases, from the effect of increasing distance.

FIG. 170.

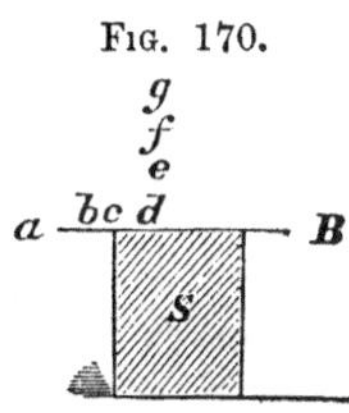

In consequence of these inductive actions, electricity when at rest is always distributed over the surface of a charged object; and therefore, for the purpose of collecting electricity, a hollow shell of conducting matter is quite as effectual as a solid mass of the same size. Many striking experiments may be given in proof of this important fact. For instance, place a metallic can, C (fig. 171, 1), upon a small insulating stand, S; communicate a charge to a brass ball, insulated by a slender glass rod, and introduce this charged ball into the interior of the can, allowing it to touch the bottom; withdraw the ball; it will be found when tested with the electroscope to have given up all its electricity. Touch the inside of the can with a *proof plane* (or small disk of paper insulated by a stout filament of shell-lac), and hold it towards the charged disk of the electroscope (fig. 161), no action will be perceived: bring the proof plane, however, into contact with any part of the outer surface of the metallic can, and an abundant charge will be obtained. No charge can be sustained towards the interior, because there is no object within towards which induction can take place; but the polarization of the air on the outside produces

FIG. 171.

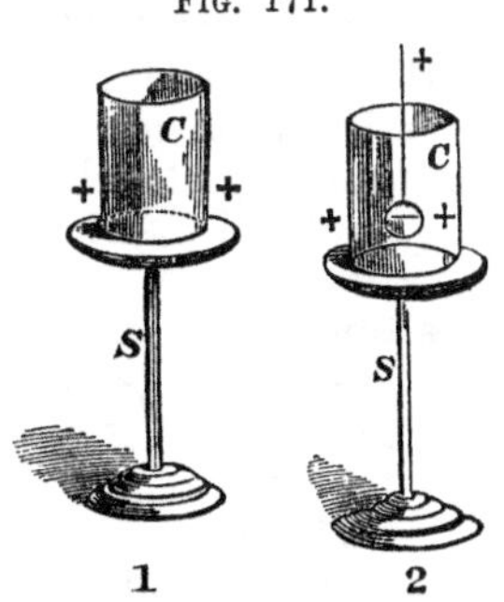

induction towards all surrounding objects.* But now, whilst the exterior still remains charged, hold an unexcited brass ball, attached to a metallic wire, in the inside of the cup, (fig. 171, 2), without, however, allowing it to touch it; if the insulated paper disk, under these circumstances, be made to touch any part of the inside of the can, it will receive a charge: the particles of the air within the can, may, under these circumstances, become polarized, because the brass ball is in a condition to become oppositely charged to the can. If the can be positive, the ball becomes negative, its positive electricity passing off to the earth by the wire.

A similar disturbance of electric equilibrium will be found whenever a charged body is brought near other uninsulated ones. If an excited glass tube be brought towards the wall of the room, and just opposite to the tube the wall be touched with the proof-plane, a small charge of resinous electricity will be carried off, and will be perceptible by the electroscope.

By increasing the surface of the conductor whilst the amount of electricity remains the same, it is obvious that the quantity upon each portion of exposed surface is diminished, and the *intensity* of the charge is said to be lowered. Thus, if a metallic ribbon, coiled up by the action of a spring, be attached to the cap of an electroscope, and a small charge be given to it, a certain divergence of the leaves will be produced; on uncoiling the ribbon, by means of a silk thread attached to it for the purpose, the leaves will partially collapse, because the same amount of induction towards the ceiling and floor of the room is now distributed over a larger surface; but on allowing the spring to exert its elasticity, and coil up the ribbon, the leaves will again resume their original divergence.

In all cases of electric excitement the charge is diffused over the surface of the conductor, but the form of that surface materially influences the mode in which the electricity is distributed. If a charged sphere be suspended in the centre of a room, the superficial distribution of the force will be uniform on all parts of its surface. But if two similar and equally excited spheres be suspended side by side, the electric accumulation will be greatest at those points of their respective surfaces which lie at the opposite extremities of a line passing through the centre of each; and, in a cylinder, the force is highest at the two ends.

This change in the distribution of electricity over the surface, which depends upon the change of form, was carefully investigated by Coulomb. For this purpose he employed his torsion balance, shown at fig. 164. The carrier-ball, *a*, of the instrument was brought into contact with that point of the conductor which was to be examined; the ball thus acquired a charge proportional to the intensity of the electricity at that spot; and the intensity was measured in the manner already described (226),

* Indeed, a delicate electrometer may be enclosed in a shell of conducting matter, which may be so highly charged as to emit sparks in all directions, though the electrometer will remain wholly unaffected.

by the angular repulsion of the needle; different points of the conductor were thus examined in succession, and the intensity at each point was compared with the others.

In this way it was found that if two spheres of unequal diameters were each originally electrified to the same degree of intensity (that is, if each sphere were so charged that the quantity of electricity upon a square inch of the surface of each was exactly equal when the two were separate) on bringing the two into contact, the greatest accumulation still occurred at the extremities of a line joining the centres of the spheres, but the accumulation was greater on the small ball than on the large one. The experiment may be carried still further: for if a series of spheres gradually diminishing in size be employed, till at last they virtually end in a point, the accumulation at length becomes so great that the point is unable to retain the charge, and dispersion ensues.

A rough idea of this effect may be conveyed by fig. 172, in which A, B, and C represent three independent spheres diminishing in size, and which in No. 1 are supposed to be charged with electricity of equal intensity, as represented by a shaded layer of equal thickness around each, while No. 2 represents the same three balls in contact. The intensity of the charge, as shown by the lines of shadow, is proportionately much greater on the smallest ball than on the largest. Points must therefore be carefully avoided in the construction of apparatus for retaining electricity. For similar reasons sharp or rough edges are equally objectionable.

Fig. 172.

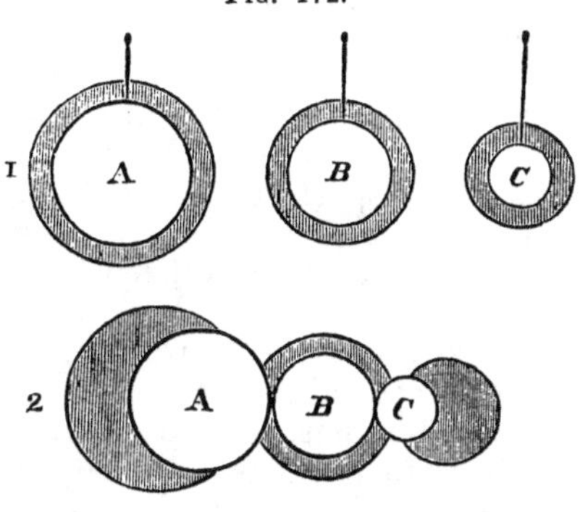

(231) *Electrical Machines.*—In order to obtain large supplies of electricity, the electrical machine is employed. Two principal forms of this instrument—viz. the *cylinder* and the *plate* machine are in general use.

Fig. 173.

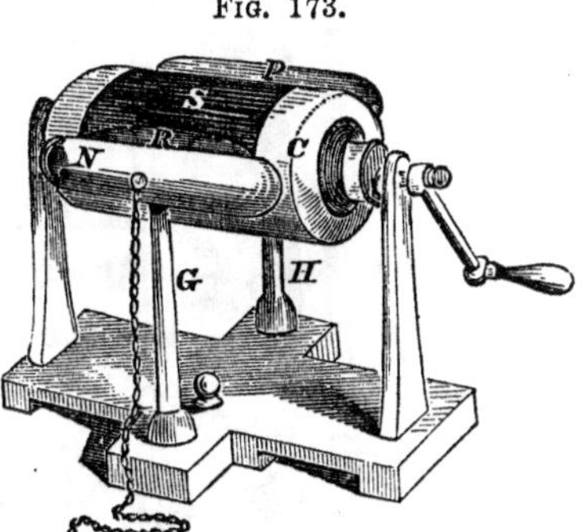

In the cylinder machine (fig. 173) a hollow cylinder of glass, C, is mounted on a horizontal axis turning by a winch in two strong wooden supports. On one side is placed a leather cushion, R, stuffed with hair and faced with silk; from its upper edge proceeds a silk flap, S, which reaches nearly round the upper half of the cylinder. N is a brass conductor for collecting electricity from the rubber. The cushion is insulated by a strong glass pillar, G. To collect the electricity from the glass, a metallic conductor, P, is mounted on an insulating stem of glass, H; this conductor, on the side next the glass, is furnished with a row of points, which, from the high degree of induction produced upon them, act as powerfully in receiving as in dispersing a charge. Before using the machine, a little of the amalgam of zinc and tin (226) is spread over the surface of the cushion. When the whole is made properly dry and warm, on turning the handle a brisk, crackling, snapping noise is heard, whilst flashes and sparks of fire dart round the cylinder from the edge of the silk flap. Sparks of two or three inches in length may now be drawn from the *prime conductor*, P, if the hand be applied to the rubber when the cylinder is turned. In order to obtain a continuous supply of sparks from the conductor, P, it is, however, absolutely necessary to maintain a conducting communication between the rubber and the ground. If the prime conductor be made to communicate with the ground while the rubber is insulated, sparks may be freely obtained from the rubber on working the machine. The electricity from the cylinder and conductor, P, however, is positive, like that from glass generally, whilst that from the rubber is negative. If the rubber and the conductor, while both are insulated, be connected by a metallic wire, no sparks can be obtained from either, however vigorously the machine be worked, the negative electricity of the rubber being exactly neutralized by an equal amount of positive electricity from the cylinder and conductor. The reason why it becomes necessary, in working the machine effectively, to connect either the rubber or the conductor, P, with the earth, is thus rendered obvious, since otherwise induction takes place between the liberated resinous electricity on the rubber and the positive electricity which accumulates on the prime conductor, and thus prevents its free discharge. No sooner, however, is the negative electricity in the rubber supplied from the unlimited stores of the earth with an equivalent amount of positive electricity, through a chain suspended to it, or through the body by placing the hand on the rubber, than the accumulated positive electricity on the conductor, P, is free to pass off in sparks to such objects as are sufficiently near.

Fig. 174.

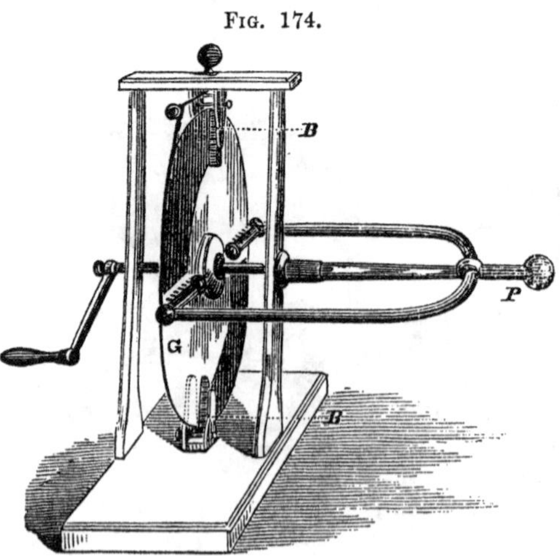

In the *Plate Machine* (fig. 174), a flat plate of glass, G, is substituted for the cylinder, C, in fig. 173. The axis of rotation passes through the centre of this plate, and the rubbers, R, R, are placed on each side of the glass along a portion of its circumference. In this form, however, it is not easy to insulate the rubbers, and to obtain negative electricity separately, though it supplies positive electricity in abundance. P is the prime conductor, insulated by a glass stem.

(232) *Extensive Operation of Induction.*—As the principle of induction already explained is one which pervades the whole phenomena of electricity, we proceed to point out a few more examples.

Every case of attraction is preceded by induction: the opposed surfaces become oppositely electrified by polar action, after which attraction ensues. The following elegant experiment by Snow Harris shows the steps of the process clearly:—Attach to a circular disk of gilt card, A, fig. 175, about three inches in diameter, one end of a slip of gold leaf, and by a rod of shell-lac fasten the disk to a light strip of wood, balanced at the other end by a weight. Suspend this freely by a thread, as represented in fig. 175; on bringing another similarly insulated charged gilt disk, B, near A, the gold leaf upon A will diverge, and then attraction of the disk will follow.

FIG. 175.

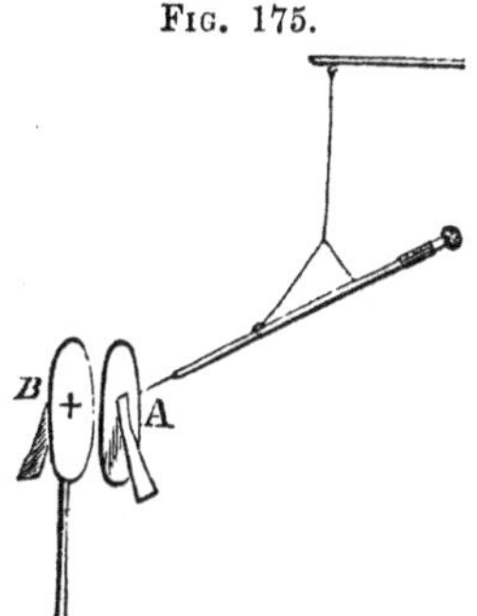

Even the phenomena of electrical repulsion may be traced to induction. If a pair of slips of gilt paper be insulated and suspended side by side as in the electroscope, they will diverge when charged; whilst in this condition a proof-plane will detect no electricity on their inner surfaces, but abundance on the outer ones: induction takes place towards surrounding objects, which attract the leaves, and they separate from each other; but if any conducting body in communication with the earth be introduced between the two leaves, induction now takes place from the inner surface of the leaves towards it, and they instantly collapse. Many amusing electrical experiments have been contrived upon the principle of induction:—light figures, placed on a conducting surface under an electrified plate, are made to dance by alternate attractions and repulsions. If a number of strips of paper be supported in the centre of a room, by attaching them to a wire which is in connexion with the conductor of a powerful machine in action, they will rise up and diverge in all directions, towards the ceiling, the walls, and the floor, under the influence of induction; if a conducting point or surface be brought near them, they will all bend over and converge towards it.

(233) *Electrophorus.*—The electrophorus of Volta is an inexpensive and portable kind of electrical machine which derives its name from ἤλεκτρὸν, and φορὸσ carrying, in allusion to the manner in which the metallic cover carries electricity: it owes

its activity to the operation of induction, which indeed it is well calculated to exemplify. The instrument (fig. 176) consists of a resinous plate, R, 12 or 15 inches in diameter, which may be composed of equal parts of shell-lac, resin and Venice turpentine, melted together and cast into a circular cake of about an inch in thickness. This cake rests on a sheet of tin-plate or metal, T; it is furnished with a moveable cover consisting of a somewhat smaller circular metallic plate, M, to which is attached an insulating handle. The resinous cake is rubbed with warm and dry fur or flannel, and on then putting down the metallic cover by its insulating handle, a spark of negative electricity may be drawn from it; on again raising it, a spark still brighter, of positive electricity, may be obtained. On replacing the cover, another negative spark may be drawn, and on raising it, another positive one, and this may be repeated for an indefinite number of times.

FIG. 176.

The action of the electrophorus may be thus explained. When the cake is rubbed, it becomes negatively electrified on its upper surface; the under surface, which is in communication with the earth through the tin-plate, becomes, by induction, positive, to a similar extent, the particles of the cake being thrown into a polar condition. It thus polarizes the metallic plate on which it rests, liberating negative electricity, and this passes off to the earth, whilst the metal preserves a positive charge, which, being retained by induction, is not perceived until the inductive action of the upper surface is directed to the metallic cover. If the metallic cover be now brought down upon the upper surface of the cake, it touches the resin on a few points only, and from the inferior conducting power of the resin receives but little direct negative charge from the contact; instead of this, the under surface of the metal becomes positive by induction from the resin, whilst upon its upper surface a corresponding amount of negative electricity is set free; this escapes in the form of a spark, if a conductor be presented. On raising the cover after the escape of the negative spark, the positive electricity, which before was attracted to the lower surface of the metallic cover and held there by induction, is in excess, and it is ready to escape as a spark when a conductor is presented near enough to it. As the resin has lost none of its charge, the process may be repeated for an indefinite number of times.* If after the resinous cake of the electrophorus has been excited in the usual manner, it be placed upon an insulating support, and the metallic cover be brought down upon it by means of the insulating handle, little or no negative electricity will be obtained from the upper plate on connecting it with the ground: but if a connexion be made

* The correctness of this explanation may be verified by substituting for the metallic cover a circular disk of tinfoil of the same diameter, and pressing it down into complete contact with the resinous plate; on removing the tinfoil it will be found to have discharged the resinous plate completely; and no charge will now be communicable to the insulated metallic cover until the surface of the resin has been excited anew by friction

between the upper and under metallic plate by touching one with each hand, a slight shock will be felt (235), owing to the neutralization of the positive electricity of the lower plate by the liberated negative of the upper. On now raising the cover, a positive spark may be obtained, and on replacing the discharged plate upon the resin, the same series of phenomena may be repeated as often as the operator pleases, without exciting the resin anew (235).

(234) *Spread of Induction.*—A remarkable peculiarity in electrical induction has yet to be noticed. When a charged sphere, A, is suspended exactly in the centre of a hollow spherical cavity, B, fig. 177, induction diminishes in every direction as the square of the distance; but it is quite otherwise if the charged ball be suspended within the hollow sphere in any other position. If we compare radiant heat with induced electricity, it will be found that the approach of a cold body, S, towards a source of radiant heat does not affect the radiations to the objects around, excepting in the case of those which are immediately sheltered by its shadow, as at B, fig. 177: not so, however, if we bring an uninsulated conductor towards a body charged with electricity. The approach of such a conductor concentrates the inductive action more or less completely upon itself, and to a corresponding extent withdraws that action which was previously directed towards the surrounding, but more distant, envelope. The fewer are the intervening particles of the dielectric air to be polarized, the higher does the polarity rise in each particle, and the more completely is the induction called off from more distant objects: consequently the smaller the distance between the charged and the disturbing body, the more complete is the diversion. The polarity of the interposed air may at last rise so high that it can sustain the tension no longer, and a spark passes between the two surfaces. The particles of the dielectric are in a forced condition, and, like the coils of a spring, tend to return to their normal state.

FIG. 177.

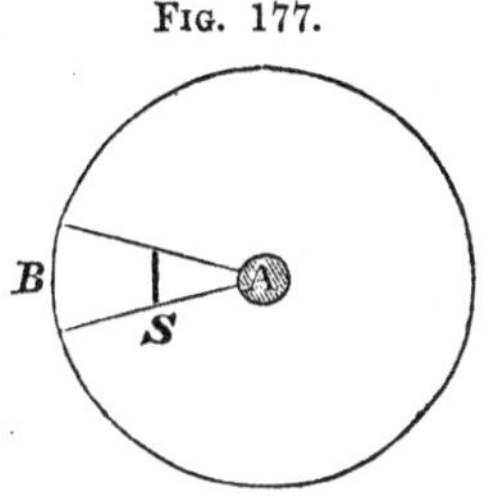

This important fact may be illustrated in the following way. Let A, fig. 178, represent an insulated circular conducting plate, connected with an electroscope. Give to the plate A a small positive charge sufficient to cause divergence of the leaves of the electroscope; then cause a second conducting plate, B, which is uninsulated, to approach the plate A. The leaves of the electroscope will gradually collapse, but they will open out again, when B is withdrawn. In this experiment a portion of the positive

FIG. 178.

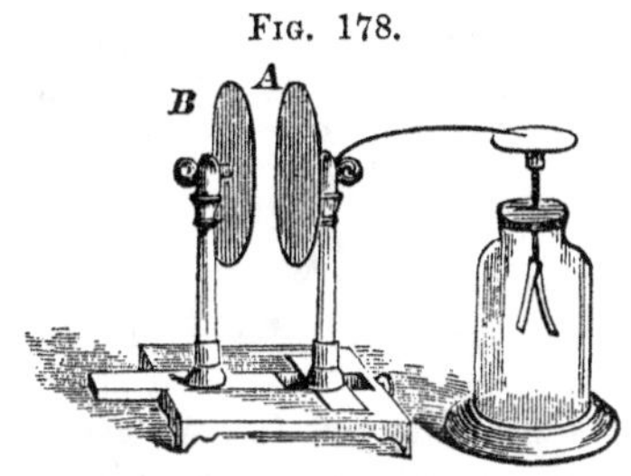

electricity of plate B, equivalent in quantity to that of the charged body, A, passes off to the earth. Owing to this lateral action, if the plate B be retained very near to A, the plate A may receive a considerable amount of charge, by repeated applications of a body feebly charged, provided that such body is freshly charged between each contact with A; by these repetitions small quantities of electricity may be accumulated, and rendered evident by suddenly withdrawing the uninsulated plate, B; the leaves of the electroscope diverge, because by such withdrawal the whole induction is directed to surrounding objects instead of being concentrated upon B. An apparatus of this kind has been called a *condenser*, from its power of collecting and rendering visible, by repeated contacts, quantities of electricity too minute to be otherwise perceptible.

(235) *The Leyden Jar.*—By substituting a solid dielectric, such as glass, for the sheet of air between the plates A and B in the preceding experiment, a much higher degree of induction may be obtained, since the fixed position of the particles of the glass prevents them from moving off when highly charged. In fact, a plate of glass between two metallic surfaces constitutes an apparatus for storing up electricity; and is, in its simplest form, the important instrument celebrated from the place of its discovery as the *Leyden Jar.* Excepting as a matter of convenience it does not signify whether the glass be flat or curved, only it is found more easy to manipulate with jars than with flat plates. The ordinary form of Leyden jar is represented at O, fig. 179. It consists of a bottle, of thin glass, with a wide neck. A coating of tinfoil is pasted upon both the internal surface, I, and the outer surface O, to within three or four inches of the neck. The upper portion of the glass is left free from conducting matter in order to preserve the insulation of the two coatings. A wire, surmounted by a brass knob, and supported by a smooth plug of dry wood, serves to convey the charge to the inner coating, with which it is in contact. Such a jar will receive and sustain a charge of much higher intensity than a simple conducting surface of brass or of tinfoil of the same extent.

Fig. 179.

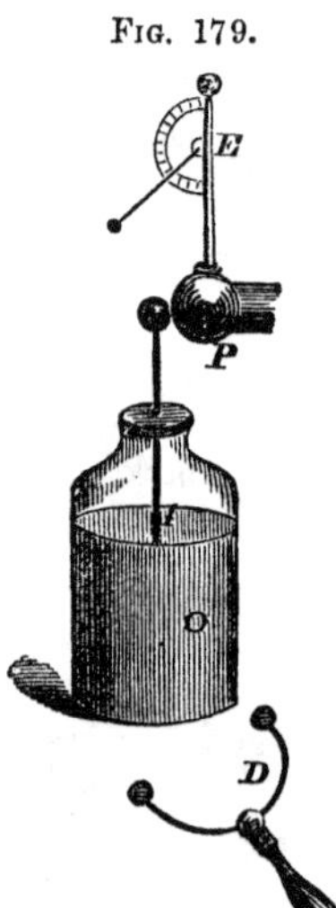

A simple experiment will suffice to show the correctness of this statement. A single turn of the machine will be sufficient to cause a straw, E, fig. 179, suspended from the centre of the graduated arc, and attached to the prime conductor of the machine, P, to assume its utmost angular repulsion; but if the knob of a Leyden jar, which need not expose a coated surface of an extent equal to the superficial area of the prime conductor, be presented as at P, it will take eight or ten turns of the machine to produce the same amount of repulsion; bright sparks will pass in rapid succession between the knob and the conductor, if the two be separated by a small interval, and on connecting the two coatings of the jar by the discharged rod, D (which is merely a jointed wire terminating in brass balls, and which for safety is insulated on a glass handle), the equilibrium is restored suddenly and completely with a loud snap and a brilliant spark. If the discharge were allowed to take place through the arms, or any part of the body, a sudden painful sensation, termed the *electric shock*, would be experienced. The power of the Leyden jar may be increased by increasing its size; and when it would be inconvenient to use jars of a large size, a similar increase in power may be obtained by placing a number of small jars side by side upon a sheet of tinfoil, or other conductor, which connects together all their outer coatings, whilst by means of wires all their inner coatings are similarly connected with each other. Such an arrangement of jars is called an *electrical battery*, and is shown at fig. 190. If the jars be of uniform thickness, the power of the battery will be in proportion to the extent of the coated surface, but the intensity of the charge will be inversely as the square of the thickness of the glass. (Wheatstone, *Government Report on Electric Cables*, 1861, Appendix, p. 285.)

That the charge of the Leyden jar depends upon an action of contiguous particles, polarization taking place across the dielectric, may be shown by taking three or four laminæ of glass, and placing them one above another between two metallic plates, thus forming them into one compound plate, and then charging the whole. If the upper plate becomes positively charged, the lower one will become negative, whilst each intermediate plate becomes polarized, and thus transmits the inductive effect.

As might be anticipated from this experiment, it is found that the charge of the jar does not reside in the coatings, which merely act as conductors to favour the distribution and escape of the electricity. If a jar be fitted with moveable coatings, and then charged, each of the coatings may be removed by a suitable insulating support; the coatings may be handled after such removal; the jar may then be replaced in them, and it will give a powerful spark when discharged in the usual manner.*

The following experiments will elucidate the action of the Leyden jar when in the process of receiving a charge. Let a jar, A, fig. 180, be placed upon an insulating stand, and let its knob be brought near to the prime conductor, P, of an electrical machine in action; under these circumstances it will be found to receive little or no charge. Now place an uninsulated conductor, C, near its outer coating; sparks will pass from P to the knob of the jar A; and for every spark that passes to the knob

* The jar, if well dried, will be found after this discharge still to retain a polar condition like the cake of the electrophorus. After the discharge, if the inner coating be withdrawn by an insulating handle, it will give off a positive spark, and, on replacing the coating, the jar may be a second time discharged; and the same series of operations may be repeated several times.

of the jar, a spark will pass from the outer coating to the uninsulated conductor C. If the jar be receiving positive electricity from the machine upon its interior, it will be found that an equal quantity of positive electricity is disengaged from the exterior. A second uninsulated jar may be placed so as to receive upon its knob the sparks from the exterior of the first; it will thus become charged to an extent equal to the charge of the first jar. Again, if three insulated jars be placed as in fig. 181, where P indicates the prime conductor, whilst the coating of the last jar is brought near to a wire, N, proceeding from the insulated rubber of the machine, for each spark that passes from the conductor, P, a similar spark will be seen to pass between each of the jars, and between the last jar and the wire N. In this way

FIG. 180.

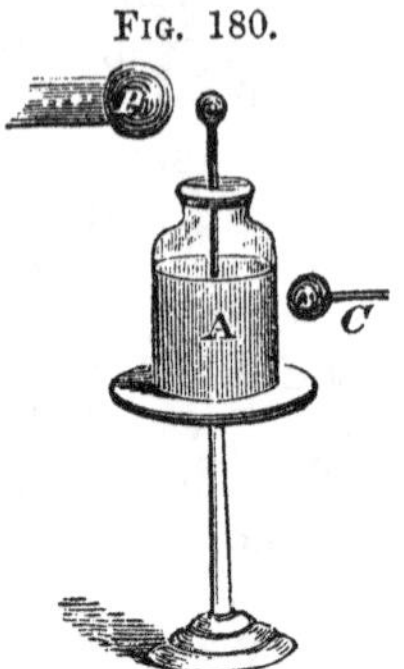

FIG. 181.

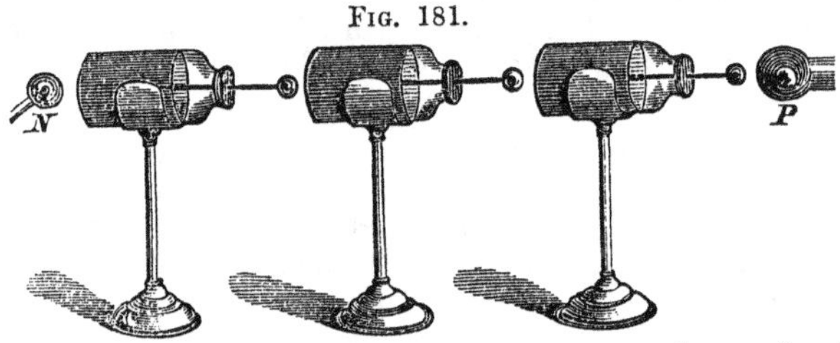

each jar will become equally and powerfully charged, although both the machine and the jars are completely insulated.

From the foregoing experiments it is plain that a jar when charged, contains no more of either electricity than it does in its neutral condition, but the distribution of the two forces is different. This statement may be illustrated by aid of the diagram, fig. 182:—Let No. 1 indicate an enlarged section of the glass side of the jar, the partially shaded circles showing its particles in the neutral state; I representing a section of the inner metallic coating, and O a section of the outer coating. Let No. 2 be a section of the same jar when a charge of positive electricity has been thrown by the machine upon the inner surface, I. In this case a corresponding quantity of negative electricity must have passed off from the same coating to the conductor of the machine, leaving the superficial layer of particles bodily charged with positive electricity, as shown by the white circles in No. 2. In order, however, that this charge of the inner layer may occur, it is necessary that the outer layer be uninsu-

FIG. 182.

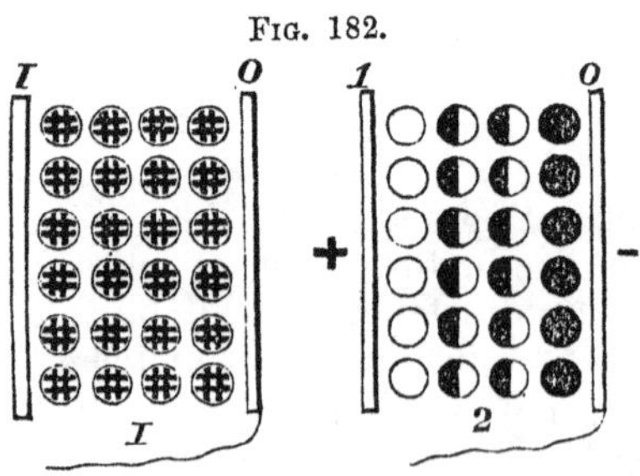

lated, for reasons which will be immediately explained. The two electricities in No. 2 are represented as being accumulated on opposite sides of each of the particles composing the layers intermediate between the inner and outer superficial layers of the glass, the white half indicating the positive electricity, the black half the negative. Polarization of each particle of the dielectric glass intervening between the two surfaces is produced, and a quantity of positive electricity is therefore disengaged from the second surface, which is exactly equal to that distributed by the inner coating, I, upon the first; but unless an escape be afforded for this excess of positive electricity from the second surface, no charge is received by the jar, for polarization becomes impossible, and no appreciable amount of electricity can enter the jar from the machine. At the same time that positive electricity is escaping from the outer superficial layer, a corresponding quantity of negative electricity supplies its place, consequently this layer becomes bodily charged with negative electricity, as indicated by the fully shaded circles.

It thus appears that the charging of a jar with electricity is totally different from the operation of filling a bottle with a liquid; the electricity is distributed not in the cavity of the bottle, but in the substance of the glass itself. Indeed, it has been already stated that a flat plate will answer equally well with the jar, but the jar, from its form, is for the sake of convenience preferred. In the experiment with the three insulated jars, an explanation similar to the foregoing one may be given: —A quantity of positive electricity passes from the conductor of the machine to the inner surface of the first jar. A corresponding quantity of the same kind of electricity simultaneously passes off from the opposite coating into the next jar, which in its turn becomes similarly polarized; and so on in succession, until, from the last jar, a quantity of positive electricity passes to the rubber, exactly sufficient to neutralize the negative electricity liberated by the machine, which is necessarily equivalent to the positive electricity accumulated on the internal surface of the first jar. It is not necessary that the last jar be connected with the rubber directly, the same object will be attained by allowing the discharge to take place into the earth, provided that the rubber also be in conducting communication with the earth. Although it is usual in the charging of a jar to connect the internal coating with the prime conductor, yet the jar may be charged equally well if its insulated *external* coating be connected with the conductor whilst the inner coating is made to communicate with the earth; in this case, however, the charge on the outer surface is positive, whilst the inner surface becomes negative.

Each jar in the series, fig. 181, thus receives a charge, though only one has been placed in connexion with the machine; the superfluous electricity upon the outer coating of the first having charged the second, and so on. If the insulations be good, and the glass of the jars thin, the last jar will be charged very nearly to the same extent as the first.

When all the jars have been thus charged, all will be simultaneously discharged if the inner coating of the first jar be connected with the outer coating of the last; but although no greater amount of electricity passes between the two extreme jars than would have passed between the inner and outer coating of a single one, the distance through which the spark passes is very much greater, and for equal charges it is found to increase as the number of jars thus discharged: if a spark of one inch in length be obtained with one jar, with two jars the spark would be 2 inches, with four, 4 inches, and so on. In practice the distance is something less, because, owing to imperfect insulation and to the resistance of the glass to receive a charge, each succeeding jar receives a somewhat weaker charge than the one which precedes it.

(236) *Measures of Electricity.*—It is upon the principles just explained that Snow Harris has constructed his *Unit jar*, for measuring out definite quantities of electricity. The unit jar is a miniature Leyden jar mounted on a slender insulating rod of glass. Attached to the outside of the jar is a wire terminating in a ball, *a*, fig. 183, parallel to the usual wire and ball which passes to the interior; on the wire connected with the inside, is a third sliding ball, *b*—this can at pleasure be brought to any required distance from the ball, *a*, which is connected with the outside: whilst the unit jar is becoming charged from the machine (say that its outer surface is rendered positive, as represented in the figure), an equal quantity of positive electricity is passing off from the interior along the wire, *w*, attached to the inside of the jar, B, which is to be loaded with a definite quantity: as soon as the charge in the unit measure rises sufficiently high, it discharges itself between the adjusted balls, *a*, *b*, without affecting the charge in the jar, B. A second charge is now given to the unit jar, which discharges itself when it rises to the same amount as before: during each successive charge of the unit jar, a corresponding quantity of positive electricity passes from its exterior into B, so that by counting the number of sparks that pass between *a* and *b*, the number of equal quantities or arbitrary units which have been given to the jar, B, is ascertained. Supposing the adjustment of the balls, *a* and *b*, to remain the same, the jar B may be made to receive, for any number of times successively, equal amounts of electrical charge, by causing an equal number of discharges of the unit jar to take place in each case.

FIG. 183.

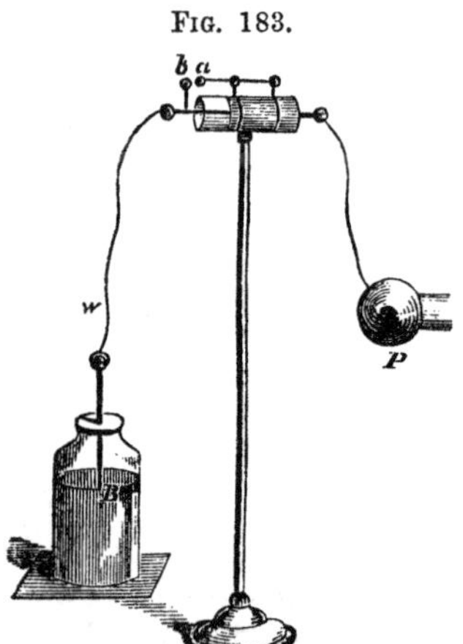

Other means have been proposed for ensuring an equal accumulation of electricity in a jar. *Lane's discharging electrometer*

is the simplest of these. One form of this apparatus is shown in fig. 184: its principle of action will be at once apparent. L is an ordinary Leyden jar, in the ball, A, of which a hole is drilled to receive the brass pin of the electrometer; a bent glass arm, *b*, carries upon its lower extremity a brass socket, *c*, through which slides an insulated rod carrying a brass knob on either extremity; one of these balls, *f*, can be placed at any required distance from the knob of the Leyden jar. A chain or wire, *w*, effects a communication between the sliding rod and the outside of the jar. If the interval between A and *f* be maintained uniform, the jar will always require the same amount of charge before the discharge takes place between these two balls, A and *f*. The quantity of electricity in the charge is proportioned to the distance between the balls: with an interval of half an inch the force would be double that required when the distance was only a quarter of an inch.

Fig. 184.

The force of attraction between two charged surfaces has been measured by an ingenious modification of the common balance devised by Snow Harris. A light disk of gilt wood is substituted, as shown in fig. 185, for one of the pans of the balance;

Fig. 185.

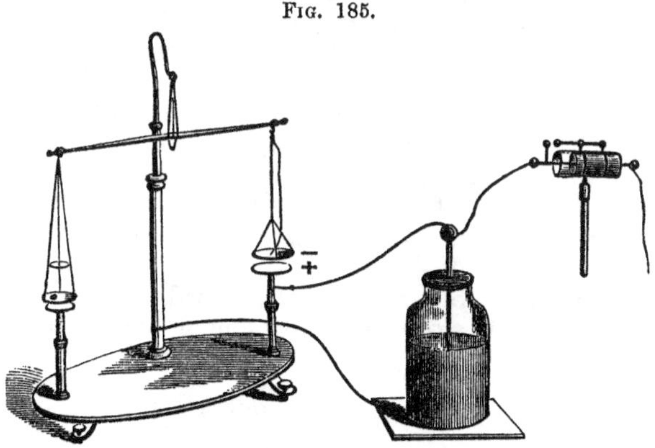

beneath it is a second similar insulated disk: the suspended disk and the balance beam, through its support, are connected with the exterior of a Leyden jar, and the lower insulated disk with the interior of the jar. By charging the Leyden jar with definite quantities of electricity by means of the unit jar, the laws which regulate the attractive force were experimentally determined. One or two of the more important results may be given as an illustration of the mode of proceeding.

If a Leyden jar charged with a certain quantity of electricity produce between the disks an attractive force sufficient to raise 4 grains, it will when charged with double the quantity raise four times the amount or 16 grains; with three times the quantity it will raise nine times the amount, or 36 grains; consequently, if the extent of charged surface continue constant, the attraction increases as the square of the quantity.

When two equal and similar jars are used instead of one jar, and the same quantity, say ten units, is distributed over them, the attractive force will be diminished to $\frac{1}{4}$, and with three jars to $\frac{1}{9}$ of what it was when a single jar was employed. For instance, a quantity which on one jar would raise 18 grains, would, if diffused over two similar jars, raise only $4\frac{1}{2}$ grains; and if diffused over three, it would raise only 2 grains. If, therefore, the quantity remain constant, the attractive force is inversely as the squares of the charged surfaces of the jars. When the distance between the disks was altered, it was found, for charges of equal intensity, that the attractive force varied inversely as the square of the distance,—the attractive force being 4 times as great at 1 inch, as it was at 2 inches, distance.

(237) *Specific Induction.*—It has been shown that the induction between two conducting plates, one of which is insulated while the other communicates with the earth, is facilitated by diminishing the thickness of the dielectric which separates them, and that the insulated plate is enabled to receive a higher amount of charge by reducing the number of particles of the dielectric which undergo polarization. It is evident from this circumstance that the polarization is attended with a certain amount of resistance. Faraday discovered that this resistance varies in amount with the material of the dielectric employed; some substances becoming polarized more readily than others. The relative facility of induction through the different bodies as compared with a common standard constitutes their *specific inductive capacity*. A plate of shell-lac, for example, of an inch in thickness, allows induction to take place across it twice as readily as does an equal thickness of atmospheric air, and sulphur with a facility equal to that of shell-lac.

The following table represents, according to Snow Harris (*Phil. Trans.*, 1842, p. 170), the specific inductive power of various bodies:—

Specific Induction.

Air	1·00	Glass	1·90
Resin	1·77	Sulphur	1·93
Pitch	1·80	Shell-lac	1·95
Bees'-wax	1·86		

The fundamental fact may be shown by the following simple experiment (fig. 186). About $1\frac{1}{2}$ inch above the cap of a gold-leaf electroscope suspend an insulated disk of metal, and communicate a small charge to the insulated disk; the gold-leaves immediately diverge by induction. Between the disk and the electroscope substitute for the dielectric air, a body the specific induction of which is greater than that of air, such, for example, as a plate of shell-lac, s, an inch in thickness, and mounted on an insulated handle; the leaves will immediately diverge more widely, because induction towards the instrument takes place more freely; on removing the shell-lac the leaves of the electroscope return to their original divergence. The effect is precisely similar to that which would be produced by bringing the charged plate nearer to the electroscope in air. Similar phenomena occur if a mass of sulphur or of resin be substituted for the shell-lac.

Fig. 186.

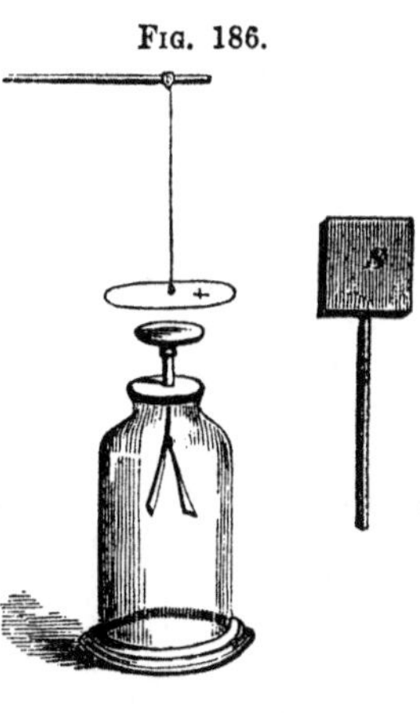

In good conductors no such polarization can be traced, and in imperfect conductors, such as spermaceti, the results become indistinct.

With gaseous bodies no difference in specific inductive power is found to exist: it is remarkable that the chemical nature of the gas has no influence; all gases having the same inductive capacity as common air. No variation in temperature, in density, in dryness, or in moisture, produces any change in this respect. The apparatus with which Faraday investigated these curious phenomena was a kind of Leyden phial (fig. 187), consisting of two concentric metallic spheres, A, A, insulated from each other by a stem of shell-lac, B. Any dielectric could in succession be placed between the spheres, whether the subject of experiment were solid, liquid, or aëriform, as by connecting it with the air-pump by means of the stop-cock, S, it could be exhausted, and the interval filled with any gaseous medium, with the same facility as with a liquid (*Phil. Trans.*, 1838, p. 9). Two of these jars having been prepared, a charge was given to one of them, after it had been filled with the body the inductive capacity of which was to be determined, and the charge was then divided with the second similar apparatus, in which the interval between the spheres was filled with air only. The intensity of the charge in each case was measured by means of a carrier-ball and Coulomb's electrometer.

Fig. 187.

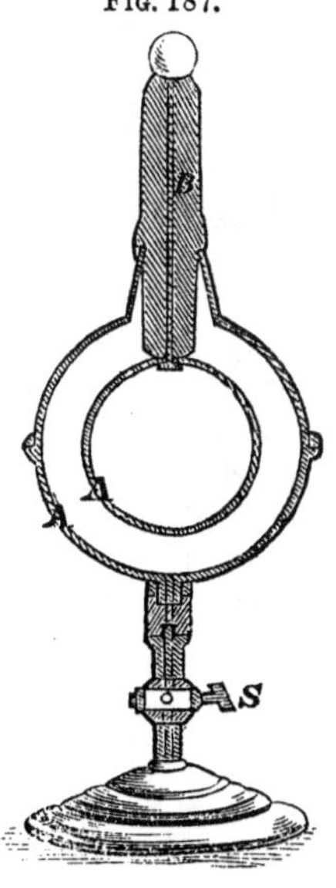

(238) *Various Modes of Discharge.*—We pass on now to consider the different modes in which the electric equilibrium is restored after it has been disturbed: this restoration may be effected in one of three ways, for the excited body may be discharged either by (*a*) *conduction*, by (*b*) *disruption*, or by (*c*) *convection.*

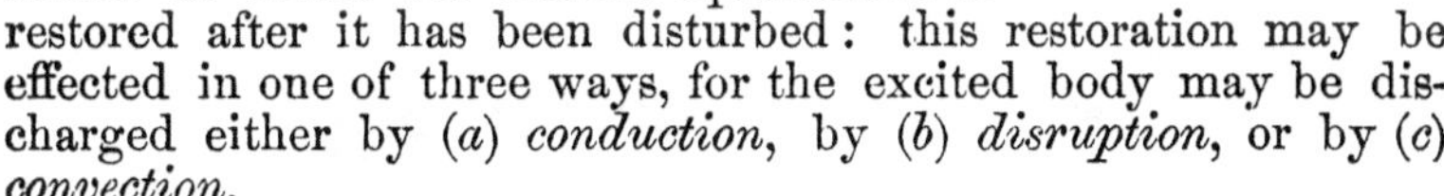

(239) *a. Conduction.*—When a charged Leyden jar is discharged in the usual way through a discharging-rod, the electri-

city passes quietly through the wire of the discharger by conduction, but traverses the interposed air by disruption, in the form of a spark attended with noise.

All bodies, shell-lac and glass not excepted, possess a certain amount of conducting power, which gives rise to the phenomenon termed the *residual charge* of a jar, or battery. If a jar be charged strongly, and allowed to remain undisturbed for a few minutes, and then be discharged, a slight apparent renewal of the charge will take place, and a second smaller spark may be obtained from it. This Faraday considers to be due to the penetration by conduction of a portion of the charge into the substance of the dielectric. Each surface of the glass acquires a weak charge, one of positive, the other of negative electricity; but as soon as the constraining power which caused this penetration of the electricity is removed, it returns towards the nearest surface and produces the slight recharge, or residual charge.

As no bodies are perfect insulators, so none are perfect conductors, for even the metals offer a certain measurable resistance to the transmission of electricity. The following experiment will serve to illustrate this point. Charge a large Leyden jar (fig. 188), and arrange a metallic wire, W, 50 or 100 feet in length, so as to act the part of a discharger; at the same time open a short path for the discharge to the outer coating, by bringing the balls *a* and *b* within a short distance of each other. Under this arrangement, a portion of the electricity takes the shorter course from *a* to *b*, and overcomes the high resistance of the stratum of air interposed between the balls, owing to the resistance experienced by the discharge to its passage along the continuous conducting wire, W.

Fig. 188.

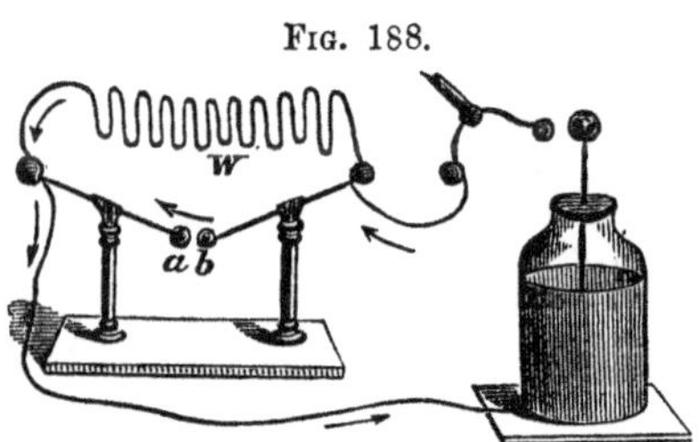

This resistance, even in good conductors, often occasions the spark to pass between two contiguous conductors, and produces what has been called the *lateral spark*, which can be elicited,

Fig. 189.

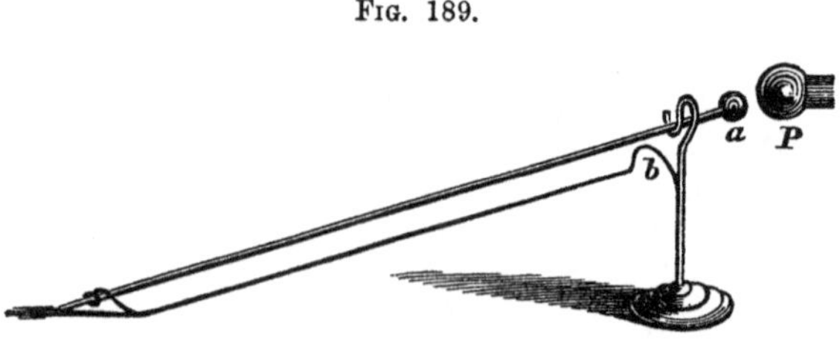

even if the conductors subsequently unite below. Thus, in fig. 189, at the moment a spark passes from P to the ball, *a*, a minute spark will be seen to pass between the wire and the loop, *b*, if they be sufficiently near each other. This lateral spark may acquire sufficient power to ignite gunpowder or other combustible matter. In fact, momentary as is the duration of the discharge, induction takes place towards all surrounding objects whilst electricity is in motion, as well as when it is at rest.

If in a darkened room a thin insulated wire be made to terminate at each extremity in a metallic ball, and on one ball large sparks be thrown, whilst from the other ball the sparks are allowed to pass off to some contiguous conductor, the air will be seen to become feebly luminous from induction along the whole course of the wire every time that a spark passes.

(240) *Development of Heat.*—The passage of electricity through conductors is attended with evolution of heat, the amount of which is inversely as the conducting power. Snow Harris (*Phil. Trans.*, 1827, p. 21), by means of an air thermometer with a large bulb, across which were passed in succession wires of different metals but of equal length and thickness, found that when equal quantities of electricity were discharged through these wires, the heating effects were as follows. The metals which stand first on the list are the best conductors, and they emit the least heat:—

Development of Heat in Metals by Electricity.

Metal		*Alloys.*		
Copper	6	Brass	=	18
Silver	6	Gold 3, Copper 1	=	25
Gold	9	Gold 1, Copper 3	=	15
Zinc	18	Gold 3, Silver 1	=	25
Platinum	30	Tin 1, Lead 1	=	54
Iron	30	Tin 1, Copper 8	=	18
Tin	36			
Lead	72			

It will be seen that by alloying the metals with each other, the conducting power is often greatly reduced. Great care should therefore be taken to ensure the purity of the metals in experiments of this nature.

If different quantities of electricity be transmitted through the same wire, it is found that the rise of temperature is proportional to the square of the quantity transmitted in equal times: for example, if the thermometer, with a given charge, rise 10°, a charge of twice the power will raise it four times as much, or 40°.

By sufficiently reducing the thickness of the conductor at one part of the circuit, the heat may be raised so far as to fuse the wire, or even to convert it into vapour.

The amount of electricity required to produce this effect, when measured by a unit jar, is found to be equally powerful whether it be diffused over a large or small surface; the *intensity* (*i. e.* quantity which passes through a given space in a given time) is the same in the wire in both cases, though the intensity of the charge on equal surfaces of the jar is very different. Where large quantities of electricity are needed, a corresponding extent of coated surface is requisite; this may be obtained either by employing a single jar of large dimensions, or several smaller ones, the inner surfaces of which are connected by wires, and the outer surfaces likewise united by placing them upon a sheet of tinfoil, or on a metallic tray. By discharging such a battery through thin metallic wires—of silver, steel, platinum, or copper, for instance—they will be fused and dispersed.

The arrangement represented in fig. 190, shows one method of employing such a battery for the deflagration of metallic wires: nine jars are in this case represented; they are enclosed in a wooden case, B, and rest on tinfoil, which communicates with the earth through the chain C. The battery is charged from the prime conductor P. The internal coatings of all the jars are connected by cross wires. In order to direct the discharge of the battery, a wire passes from its inner coating to the insulated upper arm *f*, of the discharger A, a second wire passes from the ball *b*, to one of the insulated wires on the stand of the *universal discharger* D. The wire for deflagration, *w*, is fastened to a card which is also supported on a little stand insulated by glass; and the communication with the external coating of the battery is continued by a wire connected with the other insulated support of the universal discharger D; thus the conducting communication is complete with the exception of the interval between *a* and *b*. When the battery is adequately charged, the lever *l* is withdrawn, the ball *a* and its attached wire are thus released, and fall through a hole in the metallic arm *f*, which is connected with the inner coating, and the circuit is completed when the balls *a* and *b* come into contact.

Fig. 190.

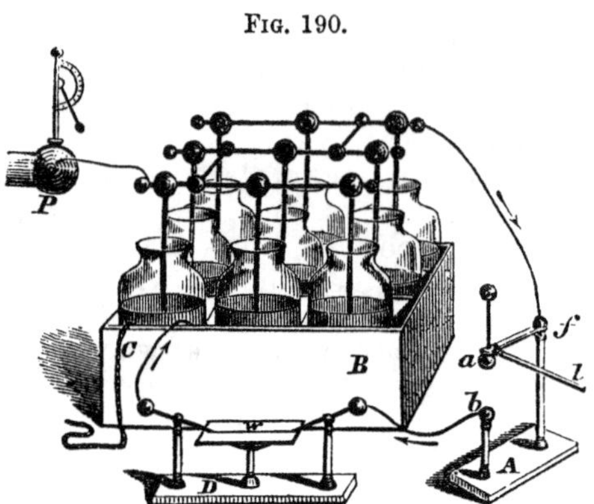

It must be observed that in all cases of conduction the charge passes through the whole thickness of the rod or wire, and is not confined to its surface: it therefore makes no difference whether the metal is in the form of wire, or is extended over a large surface as leaf. The induction at any part of the wire during the discharge is mainly from one transverse section of the wire to the contiguous section that immediately precedes and that follows it.

The dispersion of the conductor by the passage of high charges of electricity leads us to consider next what Faraday terms the *disruptive* discharge.

(241) *b. Disruptive Discharge.*—This mode of discharge is attended by sudden and forcible separation of the particles of the medium through which it occurs; and it is attended with extrication of light and heat. It is best seen between two conductors

separated by a dielectric, such as two metallic balls in air. In these cases, when a sudden bright spark passes, the discharge is as complete as if it had been effected by direct metallic communication. The particles of the intervening dielectric are brought up to a highly polarized state, until at length the tension on one particle rising higher than the rest, and exceeding that which it can sustain, it breaks down; the balance of induction is thus destroyed, and the discharge is completed in the line of least resistance.

In all these cases, portions of the solid conductors are detached, and by their ignition increase the brilliancy of the spark. This transfer of material particles by the spark is easily proved, for if sparks be caused to pass between a gold and a silver ball, the surface of the gold becomes studded with particles of silver, and *vice versâ*. If an iron chain be laid on a sheet of white paper, and a powerful discharge be sent through it, each link will leave upon the paper a stain, arising from the portions of the metal which have been detached; and if the discharge be effected over a plate of glass, particles of the metal are frequently forced into it. The experiment may be varied by suspending the chain in a dark room, and passing the discharge through it; brilliant deflagration of the iron will be seen at each link.

If the sparks be taken between wires composed of different metals, and the light of each spark be viewed through a prism, the spectrum will in each case exhibit the bright lines due to the light of the corresponding metal in the state of vapour (107).

Sparks attended with disruption may also take place in the midst of liquid dielectrics. More rarely disruption from the force of the discharge occurs in solids: occasionally this is exemplified in the Leyden jar itself, the tension upon the glass now and then rising so high that the glass is perforated. Across this fracture discharge always afterwards occurs; so that no effective charge in a battery can be maintained till the cracked jar is removed. This disruption of glass may be produced at pleasure by bending a wire so that its point may press against the side of a tube or other vessel filled with some liquid dielectric, such as olive oil. On charging the wire from the prime conductor, and applying a ball to the outside of the tube opposite the end of the wire, a spark passes, and a minute perforation is produced.

Great expansion of the air occurs from the heat developed at the moment of the discharge, as is shown in the following experiments. Paste a strip of tinfoil on glass, cutting it through in two or three places with a knife; place a few wafers or other light bodies over the interrupted points, then discharge a jar through the tinfoil, and the wafers will be immediately scattered in all directions. If a card or half quire of paper be placed in the direction of its thickness in the track of the discharge, the card or the paper will be burst outwards on both sides.

Many pleasing experiments may be made by causing a succession of discharges to occur through such interrupted conductors: a beautiful display of the electric light may thus be exhibited in a darkened room.

(242) *Velocity of Discharge.*—Of the velocity of the spark discharge some notion may be formed from the brief duration of its light, which cannot illuminate any moving object in two successive positions, however rapid its motion. If a wheel be thrown into rapid rotation on its axis, none of its spokes will be visible in daylight, but if the revolving wheel be illuminated in a darkened room by the discharge of a Leyden jar, every part of it will be rendered as distinctly visible as though it were at rest. In a similar manner, the trees even when agitated by the wind in a violent storm, if illuminated at night by a flash of lightning, appear to be absolutely motionless.

By a very ingenious application of this principle, Wheatstone has shown that the duration of the spark is less than the one millionth part of a second. The apparatus is the same in principle as the revolving wheel.

By a modification of the apparatus, Wheatstone was also enabled to measure the velocity with which the discharge of a Leyden jar was transmitted through an insulated copper wire. He estimated the rate of its passage at 288,000 miles in a second (*Phil. Trans.*, 1834, p. 589). For this purpose he employed an insulated copper wire about half a mile long, through which a Leyden jar was discharged. This insulated circuit was interrupted at three points; one of these interruptions was within a few feet of the inner coating of the Leyden jar; the second was in the middle of the wire, and the third within a few feet of the outer coating of the jar. The parts of the wire at which these three breaks in the circuit occurred were all arranged side by side on an insulated disk, so that the three sparks could be seen simultaneously. In fig. 191 a wire is represented as proceeding

Fig. 191.

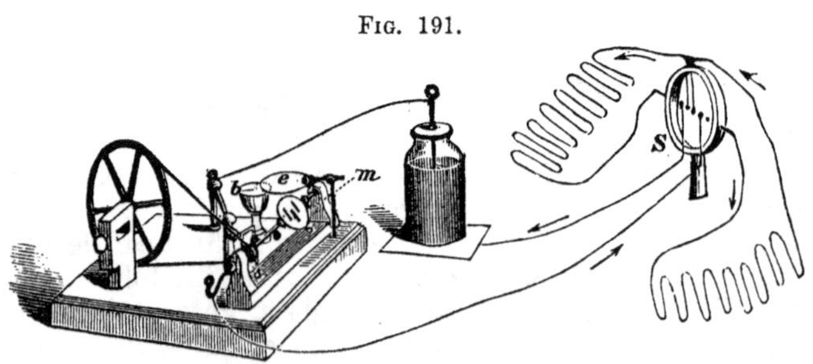

from the knob of the jar to an insulated rod; when the charge attains a certain intensity, a spark passes between this rod and a small knob attached to the axis of a revolving mirror, *m*: to one extremity of this axis, the wire which passes to the outer coating is fastened; but the discharge is made to traverse the whole length of the two intervening long contorted portions of wire, before it reaches the outside of the jar. The three sparks, if viewed by the naked eye, appear to be simultaneous. If viewed through the glass plate, *e*, in a small steel mirror, *m*, to which is given a regulated but extremely rapid revolving motion on an axis parallel to its surface, the sparks appear no longer as dots of light in the same horizontal line, but present the appearance of three bright lines of equal length. The two outer ones commence and terminate in the same horizontal line, but the middle one occurs later than the other two, and the angular position of the mirror has had time slightly to advance before the middle spark appears, which consequently exhibits an image slightly displaced. As the velocity of rotation of the mirror is recorded by the register, *b*, and the amount of this angular deviation of the image of the central spark is easily ascertained, the retardation of the discharge by the copper wire, or, in other words, the velocity with which it travels along it, can be estimated.

This experiment has another important signification, to which due weight appears hardly to have been given; for it affords a convincing proof of simultaneous action and reaction in the operations of electricity, and of its existence as a duplicate force: at the same moment that a positive influence leaves the inner coating, an equal amount of negative influence leaves the outer coating, and these two neutralize each other at the central point of the conductor, after the lapse of an extremely minute but still appreciable interval of time. It appears from this experiment that Franklin's theory (227), though in many cases a simple and convenient mode of explaining facts, is not the true representation of the phenomena. The theory of two fluids, or rather of two forces acting in opposite directions, seems by this experiment to be demonstrated.

The velocity of the electric discharge is, however, found to vary with the intensity of the charge, and with the nature of the conducting medium (Faraday, *Phil. Mag.*, March, 1854). The duration of the discharge may be prolonged by causing it to take place through bodies of inferior conducting powers. A charge of a given amount, if transmitted slowly, may, by the prolonged period through which its heating powers can be applied to a combustible, be made to ignite bodies, which the same charge, if more quickly transmitted, would only have dispersed:—for example, let two metallic wires be brought within an eighth of an inch of each other, and let a little loose gunpowder be placed over the interval—the powder will simply be dispersed if the charge of a Leyden jar be sent through the wires; but if a few inches of wet string be interposed in any part of the circuit, the discharge will be prolonged sufficiently to fire the powder.

(243) *Striking Distance.*—In air, whatever be its density, the same amount of charge produces, *cœteris paribus*, induction to the same extent. But the distance through which the discharge of equal quantities of electricity takes place in the same gaseous medium, varies inversely as the pressure. This might be anticipated, since under a double pressure double the number of particles of air would exist in the same space, and the polarity would

therefore be transmitted through double the quantity of insulating matter:—so that, if a given charge in air of ordinary density pass as a spark at 2 inches, at double the usual pressure the striking distance would be reduced to 1 inch; at a pressure of one half it would be increased to 4 inches; at one quarter, to 8 inches, and so on, until *in vacuo* theoretically it would pass through an unlimited distance. Experiment, however, has shown that a certain portion of matter, though it may be attenuated to an extent almost beyond the limits of calculation, is necessary for the transmission of the electric discharge (312). If the density of the air continue to be constant, it is found that the striking distance varies directly as the intensity of the charge. For example: if with a certain charge the striking distance be 1 inch, a double charge will discharge itself through 2 inches, and a threefold charge through 3 inches (Harris). For equal quantities of electricity the striking distance is inversely as the extent of charged surface; so that, when a single jar is charged with a quantity of electricity sufficient to produce a discharge at $\frac{6}{10}$ of an inch, on employing 2 similar jars with the same quantity, the striking distance is reduced to $\frac{3}{10}$, and with 3 similar jars to $\frac{2}{10}$ of an inch. For equal charges, the striking distance, however, varies in different gases, independently of their relative density, so that each gas has a specific insulating power. Hydrochloric acid has twice the insulating power of common air, and three times that of hydrogen of equal elasticity. This is in striking contrast to the equality of inductive capacity (237) in all gases.

This inequality of insulating power was proved by Faraday by opening to the same charge two separate paths, one of them through air, the other through a receiver filled with the gas which was to form the subject of the experiment, as shown in fig. 192. The distances between the balls were varied until the discharge took place with equal facility in both receivers; the same charge was thus found to traverse double the distance in air that it did in hydrochloric acid gas.

Fig. 192.

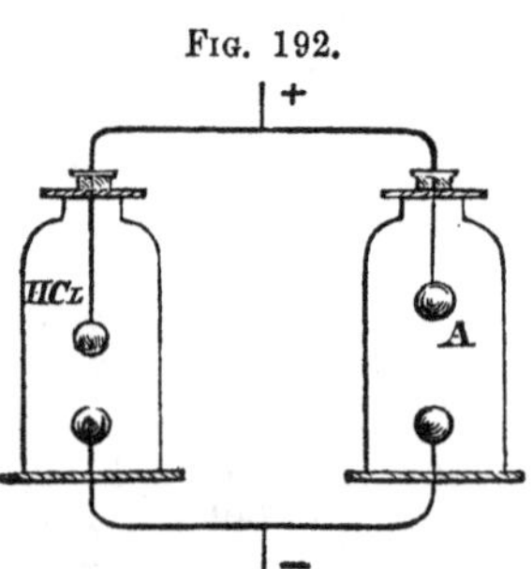

Rarefaction of air, whether effected by heat or by mechanical means, equally favours the electric discharge. A jar may consequently be discharged through several inches of a common flame, in which the air is rarefied by heat to nearly six times its ordinary bulk, the temperature of flame according to Becquerel's experiments being nearly 2200° F. A flame also acts by its pointed form in dissipating a charge with great rapidity, and its proximity should be avoided in exact experiments.

Dissipation of the electric charge in dry air according to Matteucci is not increased by agitation of the air. Further, if the gases are all perfectly dry, and at the same temperature and pressure, the dissipation of the charge takes place with equal rapidity in air, in carbonic acid, and in hydrogen. As the temperature rises, the dissipation of the charge increases in rapidity, the loss of the charge being twice as rapid at 64° as at 32° F. If the density of the air be reduced, the intensity of the charge which an insulated body will retain is reduced also, but the dissipation of the charge is very much diminished. Matteucci found, when an electroscope, feebly charged, was placed in a receiver, exhausted till the pressure was reduced to 0·118 inch of mercury, that the divergence remained unaltered after a lapse of two days.

The form and size of the spark depend upon the shape of the discharging surfaces almost as much as upon the intensity of the charge. Between the rounded parts of the prime conductor and a large uninsulated metallic ball dense brilliant sparks pass; whilst if the same ball be presented to a wire which projects three or four inches from the conductor, and which terminates in a ball an inch in diameter, a long, forked, and often branching spark, resembling a miniature flash of lightning, will be obtained.

When disruptive discharge occurs between a good conductor of limited surface and a bad one which exposes a larger surface, an intermitting and dilute spark or *brush* passes, which, when it occurs in air, consists of a rapid succession of discharges to the particles of air around: such a brush has a bright root with pale ramifications, attended with a quivering motion and a subdued roaring noise. Such brushes are well seen when, the machine being in powerful action, the conductor is made to discharge itself into the air by means of a blunt rod which projects from it. The brush is largest from a vitreously charged surface, such as the prime conductor of the machine. From a negatively charged surface this discharge occurs at a lower tension, and more resembles a bright point or star of light. The formation of brushes is facilitated by rarefying the air around the charged points.

Some remarkable differences have been observed between the positive and the negative spark: for equal intensity of charge, the striking distance, between a good conductor positively charged and an inferior conductor, is greater in air than from the same conductor negatively charged, as may be seen in using the electrophorus. The greater facility with which positive electricity traverses the air may also be shown in the following manner:—Colour a card with vermilion; unscrew the balls, *a*, *b*, from the discharger, fig. 190, and place the points on opposite sides of the card, one about half an inch above the other; discharge a large jar through the card. It will be perforated opposite the wire attached to the negative coating, and an irregular dark line of reduced mercury will be found extending on the positive side to the point of the positive wire. If the experiment be made *in vacuo*, the perforation will be formed midway between the two wires. The distinction between positive and negative electricity is also beautifully shown by what are termed Lichtenberg's figures, which may be obtained as follows:—Dry a glass plate, and draw lines on it with the knob of a positively charged jar, then sift over the plate a mixture of sulphur and minium in fine powder; on inverting the plate the minium will fall off and leave traces of the lines in sulphur. If the experiment be made with a jar negatively charged, the minium will adhere to the traces, whilst the sulphur will fall off. The explanation is very simple: by the friction in sifting, the sulphur becomes negatively, the red lead positively electric, and thus the sulphur attaches itself to the positively electrified lines upon the glass, and the minium to the negatively electrified lines, in accordance with the usual law of electric attraction. The experiment may also be varied in the following way:—Take two circular trays of tin-plate half an inch deep and 12 or 14 inches in diameter, fill them with melted resin and allow them to cool; cause sparks of positive electricity to fall in 8 or 10 places upon one plate, and sparks of negative electricity in like manner over the other; on sifting a little brickdust over the two plates, the dry powder will assume the appearance of brushes over the plate electrified positively, and of oval or circular patches upon the negatively excited plate. Other remarkable differences between the sparks from positive and negative surfaces will be mentioned when noticing the modified discharges through exhausted tubes (312).

The colour, light, and sound of the electric spark and brush vary in different gases (106), the brush being larger and more beautiful in nitrogen than in any other gas, and its colour is purple or bluish. The sparks in oxygen are whiter than in air, but less brilliant. In hydrogen they are of a fine crimson colour. In coal-gas they are sometimes green and sometimes red; occasionally both colours are seen in different portions of the same spark. In carbonic acid the sparks resemble those taken in air, but they are more irregular and pass more freely.

(244) *c. Convection.*—With a feebler charge the sonorous brush is replaced by a quiet glow, attended in this case with a continuous dispersion of the charge. The process of disruptive discharge thus gradually passes into the third method—viz., that by *convection*. When the glow is produced, a current of air, the particles of which are individually charged, passes from the charging surface. The course of this current may be exhibited by its action on the flame of a taper, which will often be extinguished if brought near an electrified point which is connected with the machine in action; and light models may be set in motion by it. If the production of the current from the point be prevented, as by sheltering the pointed wire in a varnished glass tube, the brush or glow may be converted into a series of small sparks. These currents may take place in liquid dielectrics as well as in gaseous ones. Let a piece of sealing-wax be fixed on the end of a wire and attached to the conductor of a machine in action; if it be softened by the application of the flame of a spirit lamp, it will be thrown off in filaments towards a sheet of paper held near it. Solid insulated particles may also be the medium of convective discharge, as is seen when pith-balls or other light substances are attracted and repelled by electrified objects; and

in delicate experiments even the particles of dust floating in the atmosphere are not without effect in charging or discharging the apparatus employed.

The process of convection assumes considerable importance in the phenomena of voltaic electricity, where it is intimately connected with chemical decomposition. (281 *et seq.*)

(245) *Other Sources of Electricity.*—Hitherto we have limited our attention to cases in which electricity is excited by the friction of dissimilar substances. The development of electricity by friction is, however, but a special case of a much more general law, for it has been found that, whenever molecular equilibrium is disturbed, a concomitant development of electricity takes place. The following instances will exhibit the variety of circumstances under which this observation has been made. The mere compression of many crystallized bodies is attended by electric action: a rhombohedron of Iceland spar, if compressed by the fingers, exhibits this peculiarity. It is also found that all bodies that have been pressed together, if properly insulated, offer signs of electricity on being separated; although the effect is most easily observed between a good conductor and a bad one. The two bodies are always in opposite states. Even where two disks of the same substance are pressed together, if one be a little warmer than the other, distinct excitement is produced, the warmer disk becoming negatively electrified; the intensity of the charge, *cæteris paribus*, increases in all cases directly as the pressure to which they are subjected.

Fracture is likewise attended with electric disturbance; the freshly broken surfaces of roll sulphur often exhibit this effect to an extent sufficient to produce divergence of the leaves of the electroscope when the fragments are placed upon the cap of the instrument. The sudden rending asunder of the laminæ of a film of mica in a dark room, is usually attended with a pale electrical light, and the separated portions in this case exhibit opposite electrical states. A melted substance in the act of solidifying, sometimes exhibits electric excitement. If sulphur be allowed to solidify in a glass vessel, it becomes negatively excited, whilst the glass is rendered positively electrical; ice also is frequently electric; and the same thing has been observed of chocolate as it becomes solid. These results are probably due to friction occasioned by the contraction or expansion of the solid mass in the mould, from which it detaches itself by this change of bulk.

In some instances simple elevation or depression of temperature causes electric excitement. These effects are most distinctly seen in crystallized non-conductors which are not symmetrical in form, being produced in bodies which are hemihedral. Tourmaline, boracite, and the crystals of tartaric acid, offer the best examples of this description. The tourmaline, for instance, commonly assumes the form of a three-sided prism, the *edges* of which are replaced by two narrow planes. The extremities of the crystal are formed by the three faces of the rhombohedron. No.

1, fig. 193, shows the end of the crystal which becomes positive by heat; No. 2, the opposite end of the crystal which becomes negative. If a crystal of tourmaline be gently heated, it becomes powerfully electrical whilst the temperature is rising, one extremity, termed the *analogous* pole, becoming positive, the other extremity, or *antilogous* pole, becoming negative.* When the temperature becomes stationary, the electric excitement ceases: as the crystal cools the effect returns, but the electric polarity is reversed; the end of the crystal that before was positive now becomes negative. The particles of the mineral are electrically polarized throughout the whole mass; for, if the crystal be broken while thus electrified, each fragment retains its polarity, being negative at one end and positive at the other. In fig. 194, No. 1 represents a tourmaline in which the temperature is rising uniformly; No. 2 the same tourmaline in which the temperature is falling uniformly; and No. 3 shows the effect upon a cooling tourmaline which has been broken across. If the tourmaline be delicately poised upon its centre whilst cooling, these electric states may be rendered apparent by bringing an excited glass tube near to the mineral: one extremity will be attracted by the excited glass tube, while the other extremity will be repelled. If one end of the crystal be connected with the cap of a sensitive gold-leaf electroscope, whilst the other extremity is in conducting communication with the earth, the gold leaves will diverge.

FIG. 193.

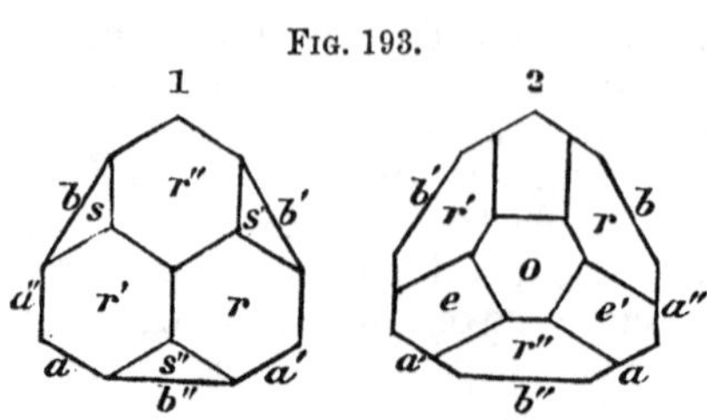

FIG. 194.

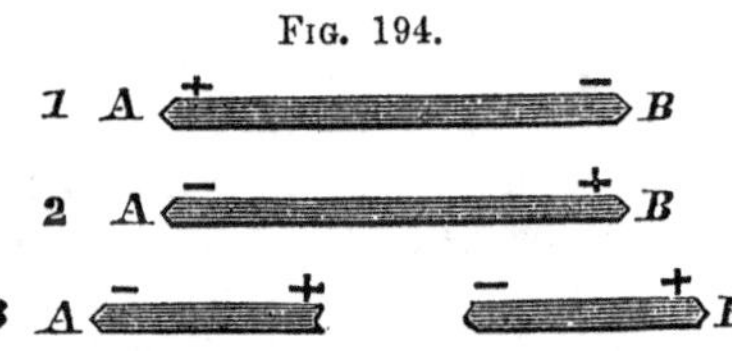

(246) *Chemical Action.*—No chemical change takes place without the development of electricity. If a clean platinum capsule be connected with a sensitive electroscope and condenser, and a liquid which has no chemical action on platinum be placed in the capsule, no change shows itself; but if any other more oxidizable metal in conducting connexion with the earth be dipped into the liquid, the *liquid becomes very feebly but positively electrified, whilst the metal which has been acted upon by it becomes negative.* The intensity of the chemical action in this form of the experiment has no influence upon the extent of electric excitement displayed. If zinc be the metal employed, and pure water the liquid, the signs of electric action are just as powerful

* The crystal must not be too strongly heated,—about 300° F. being the best point; if heated very strongly, as to 750°, or beyond, the tourmaline becomes a conductor for a time; it resumes its insulating power on cooling, but is rendered hygroscopic till after it has been washed and dried at 300°. (Gaugain.)

as if sulphuric acid were substituted for the water in the capsule; for the metal and liquid being both good conductors, almost the whole of the two electricities liberated, immediately neutralize each other, instead of passing one to the condenser, the other to the earth.

Electricity is also developed during the process of combustion; carbon, for example, becoming negatively electric, whilst the carbonic acid is positive. In like manner hydrogen in the act of burning was found by Pouillet to be negative, whilst the vapour produced by it was positive.

(247) *Electricity of Vapour.*—The act of evaporation has also been asserted to be one of the sources of electricity, but the truth of this statement is doubtful. It is true that if a few drops of water fall upon a live coal, insulated on the cap of the gold-leaf electroscope, the leaves of the instrument diverge. This, however, is due to the chemical action between the coke and the water, and not to mere evaporation; for by allowing pure water to evaporate in a clean hot platinum dish connected with the electroscope, no signs of electric disturbance occur. Pouillet found that on allowing alkaline solutions to evaporate in the capsule, the electroscope became charged positively; with acid solutions, the charge given to the electroscope was negative: but Peltier states that these electrical effects may nevertheless be due to friction, as they do not manifest themselves until the liquid is nearly all driven off, and a crepitation of the salt as it detaches itself from the sides of the capsule begins to occur. This is corroborated by Faraday's observation, that if the dish be heated to redness, and pure water be dropped in, so long as it evaporates quietly in the spheroidal form (198) no electricity is developed; but the moment that it cools down sufficiently to boil violently with friction against the metallic capsule, the leaves diverge powerfully.

In accordance with this observation, Faraday has explained the development of electricity by high-pressure steam, which occurs to so remarkable an extent under certain circumstances. This he has traced to the friction of water accompanying the steam against the orifice of the jet through which it escapes into the air. An insulated boiler from which steam is allowed to blow off at high-pressure through long tubes, in which a partial condensation of the steam occurs, furnishes, as in the *hydro-electric machine* of Armstrong, exhibited at the Polytechnic Institution, an admirable source of high electric power. In this experiment, the boiler becomes negative, the escaping steam being positive. It is remarkable that the presence of the smallest quantity of oil or of essence of turpentine in the exit-pipe reverses these electrical states. A solution of acetate of lead produces a similar effect. Indeed the purer the water that is used in the boiler, the better is it for these experiments, and the more uniform are the results. The electric condition of the steam was found by Armstrong to be also influenced by the material of which the exit-pipe was formed; glass, lead, copper, and tin, each modifying the result. Wood appeared to be the material best adapted for use in forming the orifice of the jet, as it produced the highest amount of charge by friction; some bodies, such as ivory, produced scarcely any electric effect when used as jets to the pipe.

Perfectly dry steam is in fact nearly as good an insulator of electricity as atmospheric air; but, from the facility of its condensation, it easily produces upon cold surfaces a film of conducting matter which destroys the insulation.

(248) *Atmospheric Electricity.*—Another source of electricity, the origin of which is at present shrouded in mystery, is the atmosphere itself, which affords displays of electric phenomena on the most magnificent scale. The identity of lightning and electricity had long been suspected by electricians; but the proof of it was first devised by Franklin, who, by the simple expedient of raising a boy's kite during a thunderstorm, succeeded in obtaining from the clouds, sparks of electricity, with which he charged Leyden jars, and performed some of the usual electrical experiments. Such kite-flying, however, forms a dangerous kind of recreation; and experiments on atmospheric electricity proved fatal to Professor Richman of St. Petersburg, who, a few years after Franklin's discovery, was killed by a flash from his apparatus.

No sooner had Franklin proved the identity of lightning with electricity, than he proposed his plan of averting the destructive influence of lightning from buildings, by means of metallic conducting-rods. In order to render these efficient, they must project into the air for some distance beyond the highest point of the building to be protected. They must also be sufficiently thick to carry off the discharge without fusion. This is ensured by the use of a copper rod not less than half an inch in diameter. The pieces composing these rods should be in metallic contact with each other throughout their length, and the conductor should terminate in a bed of moist earth, or better still, in a well or body of water, so as to secure free communication with the soil. If any considerable metallic mass, such as a leaden roof, form part of the building, it should be connected with the conductor by branch rods, and should also be furnished with branch conductors into the earth. The conductors are best placed exterior to the walls of the building.

The explosive power of lightning is so great that its effects may well excite our awe and amazement. A single instance may be cited in illustration of this point. In November, 1790, the mainmast of H.M. ship *Elephant*, 74 guns, was struck by a powerful flash of lightning. This mast weighed 18 tons, it was 3 feet in diameter, and 100 feet long, and was strongly bound together by iron hoops, some of which were half an inch thick and 5 inches wide; yet it was shivered into pieces, and the hoops were burst open and scattered around, amidst the shattered fragments of the mast (Harris). One of the most instructive instances recorded is that of the *Dido*, which, when off Java Head, in May, 1847, was struck soon after daylight, during a storm attended with heavy rain and little wind, by a tremendous bifurcated flash of lightning, which fell upon the main royal mast. One of the branches struck the extreme point of the royal yard-arm, and in its course to the conductor on the mast, demolished the yard, and tore in pieces or scorched up the greater part of the sail; the other part fell on the vane-spindle (the point of which showed marks of fusion) and truck, which last was split open on the instant that the discharge seized the conductor. From this point, however, the explosive action ceased, and the discharge freely traversed the whole line of the conductor, from the masthead downward, without doing further damage. One of the chief points of interest connected with this case is the entire destruction of the yard-arm, which was not supplied with a conductor, and the complete protection of the mast, which was furnished with one. It is also important as proving the incorrectness of the law of protection laid down by some French writers —viz., that a conducting-rod will protect a circular area having a radius double the height of the conductor above the highest point of the building. In all cases, the lightning will take the path of least resistance, and, from the recorded results of experience, it appears that that path of least resistance will, in about seven times out of ten, be such that the lightning will strike the highest point, if it be furnished with a good conducting line to the earth or sea; but it is quite possible that instances may occur, in which the line of least resistance may be in a different direction, or, as in the case of the *Dido*, that there may be two such lines where the resistances are equal.

If a break occur in any part of the conductor, explosion will take place at this spot when a discharge of lightning is directed upon the rod, producing, in many cases, fearful destruction. One of the most awful catastrophes of this kind occurred on the 18th of August, 1769, when the tower of St. Nazaire of Brescia was struck by lightning. Beneath this tower were vaults containing upwards of 90 tons of gunpowder, belonging to the Republic of Venice. The whole of this enormous quantity of powder exploded, destroying one-sixth part of the city of Brescia, and burying 3000 persons beneath its ruins. On a small scale the track followed by the electricity may be illustrated by sending a discharge through a series of interrupted conductors, such as gold leaf pasted upon paper. The portions of gold leaf in the line of the discharge will be burned up, whilst the contiguous portions not included in the track of the electricity remain unaltered.

The peal of thunder which accompanies the lightning flash is due, like the snap which accompanies the discharge of a Leyden jar, to the sudden displacement of air, which, in the case of lightning, sometimes extends through a distance of a mile or more. The reverberation of the peal arises chiefly from the echoes produced by objects upon the earth, and by the clouds themselves. The flash from the thunder-cloud is exactly analogous to the discharge of the Leyden jar: the cloud and the surface of the earth form the two coatings to the intervening layer of air, which, as in the case of the condenser, supplies the place of the glass, whilst a church steeple, or any projecting object, acts the part of a discharging rod.*

But it is not only during a storm that the atmosphere exhibits signs of electricity. In fine weather, if a flame, or a pointed rod, be connected with an electroscope, the instrument usually diverges positively. Before rain, the instrument often assumes a negative state: in general, the rain that first falls after a depression of the barometer is charged negatively. It frequently happens that the rain is negatively charged, although the atmosphere, both before and after its fall, exhibits signs of positive charge. Fogs, snow, and hail, if unattended with rain, are nearly always positively charged in a high degree. It appears to be probable that the clouds are almost always positive. In most cases, when negative electricity is observed in the instruments it is simply due to an effect of induction.

In winter, the atmospheric charge is usually higher than in summer. According to Quetelet, whose conclusions are based upon a series of five years' uninterrupted observations, the atmospheric electricity attains an average maximum in January, and steadily decreases till June, when it is at its minimum: from this period it again progressively increases till January, in which month the intensity of the electricity is thirteen times as high as it is in June. The electricity of the air may be stated generally to be higher in a cloudless than in a cloudy sky. Only once during the months of October, November, December, and January, has he obtained proof of negative electricity in the air.

The intensity of the charge varies likewise during each twenty-four hours; it has two maxima and two minima. The first maximum is before eight o'clock A.M. in summer, and before ten A.M. in winter; the second after nine P.M. in summer, and before six P.M. in winter. The first minimum is uniformly about four A.M., and the second about three P.M. in summer, and one P.M. in winter.

The observations made for some years at the Kew observatory by Ronalds, furnish results closely according with those of Quetelet.†

An ingenious experiment by Becquerel shows that the intensity of the charge increases with the elevation above the earth's surface, and according to Quetelet's observations, the increase in intensity is proportional to the height. This law of Quetelet has, however, been verified only for heights not exceeding 16 feet.

* These electrical accumulations are often renewed with extraordinary rapidity. On the 6th of July, 1845, about 10 P.M., after a clear hot day, in the masses of vapour forming a bank of cumuli, I counted in two minutes 83 flashes unattended by thunder; and several times during the same evening, I observed between 30 and 40 discharges from one cloud to another, per minute.

† For an interesting discussion of the theory of the development of atmospheric electricity, the reader is referred to Delarive's *Treatise on Electricity*, Walker's translation, vol. iii. p. 116, *et seq.*

Becquerel's experiment was the following:—Having ascended Mount St. Bernard, he attached one end of an insulated gilt thread to the shaft of an arrow, and connected the other extremity with the cap of an electroscope by a running knot. The arrow was then discharged in a vertical direction by means of a bow; as it ascended, the leaves expanded gradually till they struck the sides of the glass. When the full length of the thread was attained, the upward motion of the arrow detached it altogether from the electroscope, leaving the instrument charged positively. On repeating the experiment, shooting the arrow horizontally, no charge at all was obtained. Similar results may be obtained on a clear day by ascending a lofty eminence or building, to avoid the induction of near objects, and taking a gold-leaf electroscope, terminating above in a ball. The electroscope being now in a neutral state, it will, if elevated only for a foot or two, diverge with positive electricity. On bringing it back to its original position, the leaves collapse, and on depressing it below this point, the leaves again separate with the opposite electricity.

Electricity developes itself in the atmosphere in other forms; thus luminous brushes, stars, and glows, have been frequently observed in stormy weather on the extremities of the masts and yard-arms of ships, on the points of weapons, and occasionally even on the tips of the fingers. These phenomena are, in fact, cases of brush discharge upon a large scale, and are in many instances attended with a roaring noise like that of a burning portfire. Appearances of this description formerly went by the name of *St. Elmo's fire;* our own sailors term them *comazants.*

(249) *Aurora Borealis.*—Another very beautiful meteor which is sometimes seen in this country in clear frosty nights, but which is observed very frequently in higher latitudes, has probably an electrical origin. This is the *aurora borealis.* It has been supposed to be occasioned by the passage of electricity through the rarefied portions of the upper regions of the atmosphere from the poles towards the equator, but the explanation is unsatisfactory, and not adequate to account for the effects observed. The varieties of coloured light exhibited by the aurora may, however, be imperfectly imitated on a small scale by discharging a continued or an intermittent supply of electricity through a vessel partially exhausted of air.

The forms which the aurora assumes are very varied, and of extraordinary beauty; there is, however, usually some general similarity in its aspect at the same locality. Commonly, streams of light are seen shooting upwards from the northern horizon. These streams are frequently observed to meet together in the zenith, and produce an appearance as if a vast tent were expanded in the heavens, glittering with gold, rubies, and sapphires.

A remarkable connexion has been observed between the aurora and the magnetism of the earth; the magnetic needle being very generally disturbed during a display of the aurora. The arches of the aurora most commonly traverse the sky at right angles to the magnetic meridian, though deviations from this direction are not rare. Sir J. Franklin found that the disturbance of the needle was not always proportionate to the agitation of the aurora, but was always greater when the quick motion and vivid light were observed to take place in a hazy atmosphere. The aurora is most frequent and vivid in high latitudes towards either pole, but the meteor is not confined to these parts, as Dr. Hooker states that one of the most brilliant displays he ever witnessed was under the tropical sky of India; and other observers have recorded instances of its appearance in the equatorial districts of the globe.

The altitude of the aurora varies considerably; there is no doubt, however, that it frequently occurs at small elevations. Both Franklin and Perry record examples of its appearing below the level of the clouds, which they describe as concealed behind the masses of its light, and as reappearing when the meteor vanished. There appear to be two distinct kinds of aurora, one dependent upon local causes, as in the cases last mentioned, while, in the other, the causes are probably cosmical, and the auroral effects are seen at very distant points of the earth's surface. (Sabine.)

§ III. Galvanic or Voltaic Electricity.

(250) *Galvani's Discovery.*—About the year 1790 Galvani made the observation that convulsive movements were produced in the limbs of a frog recently killed, if brought into contact with two dissimilar metals, such as zinc and copper, which were themselves in contact. The experiment may be readily repeated in the following manner:—Expose the crural nerve (N, fig. 195) of a recently killed frog, touch it with a strip of zinc, z, and at the same time touch the surface of the thigh, *m*, with one end of a bit of copper wire, c; the moment that the other end of the copper wire is made to touch the zinc, the limb is convulsed: but the convulsions cease when the two metals are separated from each other, though they are still in contact with the animal tissues. Each time that the zinc and copper are made to touch each other, the convulsion is renewed. A live flounder laid upon a pewter plate shows no particular sign of uneasiness; a silver spoon may also be laid upon its back without any apparent effect: but if the spoon be made to touch the pewter while it rests on the fish, the animal becomes strongly convulsed. If a piece of zinc and a shilling be placed one above and the other under the tongue, no particular sensation is perceived so long as the two metals are kept separate, but if the silver and the zinc be

Fig. 195.

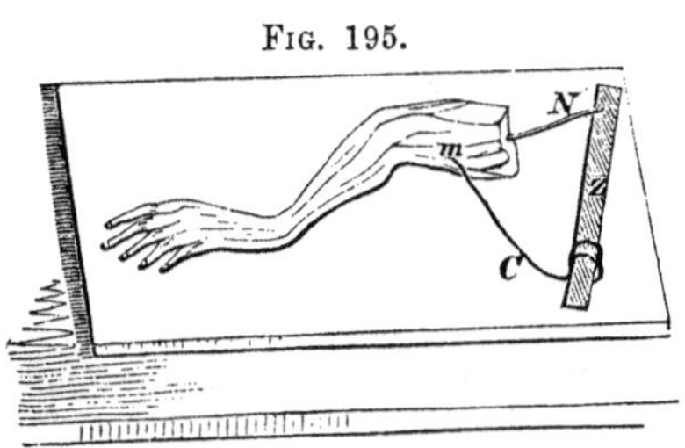

allowed to touch each other, a peculiar tingling sensation or taste is experienced; and if the silver be placed between the upper lip and the teeth instead of under the tongue, each time that the two metals are brought into contact, not only will a taste be perceived, but a momentary flash of light will appear to pass before the eye.

These phenomena are all analogous to each other, and have an electrical origin; and by tracing them to this source, a branch of electrical science has gradually been developed, which in honour of its first discoverer has been termed *galvanism*. The term galvanism, or *voltaic electricity*, as it is also called, in remembrance of the researches of Volta in this field, is applied to electricity which is set in motion by chemical action. It is usually developed by the contact of two dissimilar metals with a liquid.

(251) *Elementary Voltaic Circuits.*—These effects may be traced by very simple means. When a plate of zinc is immersed in diluted sulphuric acid, the metal becomes rapidly dissolved, and an extrication of hydrogen gas takes place, and the zinc becomes dissolved in the sulphuric acid. But if the surface of the zinc, after it has been cleansed by immersion in the acid, be rubbed over with mercury, a brilliant amalgam is speedily formed over the whole face of the zinc. Such a plate may then be plunged into the acid, and it will remain without undergoing any chemical change for hours. The cause of this inactivity of the zinc is not satisfactorily accounted for, but the fact is continually made use of in voltaic experiments. The addition of a second amalgamated zinc plate, whether it be in contact with the first, or be separated from it, produces no change. But if the second plate be of platinum, of copper, or of some metal which is less rapidly acted on by the acid than zinc is, although no action will occur whilst the two plates remain separate (as shown in fig. 196, 1),

FIG. 196.

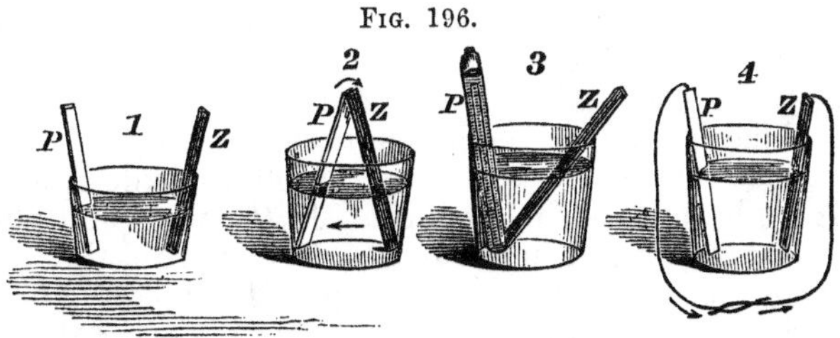

yet the moment that they are allowed to touch each other, either above (2) or beneath (3) the surface of the liquid, bubbles of gas will escape from the surface of the platinum. The platinum, however, is not acted upon chemically in this case; if the two metals be weighed before the experiment is commenced, and again after it is concluded, the weight of the platinum will be found to be unaltered; but the zinc will have been partially dissolved, and will weigh less than it did before. The gas may easily be collected by filling a tube with diluted acid, and, after introducing the platinum plate, inverting the tube in the glass, so that the lower edge of the platinum may touch the strip of zinc (No. 3). On examining the gas which rises in the tube it will be found to be pure hydrogen. It is not necessary that the two plates should directly touch each other. They may be connected by means of a metallic wire (as at 4, fig. 196), by a piece of graphite, or by any good conductor of electricity; gas will continue under these circumstances to rise from the platinum plate; but if a glass rod, a stick of shell-lac, a bit of gutta percha, or any electric insulator be made the medium of intercommunication, all signs of action will cease. The length of the metallic wire employed is comparatively unimportant; it may vary from a few inches to many miles, and in either case it will enable the action across the liquid to take place. A pair of plates of dissimilar metals in effectual communication, either by direct contact or through the medium of a wire, when immersed in a liquid which acts chemically upon one of them, constitutes a *voltaic circuit.*

(252) *Activity of the Conducting Wire.*—The wire or other medium of communication, during the time that it forms the connexion between the two metals, exhibits signs of activity which it did not before possess; it exerts a variety of influences upon surrounding bodies, and it loses these powers immediately that the contact with the metallic plates is broken. For instance, the temperature of the wire is for the time elevated. This may be proved by causing the wire to traverse the bulb of a delicate air thermometer, or by making a compound metallic ribbon, such as is used in Breguet's thermometer (140), part of the chain of communication between the plates. If a portion of the wire be sufficiently reduced in thickness, visible ignition of such portion may even be produced. Indeed the quantity of heat given out by the connecting wire may be employed as a measure of the amount of force which it is transmitting.

(253) *Action of the Conducting Wire on the Magnetic Needle.*—Another remarkable proof of the activity of the wire which connects the two metallic plates, is exhibited in the peculiar influence which it exerts over a magnetic needle freely suspended in a direction parallel to the wire. Such a needle tends to place itself at right angles to the wire. If the wire and the needle be previously arranged in the magnetic meridian, the amount of deviation in the needle affords a comparative measure of the force which is conveyed by the wire, as the needle ultimately assumes a position of equilibrium between the directive power of the earth's magnetism and that of the wire (252).

The movements of such a magnetic needle afford one of the most delicate tests of the development of galvanic electricity, or of electricity in motion. It will therefore be necessary to examine the direction and nature of these movements.

The direction of the needle under any circumstances may easily be calculated by recollecting the following rule:—*When the wire is placed in the magnetic meridian, with the end con-*

nected with the zinc plate towards the north, and the needle is placed below the wire, the marked end will deviate westward. When the needle is above the wire, the marked end will move towards the east. The first effect is shown in fig. 197, 1; the

Fig. 197.

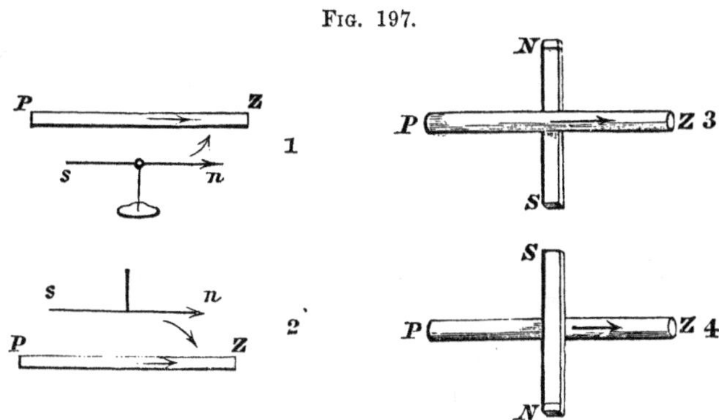

second in 2. On reversing the attachment of the wire to the plates, the phenomena will in each case be inverted. By means of a simple model, the direction of the needle under any conditions may be readily indicated:—Across a square strip of wood nail a cylindrical piece at right angles; let the square rod represent the magnetic needle, the round rod the connecting wire (fig. 197, 3 and 4), then mark upon the square rod the letters N and S, and on the round rod, P and Z, in conformity with the rule just given; by placing the model in any given position, the relative effect of the wire upon the needle under these circumstances will be shown.

Even the liquid part of a voltaic circuit acts thus upon the magnetic needle. This may be shown by suspending a needle, *n s*, fig. 198, by means of a fibre of silk, over a dish of diluted sulphuric acid. On one side of this dish a zinc plate, Z, is inserted, on the other, a plate of platinum, P. The needle must be placed so that one of its ends may point towards one plate, and the other end towards the other plate. If the two plates be now connected by a wire, as shown in the figure, the needle will be deflected, and will place itself nearly parallel to the metallic plates.

Fig. 198.

(254) *The Galvanometer.*—Since every part of the circuit acts equally upon the needle, and since it is possible to make several parts act simultaneously upon it, actions may be rendered perceptible which would otherwise be too weak to influence its motion. Fig. 199 will convey an idea of the principle upon which this is effected. Suppose the wire connecting the plates P and Z to be bent into a loop with parallel sides. If a magnetic needle be suspended

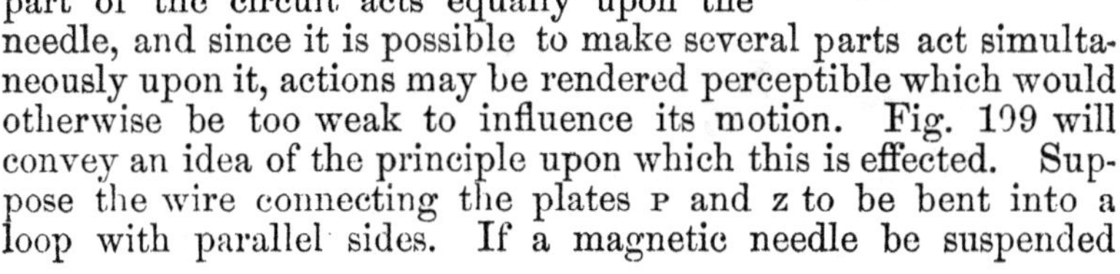

between the wires, and parallel to them, the loop and the needle being both in the magnetic meridian, with the end N pointing to the north, the marked end of the needle would be impelled westward under the influence of the force in the upper branch; and as the current returns in the reverse direction through the lower wire, this tendency of the north end westward would be doubled. By increasing the number of coils which are placed around the needle parallel to each other, very feeble actions may be rendered evident. An instrument constructed on this principle is termed a *galvanometer*.

Fig. 199.

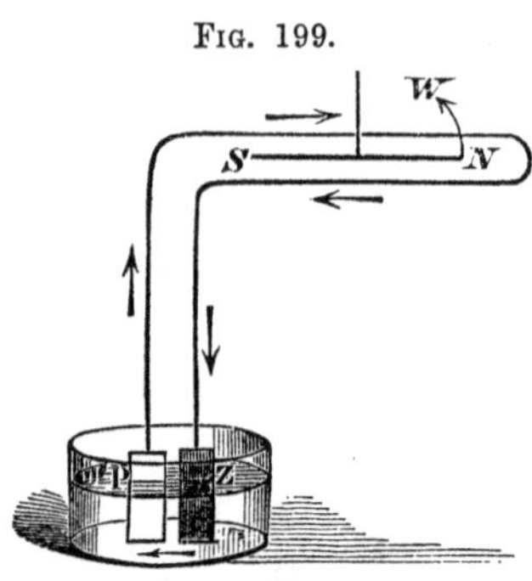

The sensibility of the galvanometer may, however, be still further increased by placing outside the coil a second magnetic needle with its poles reversed; the directive force of the earth may be thus almost exactly neutralized; its attractive power upon the north end of one needle being almost exactly counterbalanced by its repulsive action upon the south end of the needle which is parallel to it. A pair of needles thus arranged constitutes what is termed an *astatic* combination. A very feeble force will be sufficient to drive one particular extremity of such a pair of needles to the east or to the west; but the second needle being outside the coil, will be acted upon by the upper wires only, the lower ones being at too great a distance to produce any sensible effect. The action of the upper wires upon the needle above them coincides with their action upon the lower needle, with its reversed poles: and the effect of a feeble current is thus materially increased by these combined actions. The conducting wire must be covered with silk with a view to preserve each coil duly insulated from the contiguous ones.

The astatic galvanometer is represented in fig. 200. The needles, *n s*, *s n*, are suspended, one within and the other above the coil of wire, *w w*, by means of a fibre of silk, *d*, the whole being enclosed within the glass case, G. The parallelism of the two needles to each other is maintained under all circumstances, by causing each of them to pass transversely through the same piece of straw, or by connecting them together by means of a piece of fine copper wire; the fibre *d* is attached to the upper extremity of the straw or the wire. By means of a screw at *a*, the point of suspension of the silk can

Fig. 200.

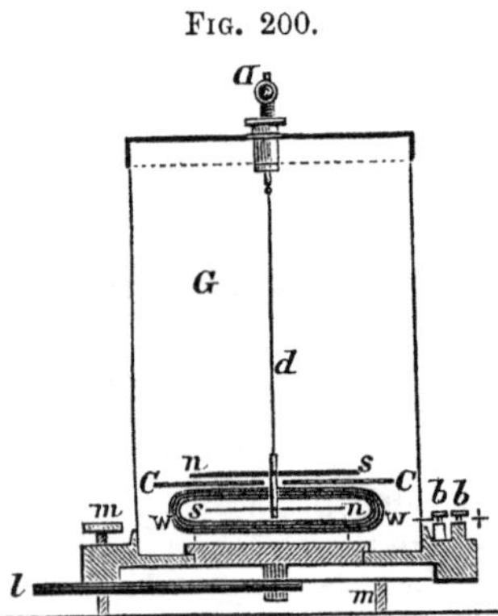

be raised or lowered without twisting it, so that when the needles are not in use their weight need not be supported by the silk fibre. C C, is a sheet of copper provided with a graduation on its margin for estimating the angular deviation of the needles; *b*, *b*, are binding-screws for connecting the extremities of the coil with the wires which transmit the current; * the apparatus can be levelled by means of the screws, *m*, *m*; and at *l*, a lever is shown by which the coil of wire *w*, can be placed accurately parallel with the magnetic needles, so as to make them coincide with the zero of the graduated circle. Such an instrument may be made not only to indicate the existence of voltaic action, but also to measure its amount. When the deviations of the needle are small, not exceeding 15° or 20°, the number of degrees of deviation gives nearly accurately the relative force; but for angles of greater magnitude, this is not the case, because the more the needle deviates from parallelism to the wire, the more obliquely and therefore the less powerfully does the force act which occasions its motion; and it becomes necessary to determine the value of the degrees by direct experiment. It would require a greater amount of power to move the needle from 20° to 25°, than from 20° to 15°: and a still greater to produce a deviation from 30° to 35°; but the force required in each case is definite, and consequently may be estimated and measured.†

* Instead of binding-screws, it is not uncommon to employ small cups containing mercury as the means of completing the metallic communication between the different parts of the circuit; the ends of the wires should be made perfectly bright before immersing them in the mercury. Copper wires may be easily amalgamated superficially by scouring them with fine emery-paper and moistening them with a solution of nitrate of mercury; the perfection of the contact is thus ensured.

† Melloni's method of graduating a galvanometer is the following, quoted by Tyndall, p. 355 of his work on *Heat considered as a Mode of Motion*:—Two small vessels, V, V, fig. 201, are half filled with mercury, and connected separately by two short wires, with the extremities, G, G, of the galvanometer. The vessels and wire thus disposed make no change in the action of the instrument, the thermo-electric current being freely transmitted as before from the pile to the galvanometer. But if, by means of a wire, F, a communication be established between the two vessels, part of the current will pass through this wire and return to the pile. The quantity of electricity circulating in the galvanometer will be thus diminished, and with it the deflection of the needle.

Fig. 201.

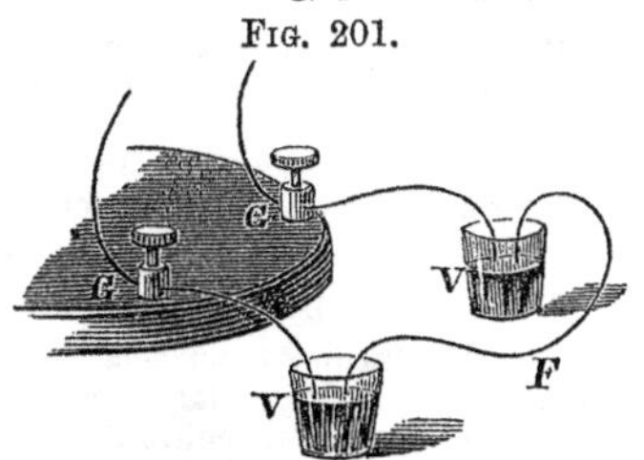

Suppose, then, that by this artifice we have reduced the galvanometric deviation to its fourth or fifth part—in other words, supposing that the needle being at 10 or 12 degrees under the action of a constant source of heat placed at a fixed distance from the pile, that it descends two or three degrees when a portion of the current is diverted by the external wire; I say that by causing the source to act from various distances, and observing in each case the total deflection and the reduced deflection, we have all the data necessary to determine the ratio of the deflections of the needle, to the forces which produce these deflections.

To render the exposition clearer, and to furnish at the same time an example of the mode of operation, I will take the number relating to the application of the method to one of my Thermo multipliers.

The external circuit being interrupted, and the source of heat being sufficiently distant from the pile, to give a deflection not exceeding 5 degrees of the galvanometer, let

(255) Allusion has already been made to the physiological action of the current, in consequence of which, if a living animal,

the wire be placed from v to v; the needle falls to 1°·5. The connexion between the two vessels being again interrupted, let the source be brought near enough to obtain successively the deflections:—

5°, 10°, 15°, 20°, 25°, 30°, 35°, 40°, 45°.

Interposing after each the same wire between v and v, we obtain the following numbers:—

1°·5, 3°, 4°·5, 6°·3, 8°·4, 11°·2, 15°·3, 22°·4, 29°·7.

Assuming the force necessary to cause the needle to describe each of the first degrees of the galvanometer to be equal to unity, we have the number 5 as the expression of the force corresponding to the first observation. The other forces are easily obtained by the proportions:—

$$1{\cdot}5 : 5 = a : x = \frac{5}{1{\cdot}5}\, a = 3{\cdot}333\, a$$

(that is to say, one reduced current is to the total current to which it corresponds, as any other reduced current is to its corresponding total current), where a represents the deflection when the exterior circuit is closed. We thus obtain—

5, 10, 15·2, 21, 28, 37·3,

for the forces corresponding to the deflections—

5°, 10°, 15°, 20°, 25°, 30°.

In this instrument, therefore, the forces are sensibly proportional to the arcs, up to nearly 15 degrees. Beyond this the proportionality ceases, and the divergence augments as the arcs increase in size.

The forces belonging to the intermediate degrees are obtained with great ease either by calculation or by graphical construction, which latter is sufficiently accurate for these determinations. By these means we find—

Degrees	13°	14°	15°	16°	17°	18°	19°	20°	21°
Forces	13	14·1	15·2	16·3	17·4	18·6	19·8	21	22·3
Differences	1·1	1·1	1·1	1·1	1·2	1·2	1·2	1·3	

Degrees	22°	23°	24°	25°	26°	27°	28°	29°	30°
Forces	23·5	24·9	26·4	28	29·7	31·5	33·4	35·3	37·3
Differences	1·4	1·5	1·6	1·7	1·8	1·9	1·9	2	

In this table we do not take into account any of the degrees preceding the 13th, because the force corresponding to each of them possesses the same value as the deflection.

The forces corresponding to the first 30 degrees being known, nothing is easier than to determine the values of the forces corresponding to 35, 40, 45 degrees and upwards.

The reduced deflections of these three arcs are—

15°·3, 22°·4, 29°·7.

Let us consider them separately, commencing with the first. In the first place, then, 15 degrees, according to our calculation, are equal to 15·2; we obtain the value of the decimal 0·3 by multiplying this fraction by the difference 1·1, which exists between the 15th and 16th degrees; for we have evidently the proportion—

$$1 : 1{\cdot}1 = 0{\cdot}3 : x = 0{\cdot}3.$$

The value of the reduced deflection corresponding to the 35th degree will not therefore be 15°·3, but 15°·2+0°·3=15·5. By similar considerations we find 23°·5+0°·6=24°·1 instead of 22°·4, and 36°·7 instead of 29°·7 for the reduced deflections of 40 and 45 degrees.

It now only remains to calculate the forces belonging to these three deflections—15°·5, 24°·1, and 36°·7—by means of the expression 3·333 a; this gives us—

The forces	51·7	80·3	122·3
For the degrees	35°	40°	45°

Comparing these numbers with those of the preceding table, we see that the sensitiveness of our galvanometer diminishes considerably when we use deflections greater than 30 degrees.

or a part of one recently killed, such as the limb of a frog, be included between a pair of plates, muscular contractions are produced; similar effects occur if a portion of the human body, such as the tip of the tongue, be included between two interrupted points of the conducting wire. But in addition to the heating, magnetic, and physiological effects, another remarkable series of phenomena, those of chemical decomposition, may be exhibited at the interrupted points of the conducting wire. These, however, are more distinctly shown when a number of pairs of plates is employed.

(256) *The Voltaic Pile.*—In prosecuting the experiments of Galvani, Volta discovered that by using a number of similar metallic pairs moistened by a saline or by a feebly acid liquid, many of the effects already described were greatly increased, and in the year 1800 he published a description of the apparatus which he had contrived, and which has perpetuated the name of its inventor under the designation of the *Voltaic Pile.* This important instrument is represented in fig. 202. It consists of a succession of pairs of plates of two dissimilar metals, such as zinc, Z, and copper, C, or zinc and silver, each pair being separated on either side from the adjacent pairs by pieces of card or flannel, F, moistened with salt and water, or with very weak acid: these plates may be supported by a frame of dry wood. The effects produced by such an apparatus were soon seen to be of an electrical character. If the ends of the pile or the wires connected with them were touched, one with each hand previously moistened, a sensation similar to that of the electric shock was experienced. Sparks could be obtained between two pieces of charcoal attached to the ends of the wires; divergence of the gold leaves of the electroscope was produced when one wire touched the cap of the instrument, whilst the other wire was in communication with the earth; and other electrical effects were obtained. In arranging the plates of metal it is necessary strictly to observe a certain order in their succession; thus, if a plate of zinc with a wire attached to it form the bottom of the pile, a piece of wet flannel must be placed upon it, then a piece of copper, then a piece of zinc, then flannel, then copper, then zinc, then flannel, and so on, till the pile terminates at the top with a plate of copper to which a wire is attached. By soldering together the zinc and copper in pairs, a considerable improvement is effected; complete contact of the two metals is insured, and the apparatus can be mounted with more rapidity. Many practical inconveniences, however, are experienced when the instrument is mounted in the form of a pile: the liquid in the flannel soon loses the power of

Fig. 202.

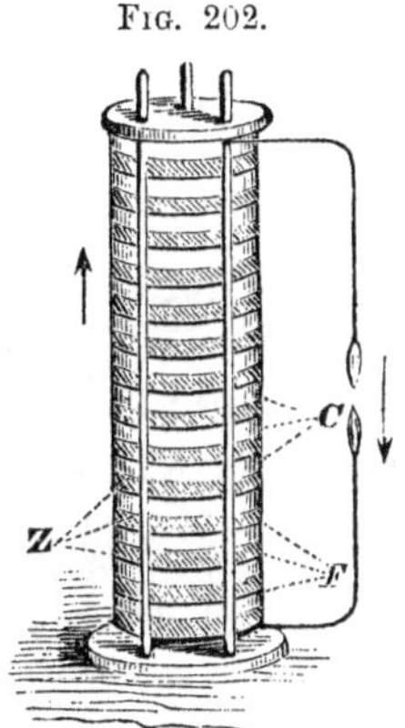

acting chemically on the zinc, and the activity of the combination rapidly declines.

Another more effectual arrangement adopted by Volta is shown in fig. 203; he termed it the *Crown of Cups*. In this

Fig. 203.

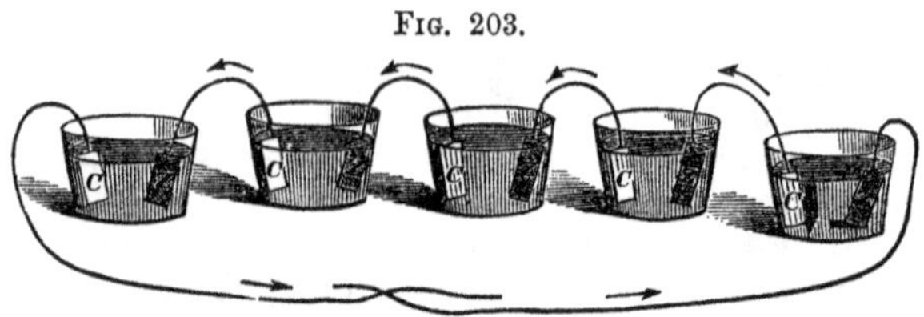

form, the liquid in the cell corresponds to the moist flannel of the pile, and the zinc of one cell being connected with the copper of the *adjacent* cell, the arrangement corresponds exactly with that of the pile, where the zinc is on one side of the flannel, whilst the copper in contact with the other surface of the flannel communicates with the zinc touching the flannel next above it, and so on. Other more efficient forms of the voltaic battery will be described further on.

The Conditions required to produce Voltaic Action.

(257) *Electric Disturbance by Contact of Dissimilar Metals.*—Having in the foregoing remarks traced the voltaic phenomena to a modification of electricity, we may now proceed to examine more particularly the conditions under which they occur.

It was early observed by Volta that when two different metals, properly insulated, are brought into contact, and then separated by means of insulating handles, each plate exhibits signs of electricity which may be detected by a sensitive electroscope such as Bohnenberger's (*note* § 298). The more oxidizable metal is found to be positive, while the less oxidizable metal is negative. If zinc filings be sifted through a piece of insulated copper-wire gauze upon the cap of a gold leaf electroscope, the leaves of the instrument will diverge. On approaching the electroscope with an excited stick of sealing-wax the leaves will collapse, thus proving that the zinc filings have acquired positive electricity. If copper filings be sifted through zinc gauze, the filings will be found to be negative. The various metals may, with reference to these electric actions, be arranged in a series in which those first in order become positive by contact with all those that follow, and negative with all those that precede: for example, potassium, zinc, iron, lead, tin, copper, mercury, silver, gold, platinum. This, it may be observed, is merely the order of the oxidability of the different metals, and Delarive contends with great probability that the development of electricity in Volta's experiment is due to an excessively minute oxidation produced by the moisture of the air upon the plate which becomes positive, though the experiments by which he attempts to prove the point are not absolutely conclusive.

Volta regarded the interposed liquid of his pile in the light merely of an imperfect conductor which allowed induction to take place through it, the electrical equilibrium being perpetually disturbed by the contact of the two metals; and he overlooked the chemical changes which the liquid is continually undergoing.

(258) *Chemical Action essential to the Production of Voltaic Action.*—It is now known that chemical changes are essential to the production of the force. Contact of dissimilar substances, it is true, is necessary to the voltaic action; because without contact there can be no chemical action. Such contact produces disturbance of the electric equilibrium in the bodies which are brought together, and thus occasions a state of tension or polarity which always precedes the discharge. Chemical action, by renewing these contacts and by furnishing appropriate conductors to the electricity thus accumulated, maintains the action and accurately measures its amount; and until chemical action occurs no current is produced. The following experiment may be cited in illustration of this point:—Let an iron wire be connected with one extremity of a galvanometer of moderate sensibility, and a platinum wire with the other extremity; immerse the ends of the wires in highly concentrated nitric acid (sp. gr. about 1·45), without allowing them to touch each other in the liquid; no chemical action will occur upon the iron, and no movement of the magnetic needle will be produced; but the addition of a little water will determine a rapid solution of the iron in the acid, and the needle, at the same moment that the chemical action commences, will receive a powerful impulse.

(259) *Polarization and Transfer of the Elements of the Liquid.*—The simple occurrence of a powerful chemical action is not alone sufficient to produce a powerful voltaic effect. The metals are all excellent conductors of electricity, and, in combining with each other to form alloys, they often give evidence of intense chemical action, but they do not produce any adequate voltaic effect. For example, if a small quantity of tin be placed in a tube bent into the form of the letter U, and be melted by the heat of a spirit-lamp, and it be connected on one side with the wire of a galvanometer, which is introduced into the melted metal in one limb of the tube, whilst into the second limb of the tube a platinum wire, connected with the other extremity of the galvanometer, is plunged, the platinum will unite with the tin with incandescence, but after the first moment of contact but a slight deviation of the magnetic needle will be observed, although a brisk chemical action is continued for several seconds. A solution of the elementary bodies, chlorine or bromine, when used as the liquid between the plates, although it acts powerfully on the zinc, produces by no means a proportionate power in the circuit.

In order that the liquid shall possess any marked power of exciting voltaic action, it must be a compound susceptible of decomposition by one of the metals, such, for instance, as dilute sulphuric, hydrochloric, or hydriodic acid, or a saline substance, such as chloride of sodium or iodide of potassium. This necessity for the employment of a compound liquid for exciting the force, appears to rise from the necessity of a peculiar polarization in the liquid in order to enable it to transmit the voltaic action. Indeed, in all voltaic actions the transfer of power is effected by a polar influence, propagated through both the solid and the liquid particles of the circuit, and the chain of conducting material must be continuous throughout, so that the force shall *circulate.*

This process of polarization may be conceived to occur in the following manner, which offers an explanation of the mode in which the platinum (or the plate of metal which corresponds to platinum) may be supposed to act:—When a plate of pure zinc or of amalgamated zinc is immersed in a compound liquid, which, like a solution of hydrochloric acid (HCl), is capable of attacking it chemically, the metal at the points of contact becomes positively electrified, whilst the distant portion becomes negative. The layer of liquid in contact with the zinc undergoes polarization, which affects each molecule of its chemical constituents; the particles (C) of chlorine become negative, and the particles of hydrogen (H) positive: but in this form of the experiment there is no communication between the distant negative part of the zinc and the positively electrified particles of hydrogen; consequently, beyond the production of this state of electric tension, no change ensues. This condition is represented in fig. 204 (1). But

FIG. 204.

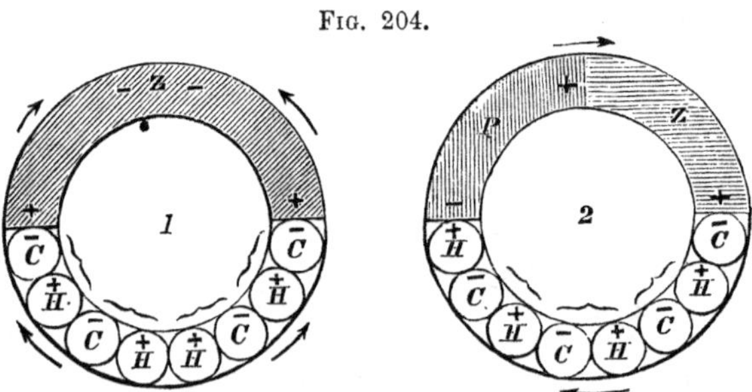

the case is entirely altered if a plate of platinum, or of some other metal which is not easily acted upon by the acid, be introduced, and made to touch the zinc. By contact with the zinc the platinum itself becomes polarized; it imparts a certain amount of positive electricity to the zinc, and receives a portion of negative in return, and transmits the polar action to the liquid. A chain of polarized particles is thus produced, as represented in fig. 204 (2); the chlorine of the particle of HCl nearest the zinc becomes negative under the influence of the chemical attraction which exists between it and the zinc, and the hydrogen becomes positive; the second and third particles of HCl become similarly electrified by induction; but the platinum, under the influence of the induction of the zinc, being negative, is in a condition to take up the positive electricity of the contiguous hydrogen. The action now rises high enough to enable the zinc and the chlorine to combine chemically with each other; the chloride of zinc thus produced is dissolved by the liquid, and is removed from further immediate action; but the particle of hydrogen nearest the zinc now seizes the oppositely electrified chlorine which lies next to it, and a new portion of hydrochloric acid is reproduced, whilst the hydrogen in the second particle of the acid is transferred to the chlorine of the adjacent particle, and the particle of hydrogen which terminates the row is electrically neutralized by its action upon the platinum, to which it imparts its excess of positive electricity, and immediately escapes in the form of gas. Fresh particles of hydrochloric acid continually supply the place of those which have undergone decomposition, and in this way a continuous action is maintained. Thus the transfer of electricity from particle to particle of the liquid is attended at the same instant by a transfer of the constituents of the liquid in opposite directions.

These changes are not successive, but are simultaneous in each vertical section of the liquid, and are also attended with corresponding changes at all points of the entire circuit. These changes when continued uninterruptedly constitute what is conveniently termed a *voltaic current*. This term, 'current,' is in general use, but it should be borne in mind that it is in this sense employed merely to signify the continuous transmission of force, not of any material substance. In every voltaic current it is assumed that a quantity of negative electricity, equal in amount to that of the positive set in motion, is proceeding along the wire in a direction opposed to that in which the positive electricity is travelling; and it is conceived that by the perpetual separation and recombination of the two electricities in the wire, its heating and other effects are produced. In order to avoid confusion, however, whenever the *direction* of the voltaic current is referred to, the direction of the positive current alone is indicated.

Fig. 205.

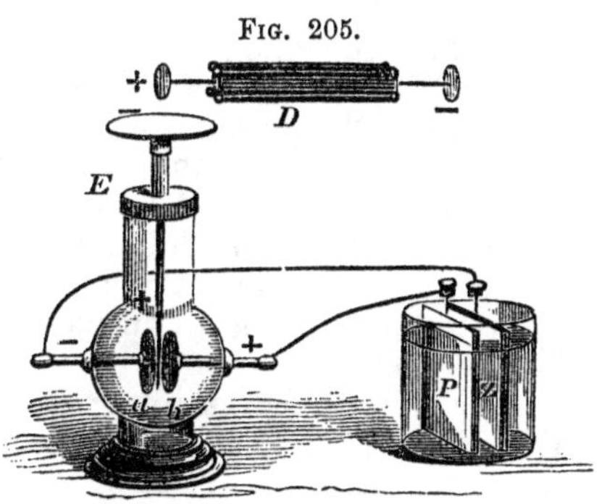

The polarization of the metallic and liquid particles composing a circuit when zinc is placed in an acid, or, in other words the occurrence of electric tension as a preliminary to the passage of the voltaic current, may be shown by the following experiment (Gassiot). A plate of platinum, P, fig. 205, and another of amalgamated zinc, Z, are immersed in dilute sulphuric acid, and the wire which proceeds from each is insulated and connected with the two gilt disks, *a*, *b*, of the electroscope, E;

these disks are insulated from each other, and from the ground by the glass of the apparatus; they slide easily to and fro in the sockets, and can be brought within a quarter of an inch or less of each other; a single gold leaf, mounted as in the ordinary electroscope, is suspended midway between them: now if the positive end of a Deluc's pile (298), D, be brought near the cap of the instrument, the gold leaf will approach the disk *a*, which is connected with the zinc plate; the leaf becomes positive by induction from the positive end of the pile, and is therefore attracted by the negatively electrified disk *a;* but if the opposite end of the pile D, which is charged with negative electricity, be presented, the gold leaf becomes negative, and is attracted by the positively electrified disk *b*, which is in connexion with the platinum plate. The amount of the electric tension increases in proportion as the number of pairs is increased. Gassiot found with a battery of 400 pairs of Grove's cells, each cell being carefully insulated, that a succession of sparks passed between the terminals when brought very near to each other; and if each end of the battery was connected with a gold-leaf electroscope, the leaves of each diverged powerfully, the wire in connexion with the platinum plate furnishing positive, that with the zinc plate, negative electricity. (299.)

(260) *Energy of the Current proportionate to the Chemical Activity.*—In order to produce a current, the two metals which are employed must be acted upon by the exciting liquid with different degrees of rapidity: thus, when two similar slips of zinc, or of any other metal, are opposed to each other, no current is excited. The galvanic action is strongest between two metals upon which the chemical action of the components of the exciting liquid differs most widely; for, from what has been already stated, it is evident that two strips of zinc would tend to produce polarization, and subsequently currents of equal intensity, in opposite directions, so that the two would necessarily neutralize each other. When zinc is opposed to tin, a current is produced, setting out through the liquid from the zinc to the tin; zinc and copper give rise to a stronger current in the same direction; whilst between zinc and platinum the current is still more powerful; and between potassium and platinum the action attains its maximum. By forming an amalgam of potassium, this last-mentioned experiment admits of easy performance; for it has been found that the voltaic relations of all amalgams are the same as those of the more oxidable metal which they contain. A good deal of the potassium is oxidized by what is termed *local* action, without contributing in any way to the production of the current. The distinction between local action and action which contributes to the voltaic effect is important, and may be illustrated by the difference in action of diluted sulphuric acid upon a slip of ordinary zinc and upon a slip of zinc from the same sheet which has been amalgamated: in the first case rapid solution of the metal will occur, although the connexion with the platinum plate may remain incomplete; in the second, the zinc will be attacked only

when the circuit is completed; but the unamalgamated zinc will produce no greater voltaic effect than an equal slip of the metal which has been properly amalgamated. In no instance is the force in circulation increased by the local action on the plates, whatever be the nature of the metal.

Wheatstone has devised a method (274) of measuring the amount of the *electro-motive force*, or energy of the voltaic power, produced by any combination; and he has by this means proved conclusively that this energy depends upon the intensity of the chemical action between the elements of the liquid and the metals which compose the circuit. He has shown that if any three of these dissimilar metals be taken in their electrical order and be formed in pairs into separate circuits, the force generated by a combination of the two extreme metals of the series is equal to the sum of the forces developed when the intermediate metal is separately combined with each of the other two in succession. For example, the voltaic energy, or electro-motive force, excited between platinum and an amalgam of potassium may be represented by the number 69: the electro-motive force between platinum and zinc, expressed in terms of a similar standard, is equal to 40; and in a similar experiment between zinc and potassium, where zinc acted the part of a negative metal towards the potassium, the number obtained was 29. Now

the amount of force between platinum and zinc	=	40
the amount of force between zinc and potassium	=	29
the two taken together	=	69

and this number, 69, is identical with that obtained by opposing platinum to the amalgam of potassium.

(261) *Direction of the Current dependent on the Direction of the Chemical Action.*—In all these cases the positive electricity sets out from the more oxidizable metal, which may be termed the positive, or generating plate, and traverses the liquid towards the less oxidizable metal which forms the negative or conducting plate: from the conducting plate the force is transferred to the wire, and thence in turn to the generating plate; and in this way the circuit is completed. Unless this circulation can take place, all the phenomena of voltaic action are suspended. Since the chemical action of any combination is thus always in one uniform direction, the motion of a magnetic needle under its influence is equally uniform: the amount of force which is thrown into circulation, whether it be measured by its magnetic or by its heating effects, is proportioned to the quantity of the positive metal which is dissolved in a given time.

Every liquid which is active in exciting a voltaic current may be regarded as consisting of two groups of substances, one of which attacks the generating or positive plate, and may be termed the electro-negative constituent of the liquid, whilst the other is transferred to the conducting or negative plate, and constitutes the electro-positive constituent.

The elementary bodies have indeed been classified upon this principle into electro-positive and electro-negative substances;

Electro-chemical Order of the Principal Elements.

Electro-negative.	
Oxygen	Gold
Sulphur	Platinum
Selenium	Palladium
Nitrogen	Mercury
Fluorine	Silver
Chlorine	Copper
Bromine	Bismuth
Iodine	Tin
Phosphorus	Lead
Arsenicum	Cadmium
Chromium	Cobalt
Vanadium	Nickel
Molybdenum	Iron
Tungsten	Zinc
Boron	Manganese
Carbon	Uranium
Antimony	Aluminum
Tellurium	Magnesium
Titanium	Calcium
Silicon	Strontium
Hydrogen.	Barium
	Lithium
	Sodium
	Potassium.
	Electro-positive.

hydrogen and most of the metals being electro-positive; oxygen, chlorine, and other substances of this nature being electro-negative. In the preceding table the more important of the elements are arranged in the electro-chemical order on the authority of Berzelius. It has been remarked that the more strongly electro-positive metals crystallize in forms belonging to the regular system, whilst the non-metallic elements, and those metals which are most electro-negative, crystallize generally in other forms.

It is probable that the order here followed is not exactly correct. Fluorine, and chlorine perhaps, ought to stand at the head of the list; there is no doubt that hydrogen should stand much nearer to potassium; and according to late experiments aluminum should take its place between lead and cadmium. It is also certain that the elements do not under all circumstances maintain the same relative order, but that in particular cases the order is altered: for example, in strong nitric acid, iron is nearly as electro-negative as platinum; again, a metal may be electro-positive when it forms the basyl of a salt, but electro-negative when associated with the elements of the acid constituent. Indeed it may be laid down as an invariable rule that whenever the chemical action is inverted the direction of the current is inverted also.

The voltaic order of the metals given above is that which is observed when diluted acids are used as the exciting liquids, but it by no means represents the order in which they stand when the current is excited by the use of a caustic alkaline solution or a sulphide of the alkaline metals. This point is well exemplified in the following results given by Faraday (*Phil. Trans.*, 1840, p. 113). The metals which stand first on each list are negative to all those which follow them. The place of iron in the strong nitric acid is that which it shows immediately on immersion; it becomes much more powerfully electro-negative afterwards:—

Dilute Sulphuric Acid.	Dilute Nitric Acid.	Dilute Hydrochloric Acid.	Nitric Acid Sp. Gr. 1·48.	Solution of Caustic Potash.	Yellow Sulphide of Potassium.
Silver	Silver	Antimony	Nickel	Silver	Iron
Copper	Copper	Silver	Silver	Nickel	Nickel
Antimony	Antimony	Nickel	Antimony	Copper	Bismuth
Bismuth	Bismuth	Bismuth	Copper	Iron	Antimony
Nickel	Nickel	Copper	Bismuth	Bismuth	Lead
Iron	Iron	Iron	Iron	Lead	Silver
Lead	Lead	Lead	Tin	Antimony	Tin
Tin	Tin	Tin	Lead	Cadmium	Cadmium
Cadmium	Cadmium	Cadmium	Zinc	Tin	Copper
Zinc	Zinc	Zinc	Cadmium	Zinc	Zinc

The relative size of the generating and conducting plates has no influence upon the direction of the current, which sets in as certainly through the liquid from a square inch of zinc to a square foot of copper as from a square foot of zinc to a square inch of copper. The spread of this force may be traced in an interesting manner by substituting a solution of sulphate of copper for sulphuric acid as a part of the exciting liquid; copper will be thrown down instead of hydrogen, and by its colour and thickness will very accurately indicate the extent and direction of the action. The experiment is easily made by taking advantage of a property possessed by porous diaphragms, in consequence of which, a piece of any animal membrane, or of unglazed earthenware, which can be thoroughly wetted by the liquids, will allow the current to traverse it without opposing any material obstruction to its passage. Diluted sulphuric acid may thus be employed upon one side of the diaphragm, and a solution of sulphate of copper upon the other side: under these circumstances a current would be freely transmitted, whilst the two liquids would be prevented from intermingling. For example, let a piece of bladder, *b*, fig. 206, be tied firmly over the lower end of a wide tube open at both extremities; place some diluted sulphuric acid, A, in the tube, and suspend a rod of amalgamated zinc, Z, in its axis; support the tube so that its lower end shall dip beneath the surface of a solution of sulphate of copper, S, contained

Fig. 206.

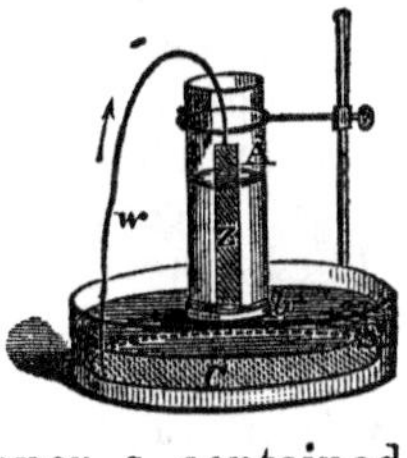

in a shallow glass dish, upon the bottom of which rests a sheet of copper, c: on connecting the zinc and copper by the wire, *w*, voltaic action will ensue, and a deposit of metallic copper will be produced upon the plate, c. It will, however, be observed that this deposit does not take place uniformly over the surface of the sheet c, but that it commences in the centre in a circular form; the layer of copper shows itself first at the point immediately beneath the extremity of the zinc rod, and it is at this point that the greatest thickness of the deposit occurs; it gradually becomes thinner towards the circumference of the circle, which, however, continues to increase in diameter as the experiment proceeds, until, if sufficient time be allowed, the plate is covered with reduced copper.

Whilst a metal is thus rendered electro-negative by voltaic action, it is no longer liable to the ordinary action of chemical agents. A beautiful application of this principle was made by Davy to the prevention of the corrosion of the copper sheathing of ships by the action of sea water. Copper is the material best adapted to preserve the timbers of the ship from the attacks of marine insects and boring animals; but this metal, when subjected, under ordinary circumstances, to the combined influence of the salts dissolved in sea water and of the atmospheric air which it also holds in solution, experiences corrosion, which in the course of a few years renders it necessary to renew the copper. It was, however, discovered by Davy, that by placing pieces of zinc, or of cast-iron, in contact with the copper under water, this corrosion could be prevented; and that a surface of zinc, not exceeding $\frac{1}{150}$ of that exposed by the copper, was adequate to the entire protection of the copper, the whole of the chemical action being transferred to the zinc; and that even when the surface of zinc was reduced until it was only equal to $\frac{1}{1000}$ of that of the copper, a considerable preservative effect was experienced. But the very success of the experiment in the direction anticipated, created difficulties of another kind; earthy matters, consisting of compounds of calcium and magnesium, were deposited from the sea water by the slow voltaic action, and they attached themselves to the surface of the copper; weeds and shell-fish found in this deposit a congenial pabulum, the bottom of the ship became foul, the sailing qualities of the vessel were necessarily impaired, and the system of voltaic protectors was abandoned. For some years past a kind of brass, introduced by Mr. Muntz, which admits of being rolled whilst hot, has, in the merchant service, been largely and advantageously substituted for copper as a material for ships' sheathing. In this case the zinc and the copper are combined in the sheet itself, which is less rapidly corroded than if composed of either metal separately. The protective influence of zinc both on copper and on iron is readily shown by exposing bright bars of these metals in separate vessels, either in sea water or in a solution of common salt containing an ounce of salt in each pint of water. If a fragment of zinc be attached to one of the bars of copper and to one of the bars of iron, these bars will remain bright, whilst the zinc is corroded; but the unprotected bars will, in a few hours, give evidence of the commencement of chemical action.

Another remarkable proof of the dependence of the current, for its direction and its force, upon chemical action, is afforded by the manner in which a voltaic circuit may be produced between two surfaces, one of which has a stronger attraction for *hydrogen* than the other possesses. For example, when two clean plates of platinum are immersed in diluted acid, and connected with a galvanometer, no voltaic action is excited; but the case is different if one of these plates be first coated with a film of some metallic peroxide, such as peroxide of manganese (MnO_2), proxide of lead (PbO_2), or peroxide of silver (Ag_2O_2). The platinum plate may be thus coated by immersing it in a solution of sulphate of manganese, of nitrate of lead, or of nitrate of silver, and connecting it with the platinum side of a weak voltaic arrangement for a few minutes, whilst the liquid is connected by a second plate with the zinc end of the battery: the plate, after it has been thus coated with the oxide, must be well washed with distilled water. If it be then opposed to a plate of clean platinum, and immersed in any diluted acid, it will originate a current which depends upon the chemical attraction of the hydrogen of the diluted acid for the second atom of oxygen in the peroxide. In a combination of this description the clean platinum becomes positive, and corresponds to the zinc plate, whilst the coated platinum becomes negative. The coated plate, although negative, thus becomes the generating or active surface, and transmits the current at once to the conducting wire.

Faraday has shown that the direct contact of dissimilar metals is not necessary to the production of the voltaic current, provided that they are connected by some liquid of sufficient conducting power. This is a point of considerable importance, as it shows that Volta's theory of the origin of the force, which is still maintained by many philosophers who have not made the chemical phenomena of the pile their especial study, is deficient in accuracy. The following is the simple experiment, which proves the point now under discussion: Z, fig. 207, is a plate of zinc, bent at a right angle; P, a platinum plate, to which a platinum wire is attached. At *a*, a small piece of blotting paper, moistened with a solution of starch and iodide of potassium, is interposed between the plate of zinc by which it is supported and the platinum wire which rests upon it; no change occurs in the solution of the iodide until the two plates are immersed in diluted nitric acid; but in a few minutes after such immersion, evidence of a current in the direction of the arrow is afforded, by the appearance of a blue spot against the platinum wire, due to the liberation of iodine, from the decomposition of the iodide of potassium by the voltaic action.

Fig. 207.

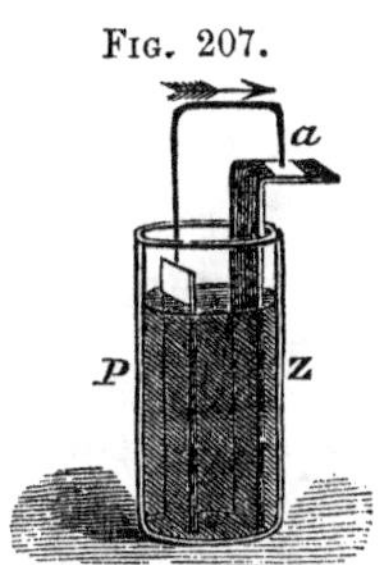

(262) *Circuits with one Metal and two Liquids.*—For the establishment of a voltaic current, it is further necessary that the body which decomposes the liquid be a conductor of electricity, in order to carry off the force generated; but it is not necessary to use two dissimilar metals, provided that one extremity of the metal be plunged into a liquid capable of acting on it, whilst the other extremity dips into a different liquid which has little or no action on the metal, but which communicates freely with the first liquid.

Take, for example, a tube bent into the form represented in fig. 208, 1. Place a plug of tow in the bend; into one limb, *a*,

FIG. 208.

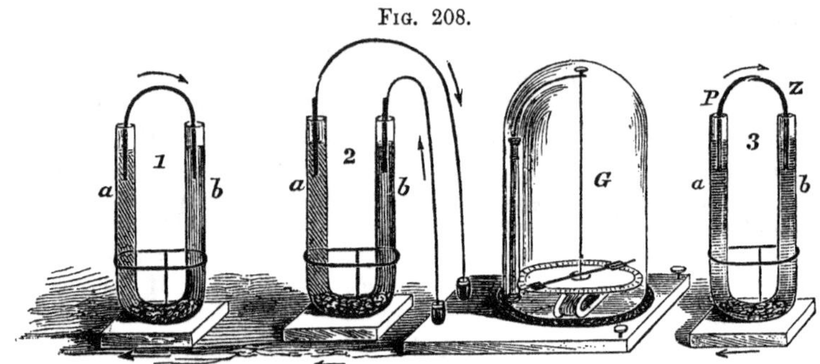

pour a solution of chloride of copper ($Cu\ Cl_2$), in the other limb, *b*, place a solution of common salt ($Na\ Cl$) (chloride of sodium). Connect the open ends of the tube by bending a strip of copper so that one end of it shall dip into the solution of copper and the other end into the solution of salt. Crystals of copper will be formed gradually upon the end of the strip which is immersed in the metallic solution, whilst the end of the strip which is immersed in the salt and water will be slowly corroded, and chloride of copper will be formed. The following diagram may assist in explaining this change:—

A

$$(1.)\quad Cu \mid CuCl_2\,CuCl_2 \mid Na_2Cl_2\,Na_2Cl_2 \mid Cu$$

$$(2.)\quad Cu\,Cu \mid Cl_2\,Cu,Cl_2 \mid Na_2Cl_2\,Na_2Cl_2\,Cu \mid$$

Let the symbol $Cu\ Cl_2$ represent the combination of chloride of copper, Na_2Cl_2 that of chloride of sodium, the line at A being used to show the position of the plug of tow. If No. 1 indicate the state of things before any change has occurred, No. 2 will represent the change after the circuit is complete.

If the strip of copper be divided in the middle, and the two ends be connected with a galvanometer, G, as shown in fig. 208, 2, a current is found to be circulating through the apparatus. A still simpler arrangement may be adopted; if a long straight tube be filled half full with diluted sulphuric acid, and the remainder with a solution of sulphate of copper, a strip of copper plunged into it will be dissolved below, while an equal amount of copper will be deposited on the upper extremity; from the extreme slowness and regularity of the action, the metal will assume the form of crystals. Becquerel, by using various liquids in the two limbs of the bent tube (No. 1) has obtained many of the metals crystallized in forms of great beauty.

By employing two dissimilar metals in the metallic arc, as P Z, (fig. 208, 3), a more powerful but equally regular action may be excited. If a solution of common salt be placed in one limb, *b*, and a solution of green chloride of iron in the other, *a*, whilst the zinc end of a compound arc of zinc and platinum is plunged into the first, and the strip of platinum is immersed in the second liquid, tetrahedral crystals of iron will in a few days be deposited upon the platinum. If a little chloride of iron be mixed with chloride of zirconium, and substituted for the chloride of iron in the limb *a*, plates of zirconium will be obtained, of a steel-gray colour, and which, by exposure to the air, become oxidized and fall to a white powder.

Becquerel has shown, that within the strata of the earth similar actions are going on; and R. W. Fox and others, by connecting the surfaces of two contiguous lodes of metallic ore by means of wires attached to a galvanometer, have succeeded in demonstrating to the eye the existence of these feeble but continuous currents which are probably the cause of the accumulation of the different metals in regular beds, and of their beautiful crystalline arrangement.

Other combinations may be produced, in which the mutual action of the two liquids originates the current, the metal merely serving as a conductor. Becquerel was the first to point out the means of obtaining circuits of this description, of which the following is a good example:—If a small porous vessel be filled with nitric acid, and be immersed in a second vessel containing a solution of hydrate of potash, on plunging two platinum plates connected with the wires of a galvanometer, one into the acid, the other into the alkaline liquid, a steady current of considerable intensity will be produced, and will be maintained for many days, in a direction passing from the potash to the nitric acid, and thence returning through the galvanometer to the alkaline liquid. A still more powerful combination was obtained by Matteucci on substituting a solution of pentasulphide of potassium for the caustic potash. A single cell of this construction decomposed acidulated water if interposed between the platinum wires, and on breaking contact a distinct spark was perceptible at the surface of the mercury employed to connect the two platinum wires. Arrott (*Phil. Mag.* xxii. 427) has described a variety of other cases of this kind. These actions, however, will be more conveniently studied in connexion with the chemical effects of the voltaic battery at a future point (289).

(263) *Summary.*—The conditions necessary to the production of a voltaic current may be shortly recapitulated as follows:—

Though the contact of dissimilar metals produces electric disturbance, chemical action is necessary to propagate the voltaic current. This chemical action must be produced by means of a compound liquid, which is decomposed in the process, one of the constituents of the liquid entering into combination with one of the metals. In the transmission of the voltaic power, a polarization of the liquid, as well as of the solid portions of the circuit, is produced, and this polarization of the liquid is attended with the separation of its constituents into two groups, one of which unites with the positive metal, whilst the other makes its appearance at the same moment upon the negative plate. The activity of the combination, or its electro-motive force, is greater, the greater the difference between the chemical attraction of the electro-negative constituent of the exciting liquid for the two metals which are opposed to each other in the particular case. The relative size of the plates employed has no influence on the direction of the current which is produced. Contact of two metals is not necessary to the production of voltaic action: circuits may be formed between one metal and two liquids, if the liquids be in liquid communication with each other, and if their chemical attractions for the metal be unequal. It is even possible to obtain a current from the mutual action of two dissimilar liquids, if these liquids exert a chemical action upon each other, by connecting the liquids through the intervention of a metal upon which they exert no chemical influence, and which therefore simply performs the part of a conductor.

Different forms of the Voltaic Battery.

(264) *Counteracting Currents: Gas Battery.*—We shall now resume the consideration of those forms of voltaic combination which are the most important in practice, and in which, generally, two dissimilar metals are employed.

It has been already stated that the amount of force set in motion in a voltaic arrangement, depends upon the difference between the attraction of the two metals for the active principle or *radicle* of the acid. Under circumstances favourable to the production of a current, decomposition of the liquid which excites the action always occurs; the elements of the liquid are separated from each other, and they either combine with the metallic plate, or else they accumulate upon its surface, giving rise to the condition of the plates which is often described under the inappropriate term *polarization* of the plates or electrodes. These adhering substances oppose the voltaic action and enfeeble it, owing to the tendency of the separated components of the liquid to re-unite. When, for example, diluted sulphuric acid is used, it becomes a desideratum to get rid of the hydrogen which adheres to the platinum, and produces a current in the opposite direction. The existence of this counter-current may be rendered evident by connecting with one end of the wire of a galvanometer a platinum plate which has been thus opposed to a plate of zinc: on attaching to the other end of the galvanometer wire a second, but clean platinum plate, and plunging both into diluted acid, a powerful deflection of the needle will be observed.

This observation has been ingeniously applied by Grove, who has constructed what he terms a *gas battery*, by opposing a plate covered with oxygen to the plate coated with hydrogen, whilst at the same time he increases the surfaces of contact between the platinum and the oxygen and hydrogen. Fig. 209 represents a cell of this battery. It consists of two tubes O and H; through the upper extremity of each passes a platinum wire, which is fused into the glass, and attached to a platinum plate sufficiently long to reach to the bottom of the tube. The surfaces of these plates are coated by means of voltaic action with finely-divided platinum, for the purpose of increasing the surfaces of contact between the metal and the gas. The tube H has double the capacity of the tube O. These tubes are supported in the vessel S, by the plug through which they pass. In order to use the apparatus, the vessel S is filled with diluted sulphuric acid, and by inverting the cell the tubes are likewise filled with the liquid. The plates in the tubes O and H are then connected by the mercury cups at top with the wires of a voltaic battery in action, so that by the decomposition of the diluted acid the tube O shall become filled with oxygen, and the tube H with hydrogen. The tubes having been thus filled, the battery wires are withdrawn. If the mercury cups at the top of the tubes O and H be now connected with the wires of a galvanometer, powerful deflection of the needle will be produced, and a current will be maintained through the apparatus in the direction of the arrows. The two gases will gradually diminish in bulk, and will in a few days entirely disappear, but the current will be maintained so long as any portions of the gas remain uncombined. By connecting 8 or 10 such cells in succession, so that the oxygen tube of one cell shall be connected with the hydrogen tube of the adjacent cell, sparks may be obtained between charcoal points, and various chemical decompositions may be effected. The polar chain by which these changes are produced, may thus be represented by symbols: $H_2\,SO_4$, indicating an atom of diluted acid, O and H_2 representing the disturbing atoms of oxygen and hydrogen:—

FIG. 209.

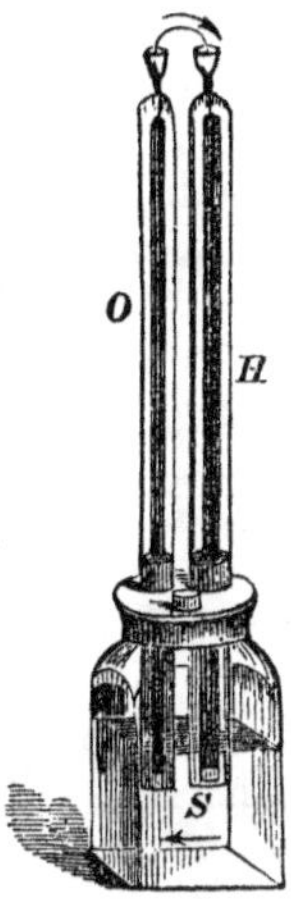

$$O\ H_2\,SO_4\ \ H_2\,SO_4\ \ H_2\,SO_4\ \ H$$

The brackets above the row of symbols are intended to show the molecular arrangement before the circuit is completed; those beneath the symbols show the action during the passage of the current.

Since no action occurs in the gas battery until metallic communication between the plates is effected, it appears that the use of the platinum plates consists in favouring the action by condensing the gases upon their porous surfaces, and in acting as conductors of the current.

It may indeed be stated generally, that the accumulation of either of the elements of the exciting liquid upon the metallic plates of a voltaic combination, always tends to produce a counter-current, and therefore reduces the efficiency of the combination, to a proportionate extent. Hydrogen is the element which, in the usual mode of experiment, principally accumulates upon the negative plate, so that any contrivance by which the adhering hydrogen is removed, exalts the energy of the circulating force. This removal of the hydrogen may be effected by means which act either on chemical or on mechanical principles. The chemical principle is the most perfect. It consists in adding to the liquid a compound which has a tendency to unite with the hydrogen; hence the energy of the current is much increased by mixing a little nitric acid (H,NO_3) with the exciting liquid, comparatively little hydrogen being set free in this case.* The same end is attained by adding to the sulphuric acid a solution of some of the metallic salts, such, for instance, as sulphate of copper (Cu,SO_4). When sulphate of copper is employed, metallic copper is deposited upon the negative or conducting plate, whilst the sulphuric acid radicle, with which it was previously united, combines with the zinc. A disadvantage, however, is experienced when the liquid which absorbs the hydrogen is in contact with the zinc, and this is particularly evidenced when sulphate of copper is used. The zinc acts at once on the solution of copper, and becomes coated with reduced copper; hence, between the particles of zinc and those of the reduced copper innumerable small circuits are produced, which occasion a violent discharge of hydrogen from the entire surface of the generating metal, or rather from the copper deposited upon it; but the zinc thus dissolved contributes nothing to the general effect; it becomes merely a case of local action (260).

This experiment with the sulphate of copper throws light upon the cause of the effervescence which takes places when common zinc is treated with diluted sulphuric acid. Commercial zinc always contains lead and other foreign metals mixed with it in very appreciable quantity; these act as discharges to the hydrogen, and give rise to numerous local circuits at all points of the surface of the zinc. Perfectly pure zinc is dissolved very slowly in acid for want of these discharging points, but the acid is not absolutely without action upon the metal. Any inequality in susceptibility to chemical action gives rise to a current between two substances suitably disposed; hence any difference in density between two pieces of the same metal may suffice to cause a current; and a piece of hammered zinc will generally act as a con-

* By the action of hydrogen on nitric acid, peroxide of nitrogen (NO_2) and water are formed, thus: $HNO_3+H=NO_2+H_2O$.

ducting plate to a piece of zinc well annealed. The adherence of a film of oxide or of fatty matter to the surface of one piece will also cause a difference, and hence two pieces of metal which may even have been cut from the same strip, may, under certain circumstances, produce a feeble current.

The inconvenience which is occasioned by local action, when nitric acid or sulphate of copper is mixed with the liquid which is in contact with the zinc, may be avoided by the employment of porous diaphragms; and if the zinc or generating plate be plunged into diluted sulphuric acid, whilst the platinum or conducting plate is made to dip into the nitric acid or into the solution of sulphate of copper, which is separated from the generating plate by means of a tube of porous earthenware, combinations of great efficiency are obtained.

(265) *Daniell's Battery.*—These important facts were first clearly enunciated by Daniell. Their application to the voltaic battery enabled him to detect the cause of the rapid decline in the activity observed in all the forms of batteries which up to that period had been devised, and they led him to the invention of an arrangement which not only obviated these defects, and enabled him to keep up a current of uniform strength for many hours, but also furnished electrical science with a battery of far greater activity for its size than any which had previously been used. Fig. 210 exhibits a section of one of the cells of Daniell's combination. The outer case, C, consists of a cell, or cylinder of copper, which is constructed so as to retain liquids, and is filled with a solution of sulphate of copper, B, acidulated with an eighth of its bulk of sulphuric acid. The solution is kept saturated with the salt by means of crystals of sulphate of copper, D, which rest upon the perforated shelf, F. In the axis of the cell is placed a tube of porous earthenware, E, filled with an acid solution, A, which consists of 1 part of oil of vitriol diluted with 7 parts of water. A rod of amalgamated zinc, Z, is placed in this tube. On making a metallic communication between the zinc rod and the copper cell, a voltaic current is established; and by employing twenty or thirty cells of this description, always connecting the zinc of one cell with the copper of the next, a combination of great power is obtained.

Fig. 210.

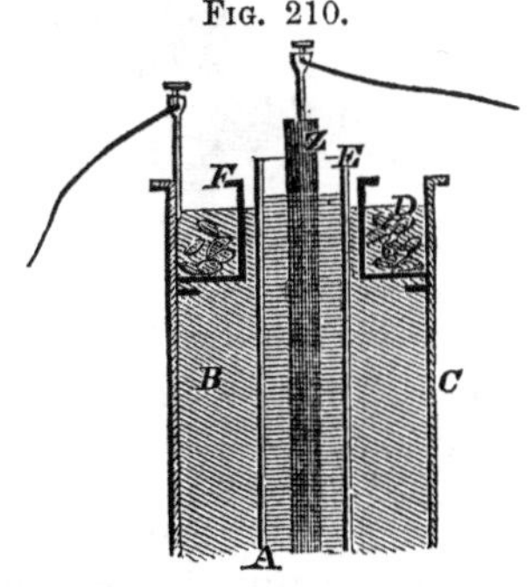

The following diagram may serve to explain the manner in which the force is transmitted through the cells:—the diluted sulphuric acid may be regarded as a compound of hydrogen with sulphur and oxygen, and is represented as H_2SO_4: whilst sulphate of copper may be looked upon as a compound of copper with the same compound of sulphur and oxygen, and is indicated by the symbol $CuSO_4$. Let the brackets above the row of symbols represent the connexion of the particles which compose the liquid before contact is made between the plates *Cu* and *Zn* at the ends. The alteration in the molecular arrangement of the liquid which occurs after the connexion is made between the copper and the zinc, may be represented by the altered position of the brackets beneath: the line A, which divides the symbols of the sulphate of copper from those of the sulphuric acid, in this case represents the porous diaphragm:—

$$Cu\ \overbrace{Cu\ SO_4}\ \overbrace{Cu\ SO_4}\ \overset{A}{|}\ \overbrace{H_2\ SO_4}\ \overbrace{H_2\ SO_4}\ Zn$$

The result of the action is, that so long as the contact between the plates is maintained, sulphate of zinc is formed uninterruptedly in the porous tubes, whilst a continual deposit of a corresponding quantity of metallic copper takes place upon the internal surface of the copper cylinder. Fig. 211 shows a convenient

Fig. 211.

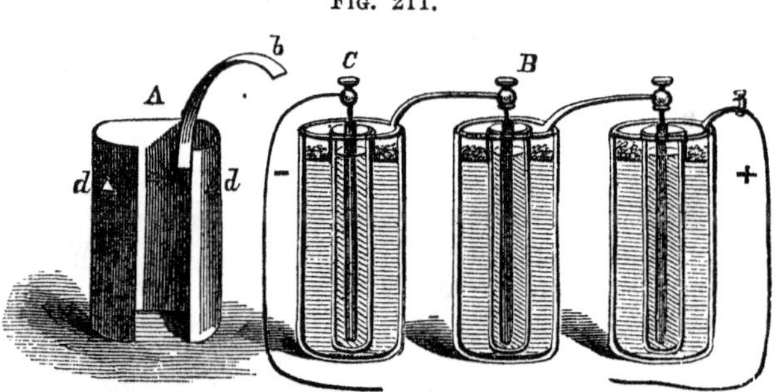

and inexpensive form of Daniel's battery. The solution of sulphate of copper is contained in glass or earthenware jars 7 inches deep, and 3½ inches in diameter. The copper plates consist merely of rectangular sheets of copper, one of which is represented at A; they are bent into a cylindrical shape and placed in the jars. By means of the strip *b*, each plate is easily connected with the zinc rod of the adjacent cell, and made fast to it by the binding-screw C. The colander, for the support of the crystals of sulphate of copper, rests upon three or four little pieces of copper, which are made to project inwards upon the sheets, at a suitable height as shown at *d*. At B, several cells of the battery are represented as arranged in a consecutive series. Twenty such cells compose a battery adequate to the performance of almost any experiments of the chemical decomposition of bodies in solution.

It is essential in mounting a voltaic arrangement of any kind, that the surfaces of contact between the metals be perfectly clean: a film of oxide will materially impede the transmission of the current, and if the force in circulation be feeble, it may even arrest it altogether. As a precaution, it is better before connecting the different parts of the apparatus, to pass a file or a piece of emery-paper over all the surfaces of the copper, the zinc, or the other oxidizable metals which are to be placed in contact with each other. Surfaces of platinum, if well washed and dried, do not need friction with emery-paper.

(266) *Grove's Nitric-Acid Battery.*—The nitric-acid battery, contrived by Grove, is a still more powerful combination on the same principle as Daniell's. It consists of a slip of platinum, P, fig. 212, which is plunged into the porous tube, N, and this is filled up with undiluted nitric acid. The outer cell, S, is filled with diluted sulphuric acid, and in this acid is placed a flat sheet of amalgamated zinc, Z, bent so as to infold the porous tube. The acid liquid in S may be conveniently made of 1 measure of oil of vitriol diluted with 4 measures of water. This combination presents in a small compass the principal desiderata for attaining intense voltaic action. Platinum is the least liable of the metals to chemical action, whilst amongst the metals that admit of being easily wrought, zinc is the one which is most readily attacked by acids; consequently the opposition of platinum to zinc furnishes a most effective voltaic combination; whilst nitric acid absorbs with ease the hydrogen liberated on the platinum, and thus forms water and nitrous acid, which remain in solution in the undecomposed acid; the resulting liquid constitutes one of the most perfect of liquid conductors. If HNO_2O in the following diagram represent nitric acid, and H_2SO_4 diluted sulphuric acid, *Pt* the platinum plate, and *Zn* the zinc one, the molecular arrangement will be indicated, before the action by the position of the brackets above, and after the action by the position of those below.

Fig. 212.

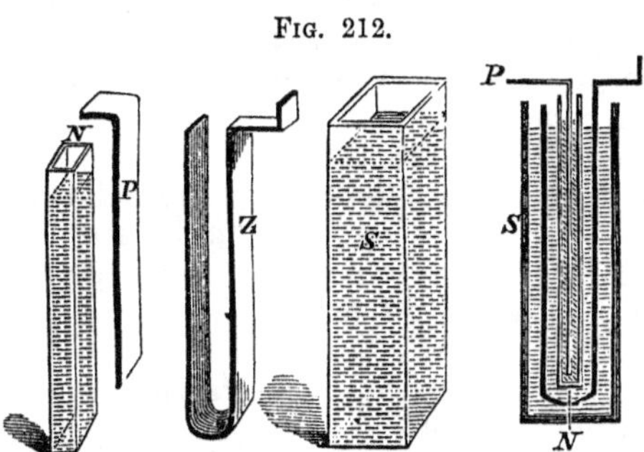

$$Pt\,\overbrace{\mathrm{H\,N}O_2O}\mid\overbrace{\mathrm{H}_2,\,SO_4}\,\overbrace{\mathrm{H}_2\,SO_4}\,Zn$$

With a battery of ten such cells, 5 inches high and 2½ inches wide, a large number of brilliant experiments may be performed, but four or five cells are generally sufficient for most purposes of electro-chemical decomposition. If oil of vitriol be mixed with the nitric acid in the porous cells in the proportion of about equal measures, a current is thus obtained, the strength of which is more uniform than when nitric acid only is used (Callan).

With a view to economy, Bunsen substitutes for the platinum plates in Grove's battery, cylinders of carbon, prepared by heating together a mixture of powdered coke and caking coal, or powdered coke moistened with a strong solution of sugar. A firm coherent coke is thus obtained. Cylinders made of this material answer well while new; but being porous, the carbon absorbs the nitric acid, which corrodes and impairs the surface of contact with the zinc. A better material is the hard carbon from the gas retorts, but it is difficult to shape it into the form of plates. Poggendorff (*Liebig's Annal.* xxxviii. 308) has employed plates either of sheet iron or cast iron instead of either platinum or carbon; in strong nitric acid the iron is totally unacted on; but if the acid become diluted till it has a specific gravity of 1·35, or less, it is liable to act upon the metal with uncontrollable violence. No combination possesses the intense energy, in union with convenience of working and comparative durability, in the same degree as that proposed by Grove. It is necessary, however, to place the nitric acid battery so that the fumes of nitric acid (which are copiously evolved during its action, especially after the battery has been in use for some time) shall pass at once into the open air; as they would otherwise seriously incommode the operator.

(267) The other mode of obviating the counteracting agency of hydrogen upon the negative plate of the battery is less perfect, and is of a mechanical nature. It was first practically applied by Smee in the construction of the voltaic battery. Hydrogen adheres to smooth surfaces of platinum and other metals with considerable force, but it passes off with ease from their asperities and edges: by multiplying their points and irregularities, as, for example, by the deposition of metal on the surface in a pulverulent form, the escape of the gas is much facilitated. Smee employs as the negative or conducting plate in his battery, a plate of silver, the face of which has been roughened by the deposition of finely divided platinum upon its surface; each side of the silver plate being exposed to a plate of zinc well amalgamated, and of equal extent, which acts as the positive plate. This pair of plates is excited by means of diluted sulphuric acid. Fig. 213 represents

FIG. 213.

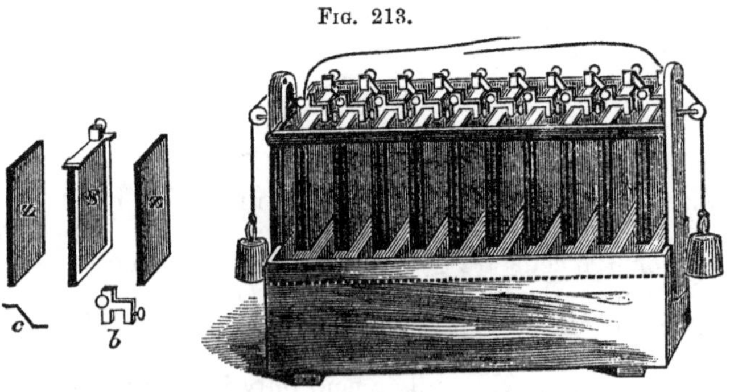

a battery constructed upon Smee's principle: a thin platinized silver plate is supported in a light frame of wood, as shown detached at s; to the upper part of this frame a binding-screw, in metallic connexion with the silver, is fastened, for the purpose of connecting the plate with the zinc plates of the adjoining cell, by means of a strip of sheet copper bent as at *c*; on either side of the silver plate a sheet of amalgamated zinc, z, z, is supported by the clamp shown at *b*; the zinc plates are prevented from contact with the silver plate by means of the wooden frame, and they are connected with the silver of the adjacent cell by a second binding-screw in the clamp shown at *b*; the separate plates are attached to a wooden frame, and being counterpoised by weights, as indicated in the figure, can be lowered into the trough of acid when wanted for use, or can be withdrawn from it when the experiment is over. The trough is divided into separate cells or compartments for each pair of plates, by glass partitions rendered water-tight by means of a resinous cement.

(268) *Resistances to the Voltaic Current.*—The amount of force which circulates in any given circuit is not dependent solely upon the energy of the chemical action which is exerted between the generating metal and the exciting liquid. The current experiences a retardation or a resistance from the very conductors by which its influence is transmitted; just as in the transmission of mechanical force, the intervention of the pivots and levers which are required for its conveyance introduces additional friction and additional weight, which require to be overcome or moved, and which thus diminish the efficient power of the machine.

The resistance to the voltaic current may be considered as of two kinds—first, that resistance which arises from the exciting liquid employed in the voltaic cell itself; and secondly, that which arises from the conducting wire and apparatus exterior to the voltaic cell. In a large number of cases the resistance offered by the exciting liquid is by much the most considerable, and it is inseparable from the combination; whilst the second source of resistance, or that which is exterior to the cell, can be increased or diminished at pleasure, and by the employment of very short and thick wires for connecting the plates, can be virtually removed altogether or annihilated. It will be advisable to consider first the resistance produced by the liquid in the active cell itself.

If plates of equal size be taken, the resistance occasioned by the liquid increases directly as the distance between the plates; the longer the column of imperfectly conducting matter which the force has to traverse, the greater is the difficulty which it will experience. If two plates be immersed in acid at the distance of an inch asunder, they will produce 12 times the effect that they would occasion at the distance of a foot from each other. On the other hand, the larger the area of the plates that are immersed, the less is the resistance. For example, if a pair of plates 1 inch broad and 12 inches long, be immersed in acid to the depth of 1 inch only, the current produced will only be equal to one-twelfth of that which would be obtained by immersing each plate for its whole depth of 12 inches in the liquid. The resistance of the liquid is therefore directly as the distance between the plates, and inversely as the surface of the plates exposed to its action. A pair of plates exposing each a square inch of surface, immersed in acid at a distance of 1 inch apart, will consequently produce an effect equal to that which would be obtained from a pair of plates which each exposed a surface of 12 square inches to the action of the liquid, if they were 12 inches apart.

A case somewhat analogous is offered when water is transmitted through pipes. The greater the length of the pipe, the more considerable will be the friction and the consequent resistance to the passage of the liquid; whilst the larger the area of the pipe the more readily will the water escape. An aperture which exposes a sectional area of two square inches will allow twice as much water to escape from it in a given time as an aperture of which the superficial area is but a single square inch.

If the two plates are of unequal size, but are immersed parallel to each other, they may, for most practical purposes, be calculated as each exposing a surface equal to the mean surface of the two. Other circumstances independent of the extent of surface exposed by the plates, and the distance between them, materially influence the resistance of different liquids to the current. Any cause that favours chemical action between the active metal and the liquid, or which diminishes the force by which the elements of the liquid are united, such as elevation of temperature, diminishes the resistance of the liquid. In most cases an increase in the concentration of the solution, provided its strength be not so great as to render deposition of crystals liable to occur, diminishes the resistance (278). The current likewise experiences a specific resistance in each liquid which depends upon the force with which its particles are united together.

Similar, but distinct resistance, though to a less extent, is offered by the metallic part of the circuit. However good its conducting power may be, it always offers some obstruction to the current. The longer the wire employed, the greater is the difficulty experienced by the force in traversing it. The resistance of each metal, like that of each liquid, is specific. Copper and silver, for instance, when wires of equal thickness and length are compared, offer far less resistance to a given amount of force than less perfect conductors, such as iron and lead. Experiment has demonstrated that with metallic conductors the same law holds good as with liquids—viz., that the conducting power is inversely as the length of the wire, and directly as the area of its section. In cylindrical wires this sectional area will of course vary as the square of the diameter of the wire; for instance, a wire $\frac{1}{10}$ of an inch in thickness will for equal lengths offer four times the resistance of a wire $\frac{2}{10}$ or $\frac{1}{5}$ of an inch thick. If wires of the same metal, and of equal lengths, be compared, the resistance will vary inversely as the weights of the wires.

In the experiment with sulphate of copper (fig. 206), the metal is deposited in greatest quantity where the force is most readily transmitted—viz., in those points which are nearest to the zinc, and where the resistance offered by the liquid, which here forms the thinnest layer, is consequently the least.

A rod of zinc supported within a cylinder of copper forms a convenient arrangement of the generating and conducting plates, because, when such a rod is placed in the axis of the cylinder, the force is evenly distributed over the whole surface of the copper.

(269) *Difference between a Simple and a Compound Circuit.*—The observations hitherto made have referred to cases in which only a single pair of metals is employed. It will be necessary now to consider in what way the results are modified by the employment of several pairs of plates. It has already been stated, when speaking of the electricity developed by friction, that when a large supply of electricity is needed, it may be obtained with equal effect either from a single Leyden jar which exposes a large extent of coated surface, or from a number of smaller jars which together expose the same amount of coated surface, all the inner surfaces of the small jars being in metallic communication with each other, but insulated from the outer coatings, all of which likewise are connected by some good conducting material (235). A similar result is also obtained in voltaic arrangements. Provided that the plates expose the same extent of surface and be kept at an equal distance apart, it matters not whether they be immersed in a single vessel of liquid, or whether they be cut up into strips and be immersed in pairs in separate vessels of the same liquid. The only requisite is that all the zinc plates shall be connected together by stout metallic wires, and that all the platinum plates shall be similarly connected by other wires. No action will occur until metallic communication between one of the platinum and one of the zinc plates is effected by means of a conducting wire; and then the whole force of the united plates will traverse the connecting wire.

These results may be exhibited to the eye in a form of battery in which the hydrogen evolved from each platinum plate admits of being collected—a contrivance proposed by Daniell, which he called a *dissected battery*. Fig. 214 shows the manner of mounting one of these cells. When in use the cells are charged with diluted sulphuric acid, and a small graduated jar, H, also filled with the diluted acid, is inverted in each of the cells over the platinum plate, P, in such a manner as to receive the hydrogen which is disengaged during the operation. The plates of such a battery can easily be connected so that all the plates of zinc, Z, shall be united by conducting wires, and all the platinum plates in a similar way by other wires; or they can with equal readiness be united so that the zinc of one cell shall be connected with

Fig. 214.

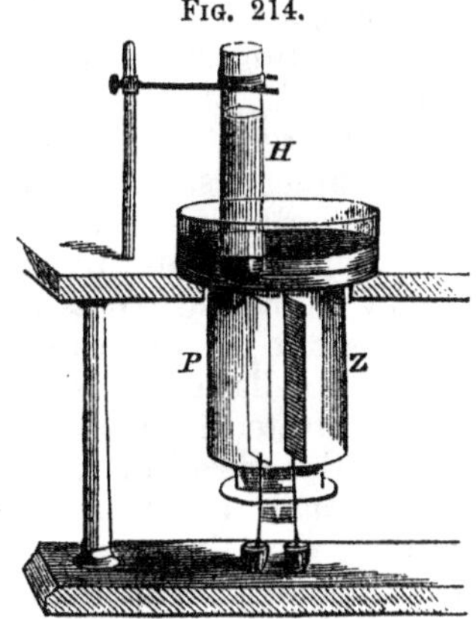

the platinum of the following cell. Suppose, for instance, two plates (Z and P, fig. 215), one of zinc, the other of platinum, each six inches square, be immersed in a vessel of sulphuric acid, at a distance of an inch apart. A current of a certain amount of power will be obtained on connecting the two plates by means of a wire, W; and in five minutes a certain quantity of zinc will be dissolved, whilst a corresponding quantity of hydrogen gas will escape from the platinum. Now if the zinc and the platinum be each cut into strips of an inch broad and six inches long, and the several pairs of zinc and platinum strips be immersed in separate vessels of diluted suphuric acid at the distance of one inch from

FIG. 215.

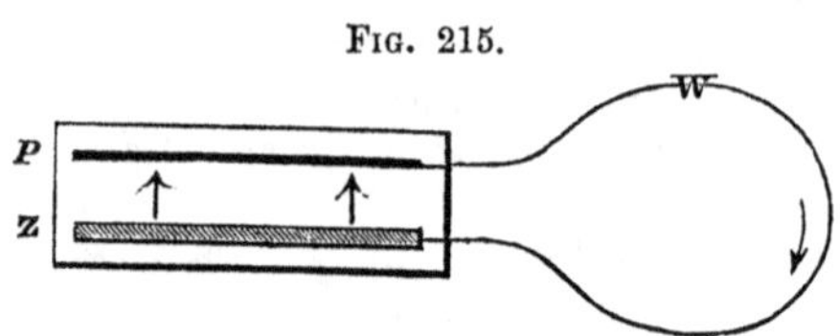

FIG. 216.

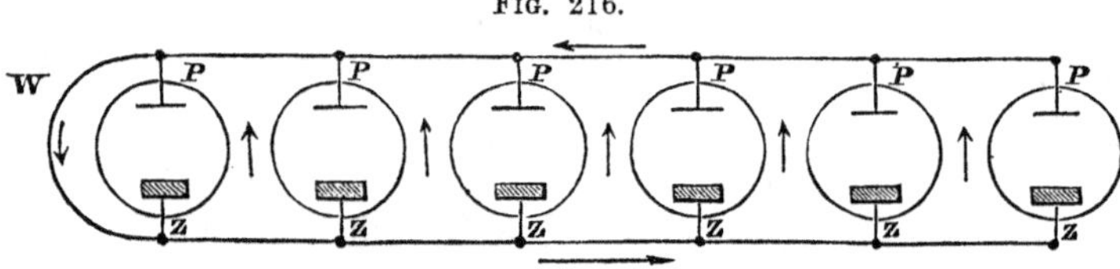

each other, and if, as in fig. 216, all the zinc strips Z, Z, be connected by wires, and all the platinum strips, P, P, be similarly united,—on connecting them together by a wire, as shown at W, the same amount of power will traverse the wire as in the first combination, and the quantity of zinc dissolved in the six plates taken together will in five minutes be the same as that which was dissolved from the single zinc surface in the first arrangement; whilst the quantity of hydrogen gas which will rise from all the six plates of platinum together will be equal to that obtained from the single plate in the former experiment (fig. 215). Such a combination, in whichever of the forms just described it be employed, may be regarded as a single pair of plates, and it constitutes a *simple voltaic circuit.*

By acting upon extensive surfaces arranged in simple circuits, the *quantity* of electricity which can be thrown into circulation is very large, though its *intensity*, that is to say, its power of overcoming resistances, is comparatively small.

The results would, however, be altered if, instead of connecting the divided plates together in the manner represented in fig. 216, they were connected as in fig. 217, in which the zinc in each cell is supposed to be connected with the platinum plate of the adjacent cell, in regular order through the series. When the extreme plates are connected by a thick wire, W, the amount of force which traverses this wire in a given time is equal to one-sixth only of the force which was thrown into circulation in the former instances; but the quantity of zinc dissolved in the six cells taken together is the same as before: and if the hydrogen be collected from the six platinum plates, the quantity will still be equal to that dis-

FIG. 217.

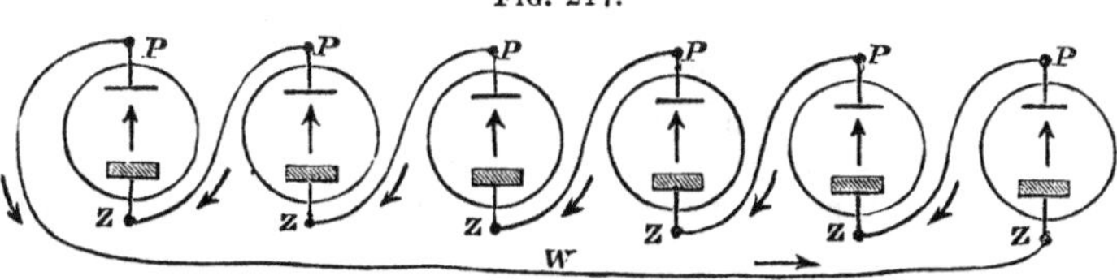

engaged in the experiments shown in figs. 215 and 216. The current has now to traverse each cell of the liquid in succession, and thus has to encounter a great additional resistance. Yet now the power starts from six separate points of origin, and each of these separate points adds its energy or impulse in driving forward the current. The electro-motive force is increased sixfold, whilst the resistance of the liquid is increased still more; in the first place it is increased sixfold, from the circumstance that the length of the column of liquid which must be traversed, is six times as great, and it is next further increased sixfold by a proportionate diminution in the breadth of the column. In the arrangement of fig. 215 there was a column of liquid six inches wide and one inch thick to be traversed; whilst in the arrangement of fig. 217 there is a liquid column six inches thick and only one inch wide to be traversed. When the plates are arranged in separate compartments, and are connected together alternately, as in fig. 217, they constitute a *compound voltaic circuit.* Volta's pile (fig. 202) and his crown of cups (fig. 203) are therefore compound circuits, and it is this form of combination which enabled him to obtain results so much superior to those of any previous experimenter. The electricity in this case is not greater in quantity than that obtainable from a simple circuit; nay, it is often much less; but it has a much higher intensity, and its power of overcoming resistances is very much greater, as a further examination will show. If, for example, 50 or 100 miles of wire, such as is used for telegraphic purposes, be introduced in a combination arranged, as in fig. 216, as a simple circuit, the effect obtained would be very materially less than if the same plates were arranged in the form of a compound circuit, as shown in fig. 217.

(270) *Ohm's Theory.*—These considerations may be much simplified, by representing the mutual action of the electro-motive forces and the resistances of any circuit, simple or compound, in the form of a fraction, in the way proposed by Ohm.

It has been found by experiment that the power of any combination is directly proportioned to the electro-motive force, or chemical energy between the active metal and one of the elements of the liquid upon which it acts; and inversely proportioned to the resistances to be overcome. The numerator of the fraction will therefore be represented by E, the electro-motive force, and the denominator by $R+r$; where R represents the resistance in the cell or the battery, (due chiefly to the attraction between the elements of the liquid for each other), and r all resistances exterior to the cell or the battery, such as the connecting wire: thus the expression $\frac{E}{R+r}=A$, would represent the effect of any combination where A indicates the amount of force actually in circulation, whether measured by its heating or by its magnetic effects. If the connecting wire be very thick, so as to offer little or no resistance to the current, r becomes evanescent, and the fraction assumes the form of $\frac{E}{R}=A$; the force of the current under these circumstances is proportional to the surface of the plates exposed to the action of the liquid.

Let it be assumed, for example, that $E=1$, and that $R=1$, when a pair of zinc and platinum plates an inch broad and six inches long is immersed in diluted acid at the distance of one inch asunder; so that under these circumstances, $\frac{E}{R}=\frac{1}{1}=1$. If a pair of plates six inches broad and six inches long, also at a distance of one inch apart, be immersed in the same acid, since the resistance is inversely as the surface of the plates immersed, the fraction becomes $\frac{E}{\frac{R}{6}}$ or $\frac{1}{\frac{1}{6}}=6$; or the power is increased sixfold, as compared with the former. If the plates be each cut into six similar strips, and be then arranged in pairs, as represented in fig. 216, the same fraction still represents the result, since the relative size and distance of the plates remain unchanged: but if the plates be arranged in succession, so as to produce a compound circuit, as in fig. 217, the fraction becomes $\frac{6E}{6R}=\frac{6}{6}=1$; the electromotive force is increased sixfold, but the resistance is increased also in exactly the same proportion. The force which under these circumstances circulates through the connecting wire is not greater than if a single cell only, containing a pair of plates one inch broad and six inches long, were employed.

But suppose now that several miles of wire, such as are employed in telegraphic communication, be introduced into the two combinations severally represented in figs. 216 and 217; r now acquires importance;—let the resistance be twentyfold greater than that of the liquid in each cell. In the first case (with the simple circuit), the fraction becomes $\frac{E}{\frac{R}{6}+r}=\frac{1}{\frac{1}{6}+20}=0{\cdot}049$; in the second (the compound circuit), the fraction is $\frac{6E}{6R+r}=\frac{6}{6+20}=0{\cdot}23$: so that although in both cases the resistance introduced most materially diminishes the amount of force which enters into circulation, the power in the compound circuit is now five times as great as that which emanates under these circumstances from the simple circuit. Indeed, in all cases where great resistances external to the battery have to be overcome, a compound battery has a great advantage over the simple circuit.*

* Let n = the number of plates in a compound circuit.
" E = the electro-motive force.
" D = the distance between the plates.
" S = the area of the plates.

(271) *Chemical Decomposition.*—It is important to remember that the force which circulates through each cell in a compound circuit is not increased by the arrangement, if the connexion between its extremities be made by means of a good conductor; if, for example, 50 similar and equal cells be connected in succession, and be united by a stout short wire, the quantity of zinc which would be dissolved in a given time in each of these cells would not be greater than that which would be consumed in a single cell of the same size in the same time, if the plates which compose it were connected by a short thick wire.

The power of a compound circuit is shown in a striking manner, when some liquid such as diluted sulphuric acid is interposed in the course of the conducting wire. The experiments which elucidate this point may be instructively performed by means of the dissected battery. If a pair of platinum plates, *a*, *b*, fig. 218,

Fig. 218.

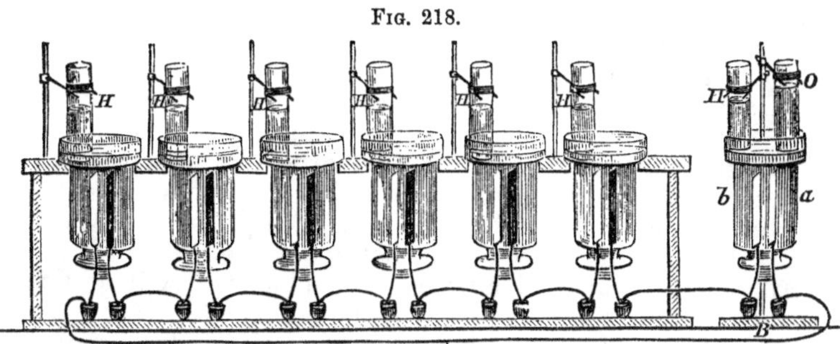

be immersed in the acid conducting-liquid at B, and connected with the wires proceeding from the compound circuit in the manner represented in the figure, the liquid will be decomposed, oxygen will be given off from one plate, *a*, and will rise in the tube O; whilst hydrogen will be given off from the other plate, *b*, and may be collected in the tube, H: but if the same cells be arranged as a simple circuit, fig. 216, no such effect is produced. By the introduction of the liquid conductor at B, the resistance is very greatly increased, such a resistance being more considerable than that of many miles of wire. But this is not all: besides this resistance, a new counteracting electro-motive force shows itself, which gives rise to a current operating in a direction the reverse of that in the battery. This force is due to the oxygen and hydrogen which are separated upon the platinum plates,

Let l = the length of the conducting wire.
" s = the area of a section of the wire.

The fraction which represents the action of a compound battery when its extremities are connected by means of a metallic wire of uniform diameter is the following: $\frac{nE}{\frac{nD}{S}+\frac{l}{s}} = A$. In this expression $\frac{D}{S}$ is substituted for R, (the resistance in each cell of the battery) to which it is equivalent; since R is directly as the distance between the plates, and inversely as their area, or surface, while $\frac{l}{s}$ represents r.

and which, as has been explained when speaking of the gas battery (264), is very considerable. Experiment shows that it is between two and three times as powerful as the electro-motive force of a pair of zinc and platinum plates excited by diluted sulphuric acid. When, therefore, the endeavour is made to decompose the diluted acid by a single pair of zinc and platinum plates, however large a surface they may present to the action of the exciting liquid, no visible action in the cell B ensues; a momentary decomposition, too small in amount to be perceived by the eye, produces a development of oxygen and hydrogen upon the two platinum plates, *a*, *b*, sufficient to oppose an effectual barrier to the transmission of the current. Even when two pairs of zinc and platinum plates are used, the energy of the current is insufficient to effect any visible decomposition: with three pairs, a few bubbles of gas show themselves; and with a more numerous series, the effects increase rapidly; till at length a point is gained, beyond which no advantage is obtained by increasing the number of cells in the battery.

It is particularly worthy of remark that in every vertical section of any voltaic circuit at a given instant, the quantity of force which traverses it is uniform: consequently, the same quantity of hydrogen makes its appearance upon the plate *b* of the cell P, which contains the liquid for decomposition, as is disengaged and collected during the same interval from each plate in the battery itself. If each zinc plate of the battery be weighed before the experiment is begun and after it is concluded, it will be found that each plate has lost weight to an equal extent. The interposition of the liquid at B, may occasion a great reduction in the amount of power which is thrown into circulation; but at every transverse section of the battery, the power that does circulate is uniform in quantity; and the measurement of the chemical action, whether it be estimated by the quantity of gas which is evolved at any one point, or by the quantity of zinc which is dissolved, may be employed as a sure indication of the quantity of power in circulation: in other words, retardation of the current by the liquid conductor is necessarily attended with an equal retardation in the conducting wire, and in each cell of the battery itself.

(272) *The Voltameter.*—The foregoing important law was discovered by Faraday. As one of its consequences he was enabled to employ a decomposing cell, such as is shown at B, fig. 218, as a measure of the voltaic power of any circuit: such an instrument is called a *Voltameter*. For each 32.7 grains of zinc dissolved in any one cell of the battery, 9 grains of water are decomposed in the voltameter, and 46·6 cubic inches of hydrogen or 1 grain, and 23·3 cubic inches of oxygen or 8 grains, at 60° F. and 30 inches Bar., are evolved upon its plates; at the same time 46·6 cubic inches of hydrogen are evolved from every platinum plate in the cells of the battery. A more convenient form of voltameter is shown in fig. 219. It consists of an upright glass cell, to the neck of which a bent tube, *c*, for the conveyance

of the disengaged gases, is fitted by grinding; the vessel is filled with diluted sulphuric acid; *a*, *b*, are the two platinum plates, each of which is connected by a wire which passes through the foot of the instrument, to a mercury cup, by means of which communication can be made with the wires which convey the current from the battery: oxygen and hydrogen are liberated by the action of the current upon the acidulated water, both gases then rise to the surface of the liquid, and are conveyed by the bent tube *c*, to the graduated jar, *d*, which stands in a small pneumatic trough.

Fig. 219.

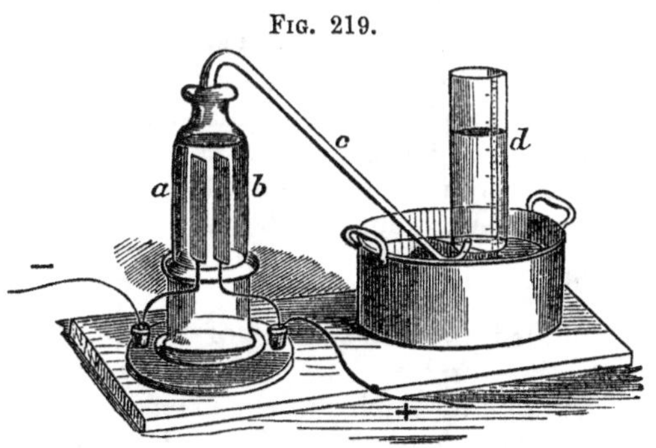

It is to be observed that the action of a simple zinc and platinum battery is not steady; it gradually declines, and before the acid has become saturated with zinc, the current almost ceases. On breaking the contact of the conducting wire with the two ends of the battery, and allowing it to remain disconnected for a few minutes, the action is partially restored; but it again gradually declines after the circuit has been completed. These effects were traced by Daniell to the action of the current upon the sulphate of zinc, which is formed in each cell of the battery during the operation; the zinc salt is decomposed in the manner shown in the subjoined diagram, in which $ZnSO_4$ represents the sulphate of zinc, and *Pt* and *Zn* the platinum and zinc plates of the cell. The brackets placed above the symbols indicate the arrangement of the particles before the current passes; those below show the change produced by the voltaic action:—

$$Pt\ \overbrace{Zn\ SO_4},\ \overbrace{Zn\ SO_4}\ Zn.$$

In this manner metallic zinc becomes reduced or deposited upon each platinum plate, and the power of the battery is arrested when the two surfaces which are opposed become virtually zinc and zinc instead of platinum and zinc. This evil may be obviated by interposing a porous diaphragm between the two plates, as in the batteries of Daniell and of Grove (265, 266); in these cases a sufficient communication between the zinc and the copper or the platinum plates, is still kept up by means of liquid through the pores of the diaphragm, but the sulphate of zinc is prevented from mixing with the liquid which is in contact with the copper or the platinum.

(273) *Further Application of Ohm's Theory.*—All the phenomena of compound circuits admit of ready calculation by the

application of Ohm's principle; for instance, if n represents the number of plates, the expression for any compound series, the cells of which are similar in nature and equal in size, becomes $\frac{n\,E}{n\,R+r}=A$; since in each cell not only is a new electro-motive force introduced, but at the same time a new resistance. Provided that the exterior resistance is such as would be offered by a metallic wire which may even be many miles in length, it is possible exactly to double the amount of force in circulation by doubling the number of cells, if at the same time the size of the plates be doubled; for $\frac{2\,n\,E}{\frac{2\,n\,R}{2}+r}=\frac{2\,n\,E}{n\,R+r}$. But if, when the number of cells is doubled and the surface of the plates also is doubled, a voltameter be employed to measure the power in circulation, instead of introducing a wire as the exterior resistance, the force measured by the voltameter is not found to be doubled, as might naturally have been expected: this difference arises from the counter current which is produced in the voltameter itself, by the accumulation of the oxygen and hydrogen upon its plates. Call this counter current e, and the formula becomes $\frac{n\,E-e}{n\,R+r}$.

The values both of e, (the counter current offered by the voltameter,) and r, which, if short thick conducting wires be used, is virtually the resistance of the voltameter itself, may be very simply estimated in the way proposed by Wheatstone. This method consists in comparing two experiments in which, the resistance remaining the same, the electro-motive forces alone vary. Upon the supposition that the voltameter merely offers an increased resistance without introducing any counteracting electro-motive force, five single cells should produce a result equal to half that obtained by the use of ten cells of double size; but by experiment, the effects as measured by the voltameter are as 6 : 20. Comparing these effects with the arrangements which produce them, we obtain the following proportion, from which, by equating, the value of e is deduced in terms of E:—

$$\frac{10\,E-e}{\frac{10\,R}{2}+r} : \frac{5\,E-e}{5\,R+r} :: 20 : 6; \text{ therefore } e=2{\cdot}857\,E.$$

The resistance r of the voltameter may be calculated with equal ease; for taking two similar batteries, each composed of ten cells, but in one of which the plates are exactly double the size of those in the other, the electro-motive forces will continue the same while the resistances alone will vary. Under these circumstances the experimental results, furnished by the voltameter in equal times, were as 12·5 : 20; and $\frac{10\,E-e}{10\,R+r} : \frac{10\,E-e}{\frac{10\,R}{2}+r} :: 12{\cdot}5 : 20$; therefore $r=3{\cdot}333\,R$. By substituting, in the formula, the values for e and r thus obtained by experiment, the results for any given number of cells may be calculated; and on comparing the values obtained by such a calculation with the numbers furnished by actual experiment, Daniell (*Phil. Trans.* 1842, p. 146) obtained the following results:—

Number of Cells..........	3	4	5	10	15	20	
Gas calculated	$\frac{5}{8}$	$3\frac{3}{5}$	6	$12\frac{18}{25}$	$15\frac{21}{25}$	$17\frac{13}{25}$	Cubic in.
Gas observed..............	$1\frac{1}{8}$	$3\frac{7}{8}$	6	$12\frac{1}{2}$	$15\frac{3}{4}$	$17\frac{1}{2}$	Cubic in.

Any alteration in the size of the plates of the voltameter necessarily alters the amount of resistance which it offers to the current, and the influence of this change in the voltameter is most perceptible when a battery consisting of a few plates which expose a large surface is employed.

The preceding considerations will render it evident that no general answer can be given to the question, 'What number of cells should a battery contain in order that it may produce the greatest effect?' The electro-motive force, E, varies in amount with the kind of battery which is used; the values for R and r will also vary with the varying circumstances of the experiment. It is found that every different arrangement requires the employment of a distinct number of cells in order to obtain from it the maximum effect with the least expenditure of zinc. This number will vary even with the same form of battery, according to the size of the battery plates, the length of wire in the circuit, and the nature of the liquid conductor in the decomposing cell. It may be stated, however, as a general principle, that the most advantageous effect is obtained when the value of A, in the formula $\frac{nE-e}{nR+r}=A$, most nearly approaches 0·5, E and R each being $=1$: in other words, the advantage is greatest when the exterior resistances, viz., those of the conducting wire and voltameter together—are equal to the sum of the resistances due to the battery itself; it may therefore be concluded that when the exterior resistance is trifling, as usually occurs when the circuit is metallic and not of very great length, little or nothing is gained by employing a large number of cells; two or three plates of large surface being the best under such circumstances; but that where a considerable chemical resistance is to be overcome, power is gained by employing a series numerous in proportion to the resistance so introduced. In no case, however, is it possible by the use of a series of plates of uniform dimensions, even if of unlimited number, to produce in any transverse section, such as an included voltameter, a chemical action greater in amount than that which would occur in a single cell of the arrangement in which the circuit was completed by a stout metallic wire.

(274) *Wheatstone's Rheostat and Resistance Coils.*—Guided by the principles which have just been explained, Wheatstone contrived an apparatus termed the *Rheostat*, by which measured amounts of resistance may be introduced into the voltaic circuit: if the effect which such added resistance has upon the amount of the current in circulation be measured, the different values of E, R, and r in different arrangements, may be deduced by a simple calculation. The rheostat is represented in fig. 220: g is a cylinder of well baked wood, $1\frac{1}{2}$ inch in diameter and 6 inches in

length; it turns easily upon a horizontal axis; on this cylinder a spiral groove is cut, the thread of which contains 40 turns to the

FIG. 220.

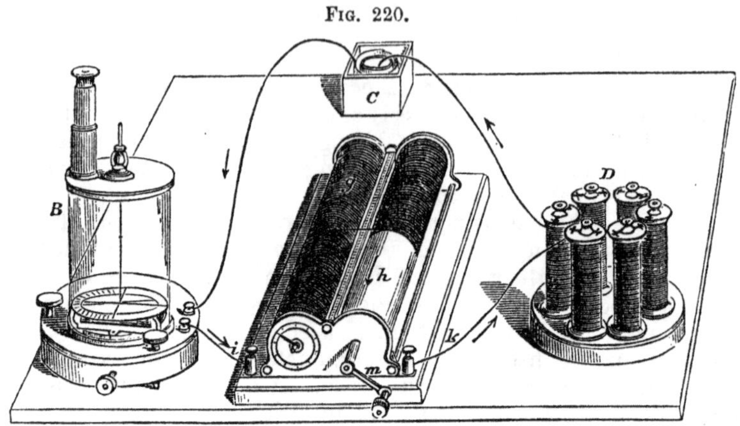

inch. This groove runs from one end of the cylinder to the other, and in it is coiled a brass wire $\frac{1}{100}$ inch in diameter; *h* is a brass cylinder, placed parallel to *g*, and equal to it in diameter; the thin wire upon *g* is connected at the end *i* with a brass ring, and at the other extremity is attached to the cylinder, *h*; at *i* is a metallic spring, one end of which is connected with a binding-screw, and the other end of which rests against the brass ring, and effects the communication with one wire of the battery: *m* is a moveable key, by which the wire can be wound upon the brass cylinder, or by transferring the key to the axis of *g*, it can be unwound from *h*, and returned to the wooden cylinder, *g*. In consequence of the non-conducting quality of dry wood, the coils of wire on the wooden cylinders are insulated from each other, so that the current traverses the whole length of the wire coiled upon this cylinder, but the coils not being insulated from each other on the brass cylinder, the current immediately passes from the point of contact to the brass spring at *k*, which is in communication with the other wire from the battery. A scale is placed between the two cylinders for the convenience of counting the number of coils unwound, and the fractions of a turn are read off upon a graduated circle, which is traversed by an index attached, as is shown in the figure, to the axis of the cylinder *g*.

Wheatstone took as his standard of resistance, the resistance produced by a copper wire 1 foot of which weighs exactly 100 grains.* It is sometimes necessary to be able to introduce an amount of resistance into a circuit much greater than can be effected by means of the rheostat. For this purpose the *Resistance Coils*, shown at D, fig. 220, are employed. These coils are

* The question of a standard of resistance is now engaging the attention of practical electricians; the conducting power of copper varies so greatly, owing to the presence of slight impurities, that it is unfitted for the purpose (276).

composed of fine copper wire, $\frac{1}{200}$ of an inch in diameter, carefully insulated by covering them with silk; two of the coils are 50 feet in length, the others 100, 200, 400, and 800 feet long. The ends of each coil are attached to short thick wires, fixed to the upper faces of the cylinders, which serve to combine all the coils into one continued length of 1600 feet of wire. Two wires proceed from the extremities of the coils, by which they are united to the circuit. On the upper face of each cylinder is a double brass spring, moveable round a centre, so that its ends can be made to rest upon the thick brass wires, or can be removed from them at pleasure. When the spring rests upon the wires, the current passes through the spring instead of through the coil; but when the spring rests upon the wood, the current must pass through the coil. In the figure, all the springs are shown as resting upon the wires; in this case none of the coils are included in the circuit, but by turning the spring of any particular coil, 50, 100, 200, or 400 yards of wire can, in a moment, be introduced into the circuit.

The following is Wheatstone's description of his method of ascertaining the sum of the electro-motive forces in any voltaic circuit or circuits:—

'In two circuits producing equal electro-motive (or voltaic) effects, the sum of the electro-motive forces divided by the sum of the resistances is a constant quantity; *i. e.*, $\frac{E}{R}=\frac{n E}{n R}$: if E and R be proportionately increased or diminished, A will obviously remain unchanged. Knowing, therefore, the proportion of resistances in two circuits producing the same effect, we are able immediately to infer that of the electro-motive forces. But, as it is difficult in many cases to determine the total resistance, consisting of the partial resistances of the *rheomotor* [or voltaic combination] itself, the galvanometer, the rheostat, &c., I have recourse to the following simple process:—Increasing the resistance of the first circuit by a known quantity, r, the expression becomes $\frac{E}{R+r}$. In order that the effect in the second circuit shall be rendered equal to this, it is evident that the added resistance must be multiplied by the same factor as that by which the electro-motive forces and the original resistances are multiplied; for $\frac{E}{R+r}=\frac{n E}{n R+n r}$. The relations of the length of the added resistances r, and $n r$, which are known immediately, give therefore those of the electro-motive forces.'—(*Phil. Trans.*, 1843, p. 313.)

Suppose, for example, it be desired to compare the electro-motive force obtained from a single pair of zinc and copper plates in one of Daniell's cells, with that of two pairs of the same combination, the following will be the mode of conducting the experiment:—Interpose the rheostat (fig. 220) and the galvanometer, B, in the circuit obtained from the single cell, C; then, by coiling or uncoiling the wire of the rheostat, bring the needle exactly to 45°. Next uncoil the wire of the rheostat, and count the number of turns required to bring the needle to 40°. Suppose 35 turns are required: this number of turns may be taken to represent the electro-motive force of the combination. Now introduce the two cells, arranged as a compound circuit, instead of the single cell at C. Bring the needle as before to 45°, interposing one or more of the resistance coils at D, if needed, by turning the spring upon the wood of the reels, and complete the adjustment by coiling or uncoiling the wire of the rheostat. Again uncoil the wire of the rheostat until the galvanometer needle stands at 40°. Seventy turns, or twice the number previously required to produce this effect, will now be needed. The electro-motive forces in the two cases are therefore as 35 to 70, or as 1 : 2. If instead of arranging the two cells as a compound circuit the zinc plate be connected with the other zinc plate and the copper with the copper, so as to form a single circuit, it would have required the interposition of a greater resistance to reduce the needle to 45° to start with than when one cell only was used; but only 35 turns of the rheostat would be needed to bring the needle down to 40°. This last experiment shows that the electro-motive force is not altered by increasing or diminishing the size of the plates.

The electro-motive power of any combination may by means of this arrangement be compared with any one selected as a standard: it was in this way that the results on the comparison of the electro-motive effects of platinum, zinc, and potassium (260) were obtained.

Processes of Voltaic Discharge.

(275) Having now reviewed the principal circumstances which influence or exalt the activity of the voltaic battery, we may proceed to examine the phenomena which are manifested when a powerful combination is brought into action by connecting its opposite extremities. Voltaic action is exhibited only during the process of discharge, for the current is a continuous succession of discharges of the electricity developed and maintained by the contact and chemical action of the materials employed in the construction of the battery. The discharge of the voltaic battery may, like that of the ordinary machine, be considered under three heads—viz., the discharge by *conduction*, as when the circuit is completed by a wire or other good solid conductor; the discharge by *disruption*, in which case a luminous appearance is exhibited through a short interval of non-conducting matter; and the discharge by *convection*, which takes place in liquids, and is accompanied by chemical action and transference of the particles of the conductor.

(276) *Conduction.*—In all cases where electricity is in motion, whether it be excited by chemical action, as in the voltaic pile, or by friction, as in the common electrical machine, the force is conveyed by the entire thickness of the conductor; the charge is not confined to the surface, as occurs when the power is stationary and produces effects by induction only. In the case of the voltaic current as well as in the momentary discharge of the Leyden battery, by far the greater portion of the induction occurs

between one transverse section of the conductor and the adjacent sections immediately before and behind it; and but a small proportion of the induction, sufficient however to be distinctly manifest, is diverted to surrounding objects. By reducing the thickness or diameter of the conducting material, a large quantity of the force is compelled to traverse a given number of conducting particles in the same time, and a great elevation of temperature is thus produced. The heat may rise sufficiently high to cause ignition of the wire, and this ignition may be produced at any point of the circuit, so as to produce the explosion of a charge of gunpowder sunk in the depths of the ocean, or buried within the recesses of a mine; the operations of blasting may thus be made to assume a degree of certainty and of safety hitherto unattained by other means, since the moment at which the discharge shall take place is absolutely under control.

Elevation of temperature diminishes the conducting power of the metals: a good experimental proof of this fact is afforded by transmitting through a platinum wire, a voltaic current of sufficient power to raise the wire to a dull red heat; and whilst the current is still passing, igniting a loop of the wire in the flame of a spirit-lamp; the temperature of the other part immediately falls, owing to the diminished amount of electricity which traverses it, in consequence of the increased resistance offered to the passage of the current by the strongly ignited part of the wire. If a loop of the wire be cooled by immersion in water, the opposite effect is produced; for in this case the reduction of temperature at one point enables a larger quantity of electricity to pass through the wire, which may thus be raised to a heat approaching its point of fusion. The power of a voltaic combination may be roughly estimated by the number of inches of platinum wire of uniform diameter, which it will heat to redness: the same quantity of electricity is transmitted in equal intervals of time through wire of the same temperature, whether it be an inch only or several feet in length; but the increased length which the stronger current will ignite measures the increase in tension and intensity of the electric discharge.

The conducting power of the different metals for electricity varies nearly in the same order as their power of conducting heat; but it is remarkable that charcoal, though so bad a conductor of heat, transmits electricity with great facility. The measurement of the conducting power of solids and of liquids for electricity has occupied the attention of many distinguished philosophers. An ingenious method was proposed many years ago by Becquerel, who constructed a *differential galvanometer*, in which the needles were surrounded by two insulated copper wires of equal length and diameter; they were coiled in the usual way, and formed two independent circuits, so that the galvanometer had four terminations instead of two. When two perfectly equal currents were transmitted, one through each wire in opposite directions, they exactly neutralized each other in their effect upon the needle, which therefore remained stationary; but if either current preponderated, a corresponding deviation of the needle was occasioned. To use the instrument, a small voltaic combination was connected with the galvanometer, two wires passing from each pole, so as to divide the current into two exactly equal portions, one being transmitted through one of the coils, the other through the second coil in the opposite direction. Wires of the different metals were then introduced into the two circuits. If into either circuit a conductor of inferior power were introduced, the current in that circuit was proportionately diminished, and the needle was disturbed; but the equilibrium could be restored by increasing the length of the wire in the other circuit; then by comparing the lengths of the two wires thus introduced, their relative conducting power could be inferred. By means of this instrument, conjoined with the use of Wheatstone's rheostat, Ed. Becquerel was enabled to measure the conducting power of a number of wires of different metals, with precision (*Ann. de Chimie*, III. xvii. 266). The relative conducting powers of the wires were obtained by ascertaining the lengths of the rheostat wire, which was required to restore the equilibrium, when wires of different metals were employed. In fig. 221 is exhibited the

FIG. 221.

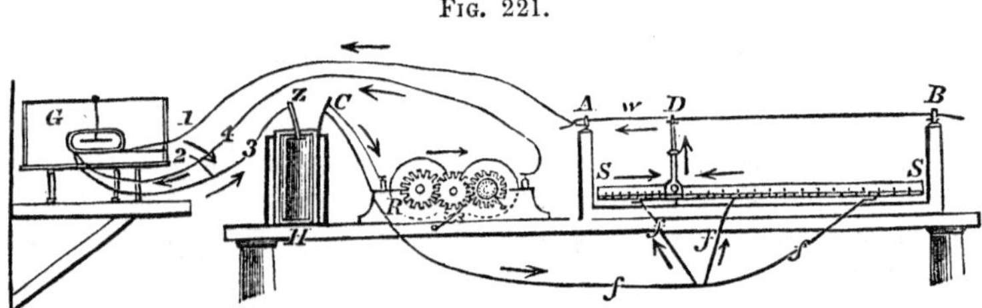

arrangement adopted in these experiments. G is the differential galvanometer with its four wires, 1 and 3 being the terminations of one coil, 2 and 4 those of the other coil; H, a voltaic pair; R, the rheostat; and *w*, the metallic wire, the resistance of which is to be measured. This wire is stretched and insulated between two binding clamps, A and B; S S, is a copper scale with linear subdivisions for measuring the length of the wire which is included in the circuit; D is a sliding clamp of copper, which can be made to move in either direction along the scale S, and can be connected with *w*, at any desired point, by the clamp at D. Suppose the resistance of a certain length of *w* is to be measured. The current from H is divided into two portions so as to send each in opposite directions through the galvanometer. One half of the battery current is made to pass along the wire *f f f*, up the clamp D, and through part of the wire, *w;* the other half is transmitted through the rheostat, in the direction shown by the arrows. By coiling or uncoiling the wire of the rheostat, the two circuits are rendered exactly equal, so that the needle of the galvanometer shall stand at 0°. Now, if D be unclamped, and it be caused to slide through a definite distance, say twelve inches towards B, the equilibrium of the galvanometer will be destroyed; since the resistance in w is increased, whilst that in the rheostat remains unaltered; but by uncoiling the wire of the rheostat, additional resistance can be introduced into the circuit of which it forms a part; the equilibrium may thus be again restored, and the resistance of twelve inches of w will be given by counting the number of coils of the rheostat required. The comparative resistance of any number of different wires introduced at w may thus be readily ascertained.

The following table exhibits the conducting power of wires of equal length and diameter of various metals as determined by this process. The mercury was placed in a glass tube of uniform diameter.

Electric Conductivity of Metals. (*E. Becquerel.*)

Metals employed.	At 32° F. Silver at 32° = 100.	At 212° F. Silver at 32° F. = 100.	At 212° F. Silver at 212 = 100.	Loss per cent. each metal being 100 at 32°.
Silver	100	71·316	100	28·7
Copper	91·517	64·919	91·030	29·1
Gold	64·960	48·489	67·992	25·4
Cadmium	24·579	17·506	24·547	28·8
Zinc	24·063	17·596	24·673	26·9
Tin	14·014	8·657	12·139	38·3
Iron	12·350	8·387	11·760	32·2
Lead	8·277	5·761	8·078	30·7
Platinum	7·933	6·688	9·378	15·7
Mercury	1·738	1·575	2·208	9·4

These metals were carefully purified and well annealed. It was found that annealed metals conducted better than those which had not undergone this process. The effect even of a moderate elevation of temperature in reducing the conducting power is very considerable, as will be evident by comparing the second column of figures in the table with the first.

Matthiessen (*Phil. Trans.*, 1858, p. 383, 1862, p. 1; and *Proceed. Roy. Soc.* xii. 472) gives the following as the conducting powers of wires of different metals of equal diameter. He considers the metals in the first table to have been chemically pure. The wires of the oxidizable metals were obtained by forcing them through an opening in a steel plate, by strong pressure, the wire as it was formed being received into a vessel filled with naphtha. The conducting power was determined by the process described by Matthiessen in the *Philosophical Magazine* for February, 1857. It is a modification of one of the methods devised by Wheatstone, in which an ordinary galvanometer is employed (*Phil. Trans.* 1843, p. 323).

Electric Conductivity of Metals. (*Matthiessen*).

Metal (pure).	Conductivity.		Conductivity at 212°.		
	Silver at 32° = 100.		Silver at 212° = 100.	Each metal compared with itself at 32° = 100.	
	At 32°	At 212°			Loss pr ct.
Silver (hard-drawn)............	100·00	71·56	100·00	71·56	28·44
Copper (hard-drawn)..........	99·95	70·27	98·20	70·31	29·69
Gold (hard-drawn)	77·96	55·90	78·11	71·70	28·30
Zinc..............................	29·02	20·67	28·89	71·23	28·77
Cadmium........................	23·72	16·77	23·44	70·70	29·30
Cobalt...........................	17·22				
Iron (hard-drawn)..............	16·81				
Nickel............................	13·11				
Tin................................	12·36	8·67	12·12	70·11	29·89
Thallium.........................	9·16			68·58	31·42
Lead..............................	8·32	5·86	8·18	70·39	29·61
Arsenicum.......................	4·76	3·33	4·65	69·88	30·12
Antimony	4·62	3·26	4·55	70·54	29·46
Bismuth..........................	1·245	0·878	1·227	70·51	29·49

Matthiessen and Von Bose conclude from these experiments that the law of decrease of electric conductivity is the same for all metals, and it will be at once apparent that the relative conducting powers of the metals continue to be the same with trifling variation, whether they be compared at 32° or at 212°, as will be evident by comparing the first and third columns of figures with each other. The numbers given for iron, cobalt, and nickel are calculated from experiments upon specimens of these metals, known to be slightly impure. In the table which follows, the metals were commercially pure, but the conductivity, when not absolutely accurate, is probably below the truth, as the addition of a second metal always diminishes the conductivity.

Metal.	Conducting Power.	Temp. ° F.	Metal.	Conducting Power.	Temp. ° F.
Silver	100·00	32·0	Iron	14·44	68·7
Copper..............	77·43	65·8	Palladium	12·64	63·0
Sodium...............	37·43	71·0	Platinum	10·53	69·2
Aluminum	33·76	67·2	Strontium	6·71	68·9
Magnesium..........	25·47	62·6	Mercury.............	1·63	73·0
Calcium	22·14	62·2	Tellurium...........	·00077	67·3
Potassium...........	20·85	68·7	Red Phosphorus...	·00000123	75·2
Lithium..............	19·00	68·0			

Matthiessen finds that scrupulous attention to the purity of the metal is essential. The presence of 2·5 per cent. of phosphorus in copper reduced the conducting power of a specimen of the pure metal from 100 to 7·52. A mere trace of arsenic in the copper reduced it from 100 to 60, and the presence of a little sub-oxide in the metal had a very marked effect in reducing the conducting power. Indeed, there are few metals more easily affected in conducting power by slight traces of impurity than copper, so that very great differences in conducting power are observed in wires drawn from different samples of what would be regarded as good commercial copper.

The conducting power of an alloy is generally below that of the mean of its component metals. This is seen in the alloy of antimony and tin; but the alloys of tin and lead, tin and zinc, zinc and cadmium give a conductivity almost exactly the mean of that of the component metals, allowing for the proportion of each that is present. A similar fact was observed by Calvert and Johnson (149) in the conducting power for heat of some of these very alloys.

Alloy.	Silver = 100.		Temp. ° F.
	Calculated Conductivity.	Observed Conductivity.	
ZnCd	24·04	23·78	69·4
ZnSn	17·13	17·43	71·6
Sn_4Pb	10·31	10·55	71·6
SnPb	9·09	9·20	70·5
$SnPb_4$	8·22	8·26	72·7
2 Antimony, 1 part Tin	11·99	0·413	77·0

Lenz found that all the metals continued to decrease in conductivity as the temperature rose to 400°, and Dr. Robinson proved that this diminution continued as they were raised progressively to a red and even to a white heat.

The non-metallic bodies appear to increase in conductivity as the temperature rises, for Matthiessen found that the conducting power of graphite and of coke was increased by heating them, the electric conductivity of gas coke rising about 12 per cent. between the ordinary atmospheric temperature and a 'light' red heat. Hittorf obtained an analogous result with selenium. Comparing the conducting power at ordinary temperatures of different forms of carbon with that of silver at 32° as 100°, Matthiessen obtained the following values:—

	F.
Pure Ceylon graphite	0·0693 at 71°6
Gas coke	0·0386 at 77°
Bunsen's battery coke.	0·0246 at 79·2

(277) If equal amounts of electricity, whether obtained from the voltaic battery or from the electrical machine, be made to traverse wires of different metals of equal length and diameter in the same interval of time, the rise of temperature in the wire is inversely proportioned to its conducting power, and therefore the better the conductor the less heat does it emit. The general truth of the fact may in the case of voltaic electricity be rudely but strikingly demonstrated by taking a wire of silver and one of platinum, each of exactly the same diameter, and forming

them into a compound wire consisting of alternate links of the two metals. A current of electricity may be transmitted through this compound wire, of such a strength as to heat the platinum to visible redness, whilst the silver links will exhibit no such intense heat, though each link of the wire, from the form of the experiment, must transmit equal quantities of the force in equal times. It has been ascertained that the heat developed at any part of the circuit is proportional to the square of the force of the current multiplied into the resistance at that particular point. For the same wire the rise of temperature is proportioned to the square of the quantity of electricity, and this is true also for liquid conductors.

Andrews (*Proceed. Roy. Irish Acad.*, June, 1840), found that when a fine platinum wire was traversed by a current from one of Daniell's constant batteries, the ignition of the wire varied in intensity by varying the gas with which he surrounded the wire. This wire was enclosed in a glass tube, which could be filled at pleasure with the different gases in succession. It was found that gaseous sulphurous anhydride and hydrochloric acid had a smaller cooling power than atmospheric air. Nitrogen, carbonic oxide, cyanogen, carbonic acid, nitric oxide, nitrous oxide, oxygen, and aqueous vapour, had nearly the same effect as atmospheric air. Olefiant gas, ammonia, the vapour of alcohol and of ether had a greater cooling power; and hydrogen, a far greater cooling power than any of the others. The same subject has also been investigated by Grove, (*Phil. Trans.*, 1849.)

The following experiment illustrates the cooling effect of hydrogen very clearly. Take three pieces of stout copper wire, bend them into the form shown at w w w, fig. 222, and attach them to a weighted board, by which the lower part of the bends can be sunk beneath the surface of water contained in a shallow vessel. At *a* and *b*, where the wires project above the surface of the water, complete the connexion by means of spirals of fine platinum wire, both spirals being equal in length, and each cut from the same wire. Each spiral will thus oppose an equal resistance to the passage of the current. When a voltaic current of a certain intensity is transmitted through the wire, w w w, each spiral, consequently, becomes heated to the same degree of visible ignition. But if two similar jars, one A, filled with air, the other, H, filled with hydrogen, be inverted over them, the wire in the jar H immediately ceases to be luminous, while that in A becomes more intensely ignited. This superior cooling action of the hydrogen is no doubt mainly due to the superior mobility of the particles of the gas over those of air. (152, 160.)

Fig. 222.

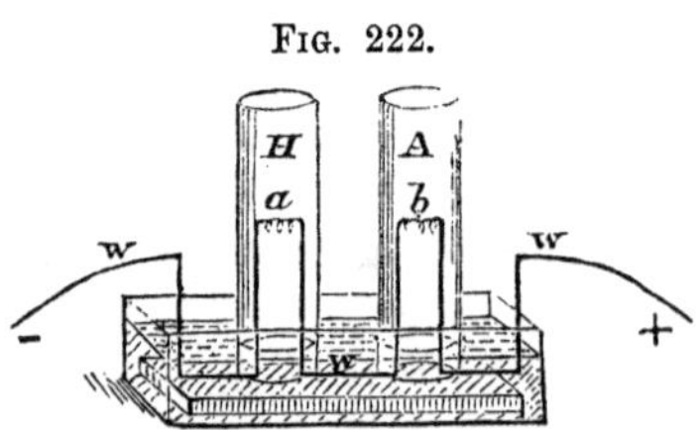

The experiment was varied by enclosing the wires *a* and *b* in separate glass tubes, and sealing them up, one in an atmosphere of air, the other in an atmosphere of hydrogen. Both were then included in the same circuit, so that they should transmit equal amounts of electricity. Before transmitting the current, however, each tube was immersed in a separate vessel which contained a weighed quantity of water, the temperature of which was accurately observed. After the current had been allowed to pass for a certain time, the temperature of the water which surrounded each wire was again observed, and it was found that the water which was around the tube which contained air was considerably hotter than that which surrounded the tube filled with hydrogen.

This result, paradoxical as it appears, and as it seems to have been regarded by Grove, must necessarily follow from the operation of two principles which have already been explained; the first of these is, that the resistance offered by a metal to the passage of electricity is diminished by reducing the temperature; and the second is, that the heat evolved by a current in passing through a conductor is inversely as the resistance which it experiences. Now, in this experiment, the primary effect of the hydrogen is the cooling of the conducting wire; and the consequence is that this cooled wire, in transmitting the same current as a similar wire in air, offers less resistance, and less heat is therefore evolved by the wire surrounded by the hydrogen than by the wire which is surrounded by air.

(278) *Electric Conductivity of Liquids.*—Liquids are very inferior to solids in conducting power; indeed, the difference between the two classes of bodies is so extreme that it is difficult to institute an accurate comparison between them. The attempt, however, has been made by Pouillet: assuming as the unit of comparison the conducting power of a solution of sulphate of copper saturated at 59°, he gives the following as the relative conducting power of the undermentioned solutions:—

Saturated solution of sulphate of copper . . .	1
Ditto, diluted with an equal bulk of water . .	0·64
Ditto, diluted with twice its bulk of water . .	0·44
Ditto, diluted with four times its bulk . . .	0·31
Distilled water	0·0025
Ditto, with $\frac{1}{20,000}$ of nitric acid	0·015
Platinum wire	2,500,000·00

The conducting power of a platinum wire, of a diameter and length equal to that of the interposed columns of liquid is probably estimated too high.

Since these results of Pouillet's were published, the subject of the conducting power of liquids has been resumed by E. Becquerel, in the paper already cited. He states that saline solutions may be divided into two classes; in the first, the conducting power increases progressively in proportion to the strength of the solution, until it becomes saturated; sulphate of copper and chloride of sodium affording instances of this kind: whilst in the second class, of which nitrate of copper and sulphate of zinc may be taken as examples, the conducting power increases with the degree of concentration up to a certain point, beyond which it diminishes as the solution becomes more nearly saturated. The salts which exhibit this peculiarity are either deliquescent or extremely soluble. The following table contains a few of Becquerel's results. The saline liquids are to be considered as saturated unless otherwise specified :—

Electric Conductivity of Liquids.

Substances used.	Density.	Temp. ° F.	Conducting power.
Pure Silver		32	100,000,000·00
Solution of Sulphate of Copper	1·1707	50	5.42
do. half the strength		”	3·47
do. one fourth the strength		”	2·08
Solution of Chloride of Sodium		56	31·52
do. half the strength		”	23·08
do. one fourth the strength		”	13·58
Solution of Nitrate of Copper	1·6008	55	8·995
do. half the strength		”	17·703
do. one fourth the strength		”	13·442
Solution of Sulphate of Zinc	1·4410	58	5·77
do. half the strength		”	7·13
do. one fourth the strength		”	5·43
Oil of Vitriol 1 measure Distilled Water 11 measures		66	88·68
Nitric Acid (Commercial)	1·31	56	93·77
Platinum		32	7,933,000·00

It is not surprising that differences so considerable should be observed between the conducting powers of liquids and those of solids; for the processes of conduction in the two cases are essentially different. In liquids chemical decomposition and free movement of the component particles are indispensable, whilst nothing of the kind takes place in solids. The effects of heat are even inverted in the two cases; for experiment shows that as the temperature rises, the conducting power of the liquid increases rapidly; according to Becquerel, the conducting power of many solutions at 212°F. is three or four times as great as that of the same solution at 32°. These phenomena, therefore, are the reverse of those presented by most solids. Exceptions, however, occur: Faraday has shown that sulphide of silver, when cold, is an insulator, but by warming it gently it begins to conduct, and when hot it affords a spark like a metal; at a point a little below redness it conducts sufficiently to maintain its conducting power by the heat of the current which it transmits. Sulphide and fluoride of lead, as well as iodide of mercury, also exhibit the same peculiarity. Glass, when cold, is an excellent insulator of the electricity developed by friction, but when heated it conducts, and when red hot it possesses scarcely any insulating power; the same thing is also true of the tourmaline. Most of these cases have been traced to a partial chemical decomposition of the compound under the influence of softening by heat (Beetz, *Phil. Mag.*, 1854, p. 191). When liquefied by heat, these compounds all undergo chemical decomposition, and allow the current to pass freely.

(279) *Electric Conducting Power of Gases.*—Gases are almost perfect insulators of the voltaic current; although some feeble indications of conducting power have been discovered by Andrews, as well as by Hankel, by E. Becquerel, and by Buff, in a highly rarefied atmosphere, between metallic surfaces strongly ignited and in close approximation; and Magnus finds that small as is the conducting power of gases, they differ in degree in this respect, hydrogen surpassing other gases and vapours.

Grove has further shown, that in flame a current of electricity is not only transmitted, but that there is evidence of its production within the flame, and he attributes its origin to chemical action. Becquerel regards it as a thermo-electric phenomenon (*Ann. de Chimie*, III. lii. 411). Becquerel's experiments, however, are not conclusive; and the feebleness of thermo-electric currents, coupled with the slight conductivity of flame, render such a view inadmissible. If two platinum wires be connected with the extremities of a galvanometer, the free ends of the platinum being twisted into a small coil, and one of the platinum wires be inserted into the root of the blowpipe flame, whilst the other is introduced just in front of the apex of the blue cone, a current will be indicated, passing from the root to the apex of the flame. By forming several jets of flame together into a compound circuit, Grove succeeded in decomposing a solution of iodide of potassium by means of the currents obtained from flame. Under certain circumstances, however, which we now proceed to notice, highly heated gaseous matter appears to transmit voltaic power of high intensity, and the phenomena thus displayed are of a most brilliant and remarkable kind.

(280) *Disruptive Discharge—Electric Light.*—When the current is greater than the conductor is able to convey, the wire melts, and is dispersed in vapour; disruptive discharge, in fact, occurs. From a powerful voltaic battery this disruptive discharge may be maintained continuously, owing to the enormous quantity of electricity in circulation.

If the air be rarefied between the interrupted conductors, the interval through which the discharge can be effected may be considerably increased. Thus the heat developed by the passage of the current between two pieces of charcoal when they are in contact, will enable them to be separated for a considerable distance without interrupting the passage of the current; this distance ranges from $\frac{3}{4}$ inch to 1 inch when a series of seventy of Daniell's cells twenty inches in height are employed. Davy, with the great battery of the Royal Institution, consisting of 2000 pairs of plates on Wollaston's construction, obtained an arc of flame, between charcoal points, four inches in length, and of dazzling brilliancy.

Despretz, by using 600 cells of Bunsen's construction arranged consecutively, succeeded when the points were placed in a vertical line with the negative pole below, in obtaining an arc of 7·8 inches in length. With 100 pairs the arc was only one inch long. The most intense light, however, is obtained when the points are separated but to a small distance, because the resistance then being less, a much larger quantity of electricity passes in a given time, and the temperature is proportionately higher. Despretz found he obtained a much more intense light by employing his 600 cells in six parallel series, so as to form 100 cells of six times the ordinary size, than when they were connected into one continuous series. He estimated the light with the arrangement of 600 in six parallel series to be nearly six times as great as when 100 cells only were employed,—a result in conformity with the anticipations of theory. The same observer found that when the charcoal points were disposed in a horizontal direction at right angles to the magnetic meridian, the length of the arc when 200 pairs of Bunsen in two parallel series were employed, was greater in the proportion of 20·8 to 16·5, when the positive pole was to the east, than when it was to the west.

During the production of this dazzling light a considerable mechanical transport of the materials composing the terminals of the pile takes place, and there can be no doubt that the ignition of the solid particles contributes mainly to the production of the intense light thus procured. A cavity is always produced in the piece of charcoal attached to the positive wire which is connected with the last platinum or copper plate of the battery; and at the same time a mammillated deposit, which continually increases in length, is formed upon the charcoal on the negative wire in connexion with the zinc plate. Attempts have been made to apply this light to the purposes of illumination, and in particular cases, as for the display of optical phenomena in the class-room, it is often of high value. Its application is, however, attended with great practical difficulties, of which the transfer of conducting material from one pole to the other is one of the most serious; and it is very doubtful if, even when the mechanical obstacles are removed, such a light can be economically or advantageously used for the general purposes of illumination. The light is too intense for the unprotected eye to endure for any length of time in its immediate vicinity, and the expense is so great, that unless the electricity can be obtained in the process of preparing some chemical compound in the battery itself which will defray the cost of production, its success as a mercantile speculation is very problematical.*

This transfer of solid particles is not confined to cases in which a porous conductor like charcoal is used. The densest metals, such as platinum and iridium, are transferred from the positive towards the negative terminal, but the arc in these cases is not

* The general appearance of the electric lamp of Duboscq is shown in fig. 223, in which T, T represent the charcoal points between which the voltaic arc is maintained. The object to be effected is to preserve these points at a uniform distance from each

so long as when more friable materials are used. When a positive coke point was opposed to a negative electrode of platinum, the arc was not more than half the length of that obtained by

other, and at the same height in the lantern, so that the source of light shall always be kept in the same position with respect to the lens.

The regulator by which this result is attained is shown at R. Within this is an electro-magnet, and a clock-movement, the principal parts of which are represented upon a larger scale in fig. 224. The clock movement is designed to bring the two

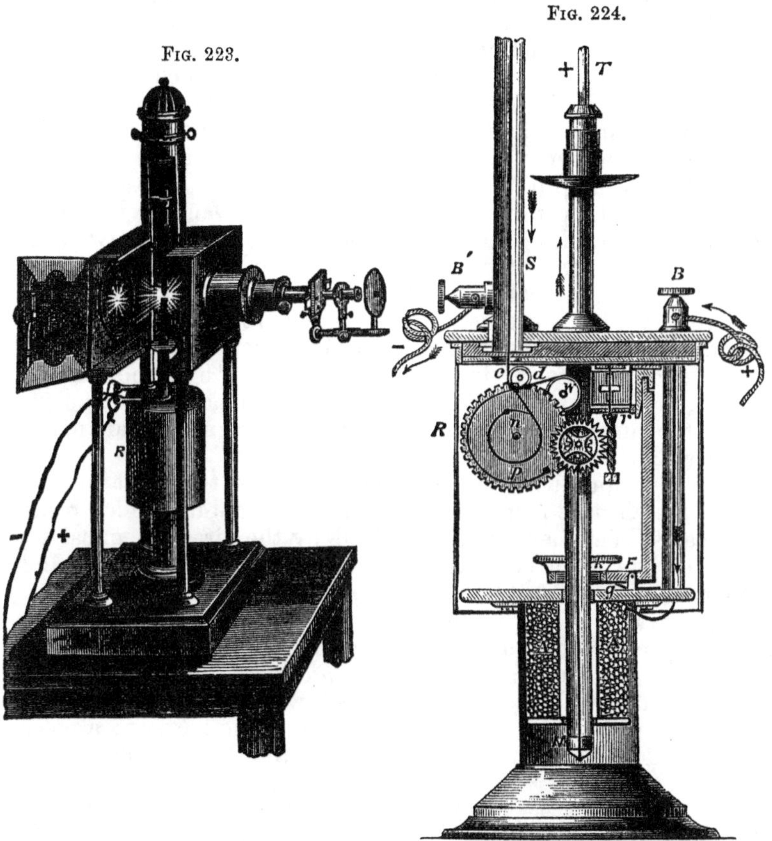

Fig. 223. Fig. 224.

points towards each other so as to compensate for the waste they experience in burning, and the electro magnet is employed to check the clock action when no longer needed. When the battery is in use the negative point is always consumed in air more slowly than the positive one; and it becomes necessary to provide means for moving each point, at a rate proportioned to the rapidity of its consumption. This is effected by making the drums *n* and *p* of unequal dimensions; the chains *c* and *d* are employed to transmit the movements of the clockwork to the points T, T'. The chain *c* attached to the upper or negative point T', is coiled upon the smaller drum *n*, and passes up the tubular support *s*. This chain is wound in the opposite direction to that of the chain *d*, which after passing over the pulley *d'*, is attached to the tube containing the lower or positive charcoal point T. Both drums are placed upon a common axis, and therefore both are moved by the clock in the same direction, so that whilst the chain *d* attached to the lower point is being wound up, the chain *c* connected with the negative point is being unwound, though less rapidly than *d*, and the negative point is allowed to de-making the coke negative and the platinum positive (De la Rive.) Grove found it to be true generally that in an oxidizing medium the brilliancy and length of the arc was greatest with the most oxidizable metals. Van Breda states that portions of the negative terminal are always transferred towards the positive wire. This was particularly evident when iron balls were made the terminals of the wires, although this transfer is much less in amount from the negative to the positive, than the simultaneous transfer from the positive to the negative wire. The light that attends the voltaic arc does not necessarily proceed from the combustion of the conducting material, for it occurs in a vessel from which air is exhausted, with a brilliancy not much inferior to that exhibited by it in the air. It may even be produced between two charcoal points which are immersed under water. In every case, however, the transference of some material particles is essential to the production of the luminous arc. Gassiot found that even when a combination of 320 cells on Daniell's construction was employed, no spark could be obtained between two platinum surfaces, connected one with one wire, the other with the opposite wire of the battery, in a high state of efficiency, although the two platinum surfaces were brought within $\frac{1}{3000}$ of an inch of each other. If, however, the transfer of some material particles be effected between the two surfaces, either by a momentary contact, or even by the discharge of a Leyden jar across the interval, the current may be established and the luminous arc maintained with a small number of pairs of plates.

The heat produced in the voltaic arc is of the most intense kind. Metals like platinum, iridium, and titanium, which resist the greatest heat that can be obtained by the direct chemical action attendant upon combustion in the furnace, readily melt and are transferred from the positive to the negative terminal by a voltaic current of high intensity. The fusion is easily accomplished by excavating a circular piece of gas coke, about an inch in diameter and half an inch thick, into the form of a crucible, which is attached by a stout copper bell-wire to the wire which is in connexion with the last platinum plate of the battery; a piece of boxwood charcoal or of gas coke about the thickness of a cedar

scend. The wires from the battery (about 40 pairs of Grove) are made fast to the binding-screws B, B′, the positive wire B being connected with one end of the coil A A of the electro-magnet M, while the other end of the coil is in electrical contact with the lower point T. The current is thus made to pass through the electro-magnet on its way to the charcoal points. When the electro-magnet is in full action it attracts the keeper *k* attached to the lower end of the bent lever working on the fulcrum F. The upper extremity of this lever, when the keeper is drawn home, locks into the ratchet wheel seen edgewise at *r*; thus arresting the clock movement, and rendering the charcoal points stationary. As soon as the distance between the points becomes too great, the current through the electro-magnet becomes reduced in power, and lets go the keeper *k*, which is forced away from the magnet by the releasing spring *q*. By this means the clockwork is immediately set free, and the points are thus made to approach each other, until the current recovers sufficient force again to attract the keeper, which once more locks into the ratchet wheel *r*. When the battery is in good action, these alternate motions of the keeper and of the clockwork recur with frequency and regularity; so that the points are maintained at a distance sufficiently uniform to prevent any sudden or material fluctuation in the amount of light.

pencil is attached to the wire connected with the zinc plate of the battery: the metal for trial is then placed in the little coke crucible, and the current from 20 or 30 pairs of Grove's battery is transmitted through it by means of the charcoal-point with which the negative wire of the battery is armed. Gassiot has pointed out the remarkable fact, of which no explanation has as yet been given, that the positive wire, or the wire connected with the platinum plate, becomes much the hotter of the two in this action. This effect is reversed in the case of the secondary current obtained from the Ruhmkorff coil (312), in which the negative terminal becomes the hottest, and from which the dispersion of solid particles almost exclusively occurs.

Favre (*Comtes Rendus*, lv. 56) has arrived at the interesting conclusion that the quantity of heat evolved by the solution of a definite quantity of zinc in any given circuit is lessened in the battery itself, in proportion as heat is evolved at any given point of the circuit, and that heat is lost when motion is produced. The quantity of heat thus lost agrees very closely with the quantity required by theory if Joule's mechanical equivalent of heat (129) be adopted. A part of the heat is thus converted into mechanical effect or motion, as must be the case if the mechanical theory of heat (130) be true. The simple solution of a quantity of zinc in sulphuric acid, equal in amount to that dissolved in the battery during each experiment, was found by previous researches to be represented by the number 18444. In these experiments Favre arranged the battery itself in a calorimeter; and in a second calorimeter he placed the conducting-wire, which was coiled in such a manner as to be applicable to the production of electro-magnetic action, the amount of which could be measured by its power of raising a weight. He then made five series of experiments. In the first of these the current traversed the battery only and a short copper wire: in the second series, it traversed the battery and the conducting-wire of the coil, the iron not being included in the coil; in the third series, the metallic core was previously placed in the axis of the coil; in the fourth series, the apparatus for rotation was set in motion, but no weight was raised; and in the fifth series a known weight was lifted to a definite height by the action of the electro-magnet. The results were as follows:—

No. of Experiments.	1st Calorimeter. (Battery.)	2nd Calorimeter. (Conducting coil.)	Heat lost for Weight raised.	Heat Units. Total.
1	18682			18682
2	18674			18674
3	16448	2219		18667
4	13888	4769		18657
5	15427	2947	308	18682

The fifth column gives the total amount of heat measured in 'units of heat' (*note* p. 208), from which it will be seen to be sensibly equal in each case.

The colour of the light emitted by the different metals when deflagrated between the wires of the battery, is peculiar for each: gold burns with a bluish white light, silver with a beautiful green light, copper with a reddish white, zinc with a powerful white light tinged with blue, and lead with a purple light; steel burns with brilliant yellow scintillations, mercury with a brilliant white light tinged with blue. If these lights be viewed separately through a glass prism, large dark intervals will be seen between a few brilliant streaks of light of different colours and of definite degrees of refrangibility (107, 108).

Chemical Actions of the Voltaic Battery.

(281) *Discharge by Convection.*—To the chemist, however, the discharge of the voltaic current by the process of convection, is even more interesting than the brilliant phenomena exhibited by the disruptive discharge, since it is in the discharge by convection that the important chemical actions of electricity are displayed.

It has already been explained when describing the voltameter (272), that if the connecting wires of a voltaic battery terminate in platinum plates or wires which are made to dip into acidulated water, decomposition of the liquid takes place, and oxygen and hydrogen are evolved at the surfaces of the platinum plates. This important discovery was made in the year 1800, by Nicholson and Carlisle, and the chemical action of the voltaic pile thus revealed, enabled Davy a few years later to decompose the alkalies and earths, which up to that time had been regarded as elements; but by showing their compound nature, he at once modified, in an important manner, the views of chemical philosophy which had prevailed up to that period.

In pursuing these experiments on the voltaic decomposition of water, it was soon observed that when copper wires, or the wires of metals which are easily susceptible of oxidation, are employed, gas escapes from one wire only; whilst if platinum or gold wires be used, gas is evolved from both. In the first case, the oxygen combines with the copper or oxidizable metal, and forms an oxide which is dissolved by the acid liquid, and therefore hydrogen alone escapes; in the second case, both gases are evolved; since neither platinum nor gold has sufficient chemical attraction for oxygen to combine with it at the moment of its liberation.

The process of resolving compounds into their constituents by electricity, is termed *electrolysis* (from 'electricity' and λύσις releasing), and a body susceptible of such decomposition, is called an *electrolyte;* the terminating wires or plates of the battery are called the *poles* of the battery. The word *electrode* is also used as synonymous with the pole of the battery, and it implies the door or path (from ὁδὸς a way) to the current by which it enters or leaves the compound through which it is transmitted.

(282) *Laws of Electrolysis.*—A great variety of bodies admit

of being decomposed by electrolysis, but the process is not applicable to all indiscriminately. It occurs under certain definite laws, which may be stated as follows:—

1. *No elementary substance can be an electrolyte:* for from the nature of the operation, compounds alone are susceptible of electrolysis.

2. *Electrolysis occurs only whilst the body is in the liquid state.* The free mobility of the particles which form the body undergoing decomposition is a necessary condition of electrolysis, since the operation is always attended by a transfer of the component particles of the electrolyte in opposite directions. Electrolysis is necessarily a process of electrical conduction, but it is conduction of a peculiar kind; it is totally different from that of ordinary conduction in solids. If an electrolyte be solidified, it instantly arrests the passage of the force; for it cannot transmit the electric current like a wire or a solid conductor; the thinnest film of any solidified electrolyte between the two plates suspends all decomposition. Many saline bodies are good conductors when in a fused condition; for example, nitre, whilst in a fused state, conducts admirably; but if a cold electrode be plunged into the melted salt, it becomes covered with a film of solid nitre, and no current is transmitted until a continuous chain of liquid particles is restored between the plates by the melting of the film; these effects are readily exhibited by including a galvanometer in the circuit. A few partial exceptions to this rule have been observed, and have already been alluded to (278); but in such cases the decomposition is always extremely limited.

3. *During electrolysis, the components of the electrolyte are resolved into two groups: one group takes a definite direction towards one of the electrodes; the other group takes a course towards the other electrode.* This direction of the *ions* (as the two groups which compose the electrolyte have been termed) depends upon the direction in which the chemical actions are going on in the battery itself. The two platinum plates in the decomposing cell may be distinguished from each other in the manner proposed by Daniell. These plates occupy respectively the position of a zinc and of a platinum plate in an ordinary cell of the battery: that is to say, if for this decomposing cell an ordinary battery cell were substituted, a rod of zinc would occupy the place of one of the platinum plates, and would be attacked by the oxygen and acid in the exciting liquid of the battery, whilst a plate of platinum or some other conducting metal would occupy the place of the second platinum plate, and would have the hydrogen of the exciting liquid directed towards it. To the plate of the decomposing cell which corresponds to the zinc rod, Daniell gave the name of the *zincode*, which is synonymous with the *anode* of Faraday and the *positive pole* of other writers. To the plate which corresponds to the platinum or conducting metal, Daniell gave the name of the *platinode*, which is synonymous with Faraday's term of *cathode*, and with the *negative pole* of other writers. Oxygen, chlorine, and the acids generally, make

their appearance at the zincode in the decomposing cell during electrolysis; whilst hydrogen, alkalies, and the metals are evolved upon the platinode.

This definite direction which the elements assume during electrolysis may be shown by collecting the gas which is evolved over two platinum plates, connected, one with the last platinum, the other with the last zinc plate, of a combination consisting of three or four pairs of Grove's battery. Hydrogen will be collected over the platinode, or the plate in connexion with the zinc end of the arrangement, and which would correspond to the platinum plate if another cell of the battery were here interposed; whilst from the zincode, or plate in connexion with the platinum of the battery, oxygen is evolved.

The following experiment further illustrates the definite direction which the components of the electrolyte assume. Let four glasses be placed side by side, as represented in fig. 225, each

Fig. 225.

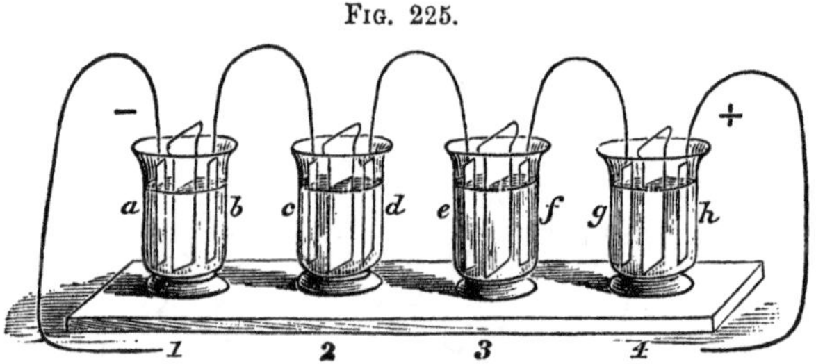

divided into two compartments by a partition of card, or three or four folds of blotting-paper, and let the glasses be in electrical communication with each other by means of platinum wires which terminate in strips of platinum foil. Place in the glass No. 1, a solution of iodide of potassium mixed with starch; in 2, a strong solution of common salt, coloured blue with sulphate of indigo; in 3, a solution of sulphate of ammonium, coloured blue with a neutral infusion of the red cabbage; and in 4, a solution of sulphate of copper. Let the plate, *h*, be connected with the positive wire, and let *a* complete the circuit through the negative wire. Under these circumstances iodine will speedily be set free in *b*, and will form the blue iodide of starch; chlorine will show itself in *d*, and will bleach the blue liquid; sulphuric acid will be seen in *f*, and will redden the infusion of cabbage; sulphuric acid will also be liberated in *h*, as may be seen by introducing a piece of blue litmus-paper, which will immediately be reddened; whilst a piece of turmeric paper will be turned brown in *a*, from liberated potash; in *c* it will also be turned brown by the soda set free; in *e* the blue infusion of cabbage will become green from the ammonia which is disengaged; and in *g* metallic copper will be deposited on the platinum foil.

4. *The amount as well as the direction of electrolysis is definite, and it is dependent upon the degree of action in the battery;*

being directly proportionate to the quantity of electricity in circulation. It has been amply proved by experiment that for every 32·7 grains of zinc which is dissolved in any one cell of the battery, provided local action be prevented, 9 grains of water are decomposed in the voltameter; or if, as in the preceding experiment, several electrolytes be arranged in succession, each compound will experience a decomposition proportioned to its chemical equivalent. For instance—if the current be made to pass first through fused iodide of lead, and then through fused chloride of tin—for each 32·7 grains of zinc dissolved in any one cell of the battery, 103·5 grains of lead, and 59 grains of tin will be separated on the respective platinodes, whilst 127 grains of iodine, and 35·5 grains of chlorine will be evolved on the respective zincodes. These numbers correspond with the chemical equivalents (not the atomic weights) of the several elements named.

Variations in the intensity of the current (*i. e.*, variations in the quantity of the force which passes through a given transverse section of the conductor in equal times) produce no variation in the amount of chemical decomposition which is effected by the arrangement. For example: if three similar voltameters, provided with plates of equal area, be arranged as at *a*, *b*, *c*, fig. 226, the first will transmit twice as much electricity in a given time as either of the others. The current will therefore have twice the intensity in *a*; but the total quantity of gas collected from *b* and *c* together will be exactly equal to the total amount yielded by *a* in the course of the experiment.

FIG. 226.

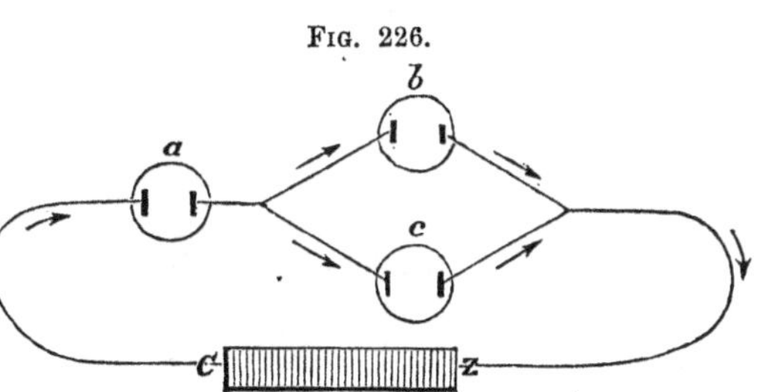

Hence it follows that the quantity of electricity which is separated from a given weight of matter in the act of combination is able, irrespective of its intensity, when thrown into the current form, to produce the decomposition of an *equivalent quantity* of any compound body which is susceptible of electrolysis; and hence it has been concluded that the equivalent weights of the simple bodies are those weights of each substance which are associated with equal quantities of electricity, and have naturally equal electric powers.

To these laws may be added a fifth—viz.:—

5. *Those bodies only are electrolytes which are composed of a conductor and a non-conductor.* The conductors accumulate on the platinode, the non-conductors on the zincode. For example, iodide of lead when melted, conducts the current; metallic lead, which is a conductor, accumulates at the platinode; whilst iodine, which is a non-conductor even when melted, collects at the zinc-

ode. On the other hand, red chloride of sulphur (SCl_2) is not an electrolyte, although composed of single *equivalents* of its components; and melted sulphur, and chlorine, when the latter is liquefied by pressure, are both insulators of electricity. A compound composed of two conductors is equally unfit for electrolysis. For instance, a metallic alloy, such as plumber's solder, composed of two parts, or one equivalent, of lead, and one part, or one equivalent, of tin, when melted, conducts the current perfectly, but no separation of its constituents is effected.

(283) *Relative Decomposability of Electrolytes.*—Every electrolyte, since it can transmit a current, is also capable of generating a current if it be employed to excite action in the battery itself. Comparatively few electrolytes, however, are practically available for this purpose. It is necessary that the deposited compounds be dissolved as fast as they are produced; otherwise the crust of insoluble matter introduces a mechanical obstacle by which the action is speedily checked.

Great differences occur in the facility with which different electrolytes yield to the decomposing action of the voltaic current. Generally speaking, the greater the chemical opposition between the elements of a compound, the more readily it yields to electrolysis. The following table exhibits the order in which, according to Faraday, the different compounds which are enumerated yield to electrolysis; those which are most readily decomposed standing first on the list:—

Solution of iodide of potassium
Fused chloride of silver
Fused chloride of zinc
Fused chloride of lead
Fused iodide of lead
Hydrochloric acid
Diluted sulphuric acid.

(284). *Electro-chemical Actions.*—The suspension of chemical action which occurs under the influence of electrical induction is one of the most interesting illustrations of the correlation of forces. This suspension is well shown in the way in which zinc when placed in contact with copper beneath the surface of sea-water, acts in preventing the corrosion of copper, and transfers to itself the chemical energy which would otherwise be manifested upon the copper (261). A similar suspension of chemical action is produced in the ordinary case of the decomposition of water between two platinum electrodes by the voltaic current: here the electricity appears to act by weakening, or rather by partly neutralizing, ordinary chemical attraction in one direction, whilst it strengthens or adds to it in the opposite, and hence the particles which were previously in combination with each other lose their attraction one for the other, and acquire it for those particles which are next adjacent to them in the liquid; thus, if the brackets above the subjoined formulæ indicate the state of combination of the elements of hydrochloric acid before the passage of the current, the brackets below would indicate the effect produced after its transmission, thus:—

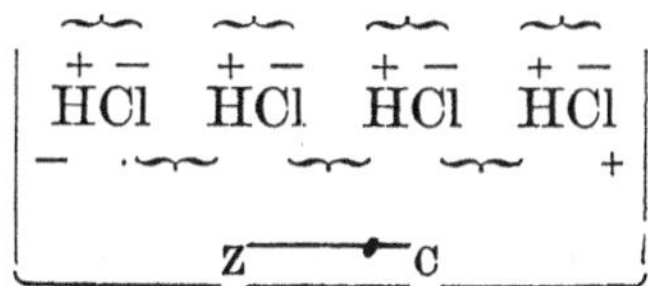

Here z c is supposed to represent the battery, and + and — the terminal wires of the arrangement: the positive electricity seems to detach the chlorine adjacent to it from the hydrogen with which it was previously in combination, whilst the negative electricity produces a similar effect upon the contiguous particles of hydrogen, and the intermediate portions are polarized in the manner above represented.

The following modification of this experiment also shows in a striking manner the remarkable influence of electric polarity upon chemical attraction:—If two separate glasses filled with diluted sulphuric acid be placed side by side, and into one glass the negative wire of the battery is plunged, whilst the positive wire dips into the other cell, no decomposition will ensue; but if a connexion be established between the two glasses by means of a slip of platinum foil, one end of which is made to dip into each, the current will be immediately transmitted: hydrogen will be evolved upon the platinode in one glass, and oxygen upon the zincode in the other glass; whilst, owing to the polar condition into which the connecting slip of platinum is thrown, hydrogen will be given off from one end of the slip, and oxygen will be evolved upon the other extremity of it, although the metal itself experiences no sensible change beyond a slight rise of temperature.

(285) *Electrolysis of Salts.*—It has already been stated (282) that when a binary compound, such as a fused chloride, or an iodide, is submitted to electrolysis, the ions or components of the compound are separated at the respective electrodes in equivalent proportions: the metal appearing at the platinode, whilst the chlorine, or corresponding element, is deposited at the zincode. If the zincode of the battery be formed of a substance capable of combining with the chlorine or corresponding element, an equivalent amount of the chloride or other compound of this metal will be formed there; and when the metal of the zincode is the same as that contained in the compound which is undergoing decomposition, the original compound is reproduced. Thus, if a quantity of fused chloride of silver (AgCl) be decomposed by a current which is conducted into it by means of silver wires, the quantity of the chloride will undergo no alteration; for in this experiment, as fast as the silver is deposited upon the negative wire, a corresponding amount of silver will be dissolved from the positive wire, since the latter wire combines with the

equivalent quantity of chlorine which is liberated at this point. Let Ag+ represent the positive silver wire, or zincode, by which the current is conveyed into the melted chloride, and —Ag the negative wire: if the brackets in the upper row of symbols which follow indicate the combination before the passage of the current, the lower ones will show the arrangement after the occurrence of the decomposition:—

$$-\text{Ag} \mid \overbrace{\text{AgCl}}\ \overbrace{\text{AgCl}}\ \overbrace{\text{AgCl}} \mid \text{Ag}+$$

$$\text{AgAg} \mid \overbrace{\text{ClAg}}\ \overbrace{\text{ClAg}}\ \overbrace{\text{ClAg}} \mid$$

An examination of the products furnished by the electrolytic decomposition of aqueous solutions of the oxysalts (or salts formed from acids which contain oxygen), exhibits results which appear to be at variance with the statement that the components of an electrolyte are separated in equivalent proportions—but further investigation shows that they are strictly in accordance with it; these experiments also lead to very interesting conclusions which have an important bearing upon the theory of salts in general.

When a solution of an oxysalt such as sulphate of sodium is submitted to electrolysis, a quantity of acid accumulates around the positive plate, and of alkali around the negative plate; whilst at the same time both oxygen and hydrogen are set free. The proportions of each may be determined by means of a diaphragm apparatus, in which the products of decomposition can be kept separate from each other, and the gases which are evolved can be separately collected. Such an apparatus was contrived by Daniell, and is represented in fig. 227. A and C are the two

Fig. 227.

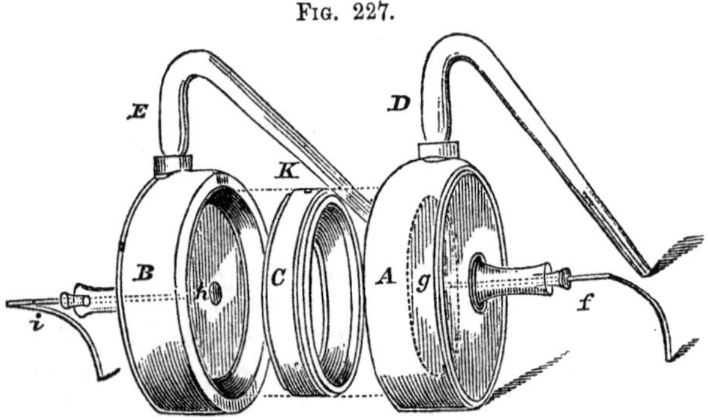

halves of a stout glass cylinder, which are fitted by grinding upon a hollow ring of glass, C; the two rims of this ring are ground down to a grooved shoulder, so as to allow a thin piece of bladder to be tied over each end of the ring, which thus constitutes a kind of drum; at K is a small hole through which the cavity thus formed can be filled with liquid; D and E are two bent glass tubes for carrying off the gases evolved during electrolysis; *g* and *h* are two large platinum electrodes, which pass through corks in the necks of the cylinder, and can be connected with the battery by means of the wires, *f*, *i*. The apparatus thus forms three compartments, which may be filled with the liquid for experiment, and the whole may be supported in a frame of wood. By the employment of this apparatus, it is found that while a quantity of acid accumulates at the zincode, an equivalent amount of alkali is set free at the platinode. At the same time, a quantity of gas is also emitted from each electrode, that from the zincode being oxygen, and that from the platinode, hydrogen. Upon placing a voltameter in the course of the circuit, it is found that a quantity of gas is emitted from the saline liquid, exactly equal to that obtained from the voltameter; and upon neutralizing the acid and alkali, they likewise are in equivalent proportions to the gas which is emitted (Daniell, *Phil. Trans.*, 1839 and 1840).* Suppose that the gas collected in the voltameter amount to 71 cubic inches (or the quantity yielded by 9 grains of water at 60° F., Bar. = 30 inches), the united quantity of oxygen and hydrogen from the solution of sulphate of sodium would be the same,—and, in addition, one equivalent in grains, or 71 grains of sulphate of sodium would be decomposed; 31 grains of soda (Na_2O) would apparently be liberated at the platinode, and 40 grains of sulphuric anhydride (SO_3) at the zincode. Upon substituting a voltameter of fused chloride of lead in the circuit for one containing diluted sulphuric acid, and still continuing to transmit the current through the solution of sulphate of sodium, it was found that for every equivalent of chloride of lead which was decomposed, 1 equivalent of the mixed gases was evolved from the saline solution, and at the same time 1 equivalent of the sulphate was decomposed. What is observed in the case of sulphate of sodium holds good also with the oxysalts of the alkalies and earths generally.

(286) *Bearing of Electrolysis on the Binary Theory of Salts.*—It is a fundamental law of voltaic action, that the amount of force circulating in any circuit at the same time is equal in every vertical section of the circuit, and consequently its decomposing energy in each section must also be equal; yet in the case of the sulphate of sodium, there appears to be in the saline solution twice the amount of decomposition that occurs in the adjacent voltameter, though both are transmitting the entire current from the battery. A satisfactory and complete explanation of this anomaly is, however, effected by the *binary theory* of salts in the following manner:—

Upon the binary theory of salts, the component ions of sulphate of sodium are not soda and sulphuric anhydride (Na_2O, SO_3)

* This observation is *strictly* true, as I have found by numerous careful repetitions of these experiments, although, as Magnus (*Pogg. Annal.* cii. 1) has pointed out, when the quantity of acid and alkali becomes considerable in the two cells, the liberated acid and alkali each transmit a portion of the current as well as the sulphate of sodium, so that if the experiment be unduly prolonged, the proportion of the acid and base set free is less than that which theory requires.

but sodium and sulphion (a compound of 4 atoms of oxygen and 1 of sulphur), the compound being *sulphionide of sodium* (Na_2SO_4); and such it proves to be under the influence of electrolysis, sodium being liberated at the platinode, whilst sulphion appears at the zincode. Sodium, however, cannot exist in the presence of water; the metal immediately takes oxygen, and becomes converted into soda; Na_2+H_2O yielding Na_2O+H_2: the alkali is dissolved in the liquid, whilst the hydrogen escapes as gas. Sulphion is equally unable to exist in the separate form; it combines with hydrogen, H_2O+SO_4 becoming $O+H_2SO_4$, while oxygen escapes, and sulphuric acid is formed: and as both sodium and sulphion are liberated in equivalent proportions, the quantity of water decomposed is also equivalent to the quantity of salt electrolysed.

On the foregoing view, therefore, the evolution of oxygen and hydrogen during the decomposition of saline solutions is a secondary action. If a solution of salt of a metal which, like copper or lead, does not decompose water at ordinary temperatures, be substituted for one of sulphate of sodium as the electrolyte, no hydrogen should be evolved, but the metal itself should appear upon the platinode; whilst if the other constituent of the salt be one which, like chlorine, is unable to take hydrogen from water at common temperatures, no oxygen should be emitted. Accordingly, upon making the experiment with a solution of chloride of copper or of chloride of lead, the salt is resolved into metallic copper or metallic lead, and chlorine gas, but no oxygen or hydrogen, is liberated. These observations will explain the reason that although water, when pure, is scarcely decomposed by the current from 100 cells or upwards, yet it appears instantly to become a good electrolyte on the addition of a few drops of acid, or of solution of a salt of an earth or an alkali; for upon the addition of the salt it is this body which is decomposed, and the water is then resolved into oxygen and hydrogen by a secondary action in the manner already explained. Sulphuric acid in solution is in like manner resolved into hydrogen and sulphion, H_2SO_4. In neither case is the water directly electrolysed. This observation also explains a circumstance which much perplexed the earlier experimenters upon the chemical action of the voltaic pile. In all experiments in which water was decomposed, both acid and alkali were invariably found to be liberated at the electrodes, although distilled water was employed; and hence it was believed for some time that the voltaic current had some mysterious power of generating acid and alkaline matter. The true source of these compounds, however, was traced by Davy (*Phil. Trans.*, 1807), who showed that they proceeded from impurities contained either in the water employed, or in the vessels made use of, or in the atmosphere itself. Having proved that ordinary distilled water always contains traces of saline matter, he redistilled it at a temperature below the boiling-point, in order to avoid all risk of carrying over salts by splashing: he found that when he used marble cups to contain the water for decomposition, the acid was the hydrochloric and the alkali was soda, both derived from chloride of sodium present in the marble itself; when agate cups were used to contain the water, he obtained silicia; and when he used gold vessels, he procured nitric acid and ammonia, which he traced to atmospheric air; by operating *in vacuo*, the quantity of acid and alkali was reduced to a minimum, but the decomposition then was almost arrested, although he operated with a battery of 50 pairs of 4-inch plates. Hence it is manifest that water itself is not an electrolyte. but it is enabled to convey the current if it contain only faint traces of saline matter.

The following table will illustrate the manner in which saline bodies may be classified in relation to their mode of electric decomposition; the *anion* indicating the electro-negative, the *cathion* the electro-positive component.

A, Simple		Simple Anion Simple Cathion	Ag,Cl.
B, Complex	I. Monobasic.	1. Simple Anion Compound Cathion	H_4N,Cl.
		2. Compound Anion Simple Cathion	K,NO_3.
		3. Compound Anion Compound Cathion	H_4N, $C_2H_3O_2$.
	II. Polybasic.	1. Compound Anion Simple Cathions	Na_3PO_4.
		2. Compound Anion Simple and Compound Cathions	(Na,H,H_4N),PO_4.

When *monobasic salts* are the subjects of electrolysis, the proportion of acid and of base liberated is in single equivalents: thus, nitrate of potassium yields 1 equivalent of potash and 1 of nitric acid for each equivalent of fused chloride of silver which is decomposed in the voltameter.

When a *polybasic salt* is submitted to electrolysis, for each atom of fused chloride of lead ($PbCl_2$) which is electrolysed in the voltameter, 2 atoms of base appear at the platinode: for example, when 2 atoms of the tribasic phosphate of sodium are decomposed, 3 atoms of chloride of lead are reduced in the voltameter; and in the diaphragm cell 2 (Na_3PO_4) yield 3 $Na_2O+3\ H_2$ at the platinode, whilst 2 (H_3PO_4)$+3\ O$ are liberated at the zincode. When the pyrophosphate of sodium ($Na_4P_2O_7$) is electrolysed, 2 atoms of chloride of lead are decomposed in the voltameter, whilst 2 $Na_2O+2\ H_2$ make their appearance at the platinode of the diaphragm cell, and $H_4P_2O_7+O_2$ are set free at the zincode. When 2 atoms of metaphosphate of sodium 2 (Na,PO_3) are decomposed, 1 atom of chloride of lead is electrolysed in the voltameter, whilst Na_2O+H_2 appears at the platinode of the diaphragm cell, and 2 HPO_3+O is liberated at the zincode. In each case the phosphoric acid thus transferred preserves its tribasic, dibasic, or monobasic character, according to the nature of the salt which was electrolysed.

The results of the electrolysis of the monobasic and polybasic oxysalts, it will thus be seen, admit of a simple explanation upon the binary theory. The results of the decomposition of the basic salts are not, however, so easily reconciled with this view. According to E. Becquerel, when basic salts are decomposed,—for each atom of chloride of lead in the voltameter, 2 atoms of a monobasic acid are liberated at the zincode, whilst all the atoms of base which were previously in combination with the acid are liberated at the platinode. My own experiments upon this point confirm this view, although from a numerous series of trials on the basic nitrites, basic nitrate, and basic acetates, of lead, I always obtained a smaller quantity of oxide of lead and of metallic lead than was required by theory, if this law held good; probably this deficiency was due to the secondary action of the solution upon the liberated oxide. When, for example, the tribasic acetate of lead ($Pb\ 2\ PbO,\ 2\ C_2H_3O_2$) was decomposed, employing as the electrodes plates of lead instead of plates of platinum, for every 2 atoms of acetic acid radicle which appeared at the zincode, somewhat less than 1 atom of metallic lead and 2 atoms of oxide of lead appeared at the platinode: so that the salt appeared to have undergone decomposition into $Pb+2PbO$ and $2\ C_2H_3O_2$. It is difficult to reconcile the idea of an ion consisting of $Pb+2\ PbO$* with the binary theory. The most probable explanation appears to be this: viz., that the oxide of lead is attached to the normal acetate in a manner analogous to water of crystallization, and that the normal acetate is the true electrolyte, whilst the oxide is left upon the electrode in the insoluble form as soon as the acid which kept it in solution is removed. A similar explanation may be applied to the case of other soluble basic salts.

Faraday's 'principle, that if the same pair of elements unite with each other to form more than one compound, it is only the compound which contains one atom of each element that admits of electrolysis,' although generally true, cannot, however, be laid down as a law of electric decomposition. It occasionally happens that two different electrolytes containing the same elements exist. Both cupric chloride ($CuCl_2$) and cupreous chloride ($CuCl$), for example, are electrolytes. When a current of given strength is transmitted successively through, 1, a solution of sulphate of copper; 2, a solution of cupric chloride; and 3, fused cupreous chloride,—decomposition takes place simultaneously in each: but for each atom of sulphate of copper resolved into Cu and SO_4, one of cupric chloride is decomposed into Cu and Cl_2 and two of cupreous chloride into $2\ Cu$ and Cl_2; so that for each atom of copper separated at the platinode from the solution of the sul-

* E. Becquerel considered that he had obtained a new suboxide of lead by the electrolysis of its basic salts, but this appears to be an error. It is a mere mixture of metallic lead with oxide of lead, for the solution of neutral acetate of lead quickly dissolves the oxide and leaves the metallic lead; and the proportion of oxide to the metallic lead varies according to the nature of the salt operated upon.

phate and from the cupric or ordinary chloride, 2 atoms of copper are liberated from the cupreous chloride.

If sulphate of copper be used as the measure of the voltaic action, Buff (*Liebig's Annal.*, cx. 257) considers when fused molybdic anhydride is electrolysed, that for each atom of sulphate of copper resolved into Cu and SO_4, 1 atom of molybdic anhydride (MoO_3) furnishes 1 atom of oxygen and 1 of MoO_2, and in like manner 1 atom of fused vanadic anhydride (VO_3) furnishes 1 of oxygen and 1 of VO_2. Fused bichromate of potassium ($K_2Cr_2O_7$, or K_2CrO_4,CrO_3) is also an electrolyte, and it is decomposed partially into K_2 and CrO_4, and partially into Cr_2O_3 and O_3.

The same current which liberates 3 atoms of metallic copper from 3 of sulphate of copper, will successively resolve one atom of chloride of aluminum (Al_2Cl_6) into Al_2 and Cl_6, 6 of cupreous chloride, 6 ($CuCl$), into Cu_6 and Cl_6, and 2 of chromic anhydride, 2 (CrO_3), into Cr_2O_3 and O_3.

When more than one salt is present in a solution, the current, when below a certain strength, decomposes only one of them, the best conductor being decomposed when the current is feeble; but when the intensity of the current passes a certain limit, a portion of the inferior conductor experiences decomposition. This limit to the intensity of the current, according to Magnus (*Pogg. Ann.*, cii. *loc. cit.*), varies with the size of the electrodes, and with the distance between them, as well as with the proportion in which the different electrolytes are mixed.*

(287) *Unequal Transfer of Ions during Electrolysis.*—A curious circumstance in relation to the proportion in which the ions of the electrolyte travel towards the respective electrodes, was remarked in the course of these investigations on the decomposition of saline solutions. It was perhaps natural to expect that, if a solution underwent electrolytic decomposition, for each equivalent of the compound decomposed, its component ions should be *transferred* to each electrode in the exact proportion of half an equivalent of each, although a whole equivalent was *liberated* in the manner shown at No. 2 in the scheme which follows:—

			A	
(1)		Cu Cu SO_4SO_4	Cu Cu SO_4SO_4	
(2)	—Cu	Cu C SO_4 S	u Cu O_4 SO_4	+ SO_4
(3)	—Cu	Cu SO_4	Cu Cu SO_4SO_4	SO_4+
			A	

In this scheme it is supposed that sulphate of copper is the

* The results obtained by Magnus upon the decomposition of iodic acid, perchloride of tin, and some other bodies, appear to be only secondary actions, not produced by the direct electrolysis of these compounds, and consequently they do not admit of being applied to the general theory. This, indeed, has already been pointed out by Buff.

electrolyte, each particle of copper represented by the symbol Cu being in combination with the particle of sulphion represented by SO_4 immediately beneath it. Let A A indicate the position of a diaphragm of bladder separating two equal quantities of the solution which in No. 1 are supposed to be in their normal state. Let No. 2 represent the same solution after it has undergone electrolysis; an equivalent of copper having been set free at the platinode, and one of sulphion at the zincode. It was not unnatural to expect that this result would have been attained by the transfer of half an equivalent of copper into the division containing the platinode, whilst half an equivalent of sulphion passed towards the zincode in the manner represented. Experiment, however, shows that such a supposition is erroneous, and that the decomposition more commonly happens in the mode represented in No. 3, in which case a whole equivalent of the anion is transferred to the zincode, leaving a whole equivalent of cathion uncombined, at the platinode. Sometimes when the oxide of a metal is soluble in water, the transfer of a small quantity of the cathion takes place towards the platinode, but the quantity of the cathion and the anion *set free* are always in equivalent proportions to each other (Daniell and Miller, *Phil. Trans.*, 1844, p. 16). Acids, whether they be soluble in water or not, always travel towards the zincode in proportions larger than the metals which are united with them pass towards the platinode.

D'Almeida (*Ann. de Chimie*, III. li. 257) attributes these remarkable irregularities, which occasion much inconvenience in electro-plating, to the development of free acid around the zincode. He considers that the acid, owing to its superior conducting power, conveys a large proportion of the current, and that the metal is then reduced upon the platinode by the hydrogen, at the moment of its liberation. He finds that when the solutions are strictly neutral the inequality of transfer is scarcely perceived. Strictly neutral solutions of copper and zinc, when decomposed between electrodes of copper or zinc respectively, become acid during the operation, because the metal at the zincode is not dissolved quite so rapidly as it is separated at the platinode, and consequently a little free acid accumulates around the zincode, and occasions the irregularity in transfer of the ions which we are now considering. When a current traverses a saline solution kept constantly acid in the zincode cell, whilst the platinode is maintained constantly neutral, the salt is transferred unequally, the zincode becoming least impoverished; but if the solution be kept neutral around the zincode whilst it is maintained alkaline around the platinode, the result is reversed, and the impoverishment of the platinode is the least marked.

This explanation of D'Almeida is confirmed by the subsequent researches of Magnus. Hittorf (*Pogg. Annal.*, lxxxix. 177, and xcviii. 1) gives a different, and, as it appears to me, an improbable and complicated theory for the explanation of these results; but his experiments appear to be consistent with those already quoted.

(288) *Electrovection*, or *Electrical Endosmose.*—It was observed many years ago by Porrett, when water was placed in a diaphragm apparatus, one side of which was connected with the positive, and the other side with the negative electrode of the battery, that a considerable portion of the liquid was transferred from the positive towards the negative side of the arrangement. It has since been found that the same result occurs in a minor degree when saline solutions are electrolysed, and, generally, the greater the resistance which the liquid offers to electrolysis the greater is the amount which is thus mechanically carried over. From numerous experiments I have found that in all these cases the water carries with it a proportion of the salt which it holds in solution. It appears from the researches of Wiedemann (*Pogg. Annal.*, lxxxvii. 321), which have been confirmed by those of Quincke, that the amount of liquid transferred, *cæteris paribus*, is proportioned to the strength or intensity of the current; that it is independent of the thickness of the diaphragm by which the two portions of liquid are separated; and that when different solutions are employed, the amount transferred in each case, by currents of equal intensity, is directly proportional to the specific resistance of the liquid.

This transfer has been minutely studied by Quincke, who seems to have explained the steps which attend its production:—

If a capillary tube, bent into the form of the letter U, filled with an imperfect conductor, such as alcohol or distilled water, be connected by platinum wires with the inner and outer coatings of a charged Leyden jar, the level of the liquid is raised in the negative limb, and depressed in the positive limb. The quantity of liquid which is thus carried over is proportioned to the electromotive power of the arrangement, and is independent of the length of the tube: he has also found that the quantity of liquid carried over for equal charges is inversely as the square of the diameter of the tube. In a tube of one millimetre diameter with a single cell of Grove's battery, distilled water rises 0·000061$^{mm.}$ in the negative tube.

If oil of turpentine or bisulphide of carbon be substituted for water, and the two platinum wires be connected with the positive and negative conductors of the electrical machine, the movements are reversed, the fluid rising in the positive bend. The motion of oil of turpentine may, however, be reversed if the tube be lined with sulphur. If a diaphragm apparatus with a porous clay septum be used, the essence of turpentine is transferred towards the positive electrode, but if a diaphragm of flowers of sulphur, compressed between two pieces of silk, be used, the transfer is towards the negative electrode. It is obvious that this transfer is connected with the particular electrical condition assumed by the containing vessel or diaphragm, in relation to the liquid which is set in motion.

It has been observed by Jürgensen, that light particles of various solids in suspension in water are transferred in the direction opposite to that in which the water is carried under the influence of the current; and these motions are diminished by the addition of any salt or other substance which increases the conducting power of the liquid.

Into a straight piece of capillary tube $0{\cdot}4^{mm.}$ in diameter, let distilled water containing a few granules of starch in suspension be placed, and let the liquid be connected with the positive and negative conductors of the machine, by means of platinum wires sealed into the tube. It will then be seen that the granules in the centre of the tube pass towards the negative electrode, whilst along the sides of the tube is a return current towards the other electrode. By increasing the rapidity of the rotation of the machine, the central current becomes increased in rapidity, whilst that on the surface becomes slower, and at length the movement of the suspended particles is reversed, so that all move towards the negative electrode. The wider the tube, the more difficult it is to produce this reversal of the current of the particles at the surface. Solid particles of the most varied description exhibit these phenomena, and always in the same order when water is employed. Thus, whether finely-divided gold, platinum, copper, iron, graphite, quartz, felspar, oxide of manganese, asbestos, emery, baked clay, sulphur, lac, silk, cotton, lycopodium, carmine, quill, paper, ivory, air-bubbles, small drops of oil of turpentine or of bisulphide of carbon, be used, the phenomena are in each case similar.

If oil of turpentine be substituted for water, the same bodies all move, but the motions are now towards the positive electrode, with the single exception of sulphur.

Quincke seems to have found the key to these remarkable phenomena. By employing granules of lycopodium, which are sufficiently uniform in size, and very nearly of the same density as water, he ascertained by watching their motion under the microscope, that the velocity of a particle near the axis of the tube is proportional to the intensity of the current. The following is his explanation:—

The water near the sides of the tube is transferred towards the negative electrode, while all the suspended particles are impelled towards the positive electrode. These two motions are effected with a speed proportioned to the intensity of the current; but the water returns along the axis of the tube, as there is no other course open to it, and assists the motions of the suspended particles. The water on the sides of the tube, on the contrary, carries the particles in a direction opposite to that in which they are tending. When the intensity of the electricity increases, the rapidity with which the particles move increases more rapidly than the motion of the liquid, because of the increasing influence of the friction of the sides upon the moving water; so that at length a point is reached in which the solid particles move faster than the opposing current of the water.

In these phenomena water acts partly as a conductor, partly as an insulator. As a conductor traversed by a current, the cylinder of water on its surface acquires a quantity of free electricity, the density of which varies from one section to another; but inasmuch as the conducting power of water is imperfect, time is required for the communication of the electricity of one particle to the adjacent particles. Now a particle of water near the side of the tube becomes positively electric by contact with the glass, and its positive electricity tends to move in the same direction as the positive electricity of the current; but since the particle of water cannot instantaneously part with its electricity, it is carried forward in the direction of the positive current: and these motions can only occur in imperfect conductors, which retain their charge for a sensible time. If a foreign substance, such as a grain of starch, be suspended in the water, it becomes negatively electric by simple contact with the water, and independently of the current from the machine,—water having been shown, by Faraday and others, to become positively electrified by friction with every substance hitherto tried; and the electricity evolved by contact follows the same law as that produced by friction. If a conducting liquid be added to the water, these conditions of the development of electricity by contact are altered, and the motion of the particles is arrested.

Oil of turpentine, on the contrary, becomes negative by friction and by contact with all substances hitherto tried, except sulphur, and consequently the direction of the movements is reversed. (Quincke, *Ann. de Chimie*, III. lxiii. 479.)

(289) *Secondary Results of Electrolysis.*—The explanation already given of the mode in which the oxysalts are electrolysed was happily applied by Daniell to the elucidation of the origin of the voltaic power, in a combination contrived by Becquerel (262), which presents many interesting peculiarities. If a porous tube filled with nitric acid be plunged into a vessel containing a solution of potash, and the wires of a galvanometer, armed with platinum plates, be plunged one into the nitric acid, and the other into the alkaline solution, a current will circulate; oxygen will be emitted from the plate immersed in the potash, and nitrous acid, owing to the absorption of hydrogen by the nitric acid, will be formed around the other plate, whilst nitrate of potassium is slowly produced by transudation of the two liquids through the pores of the diaphragm. By connecting several of these cells together in succession, upon the principle of the ordinary battery, the power may be considerably augmented. The decomposition which appears to occur is represented by the following symbols, in which H,NO_3 indicates the nitric acid, and K,HO the hydrate of potash: the position of the brackets above the symbols indicates the arrangement before the current is established, whilst, after its passage, the arrangement is supposed to be that indicated by the brackets beneath:—

$$H,NO_3\ H,NO_3 \mid K,HO\ K,HO.$$

It is particularly to be observed that no development of oxygen or of hydrogen occurs upon the platinum plates until the two plates are united by a conducting wire, and it ceases as soon as the conducting communication between the plates is interrupted: in the latter case the polar arrangement of the particles is interfered with, although the reaction of the hydrate of potash upon the nitric acid continues. The secondary action of the nitric acid on the hydrogen which is set free is necessary to the development of the current. If sulphuric acid be substituted for the nitric, the hydrogen is not absorbed and no current is obtained, probably because it is neutralized by the counter current which the accumulation of the hydrogen upon the platinum plate tends to produce (264).

The secondary actions of the voltaic current are often of great importance; they require to be carefully distinguished from its primary effects. Secondary results are, in some instances, produced by the action of the liberated components of the electrolyte upon the materials employed as electrodes: thus if a slip of copper be substituted for one of platinum, as the zincode of the battery, and be immersed in diluted sulphuric acid, sulphate of copper will be formed by the combination of the copper with the disengaged sulphion. At other times, the secondary results are manifested by the reaction of the ion upon the liquid in which the electrolyte is dissolved, as when the potassium or sodium, set free at the platinode in an aqueous solution of its salts, liberates hydrogen by its action upon the water; $K+HHO=H+KHO$. In the cases just cited, the chemical attractions of the disengaged ions are very intense, and the secondary action is exactly proportioned to the primary, so that it may be employed as a measure of the current: but when the tendency to combination is more feeble, the proportion of these secondary actions to the primary one is greatly influenced by the extent of surface exposed by the electrode to the liquid, and the energy of the current, and consequent quantity of the ion disengaged at once. Generally, the slower the action, and the larger the surface of the electrode, the more uniform and complete is the secondary action. These results are well exemplified by Bunsen's researches on the isolation of the more oxidizable metals by the voltaic current. If a thin platinum wire be used as the platinode in a solution of chloride of chromium, to convey the current from 4 or 5 cells of the nitric-acid battery, metallic chromium may be obtained without difficulty; but if a plate of platinum be employed, oxide of chromium, mixed with a certain amount of hydrogen, is liberated; in the latter case the metal has time to decompose the water before fresh particles of chromium are deposited upon its surface.

In consequence of these secondary actions the same element may sometimes appear at one electrode, sometimes at the other, as is seen in the case of nitrogen: if, for instance a solution of sulphate of ammonium be submitted to electrolysis, it yields ammonia and hydrogen at the platinode and a mixture of nitrogen with oxygen is set free at the zincode. The nitrogen in this case is liberated as a secondary result of the combination of a portion of the oxygen with the hydrogen of the ammonia. If nitrate of ammonium be substituted for the sulphate, nitrogen appears among the gaseous products at both electrodes, the nitric acid being deprived of its oxygen by the hydrogen evolved at the platinode, and the ammonia of its hydrogen by the oxygen set free at the zincode.

If a solution of acetate of lead be employed as the electrolyte, the acetic acid undergoes partial decomposition from the action of the oxygen upon it at the moment of its liberation at the zincode, but at the same time a portion of the oxygen also enters into combination with some of the oxide of lead contained in the liquid, and, as Warington proved, a deposit of peroxide of lead is produced. Nobili, who first observed this phenomenon, found that if a polished steel plate be employed in such a solution as the zincode to the battery (4 or 6 cells of Grove's may be employed), the deposit assumes the form of a thin film, which exhibits the iridescent tints of Newton's scale,—the tints varying according to the thickness of the film produced. Other experimentalists have modified the patterns which may be obtained by these *metallochromes*, which have been applied by Becquerel even to the imitation of the tints of flowers; and by varying the strength of the battery and of the solutions employed, he has succeeded in producing some effects of great delicacy and beauty. Salts of manganese or of bismuth may be substituted for those of lead, with similar results.

Many of these secondary actions are very interesting: Kolbe has devoted particular attention to the effects of oxygen when liberated during electrolysis (*Proceed. Chem. Soc.*, iii. 285, and *Q. J. Chem. Soc.*, ii. 157). Hydrochloric acid, especially when previously mixed with sulphuric acid, is in this manner partially converted around the zincode into chloric and perchloric acids; and in an acid solution of chloride of potassium, chlorate and perchlorate of potassium are formed. Cyanide of potassium in solution, when subjected to the voltaic current, is in like manner converted into the cynate. A concentrated solution of chloride of ammonium evolves hydrogen at the platinode, but the chlorine instead of being liberated at the zincode, acts upon the chloride of ammonium, and forms oily drops of chloride of nitrogen, which explode when touched by the opposite electrode. Smee has shown that by means of the voltaic current the ferrocyanide may be converted into the ferricyanide of potassium. Kolbe has, further, ascertained the effect of the liberated oxygen upon various organic compounds, and by submitting valerate of potassium to electrolysis he decomposed the valeric acid ($HC_5H_9O_2$) which it contains, and succeeded in obtaining from it a new substance, *valyl* ($(C_4H_9)_2$), (or more properly *tetryl*); a new ether, ($C_8H_{18}O$) *tetrylic ether*, and a hydrocarbon (C_4H_8), apparently identical with oil-gas: and by a similar process from acetic acid ($HC_2H_3O_4$) he obtained methyl $(CH_3)_2$, the homologue of tetryl. Particular interest is attached to these researches, owing to the circumstance that in each case the compounds obtained by the electrolysis belong to a series related to an alcohol different from that which was submitted to decomposition. The valeric acid thus yields an ether of the tetrylic series; and acetic acid, which is a derivative of wine-alcohol furnishes the hydrocarbon which belongs to the wood-spirit series.

(290) *Nascent State of Bodies.*—It is obvious, from the powerful effect which oxygen produces at the moment of its liberation from compounds during electrolytic decomposition, that such oxygen must be in a condition very different from that in which it exists when once it has assumed the gaseous form. Oxygen is not insoluble in water, and it is therefore possible to bring it in small quantities at a time into chemical contact with salts or other bodies which water may hold in solution. Oxygen gas may, however, be transmitted for an unlimited time through a solution of chloride of potassium without effecting the conversion of any portion of the chloride into chlorate, or into perchlorate of potassium; and yet, as has been mentioned in the foregoing paragraph, this change is easily effected by oxygen as it escapes during the electrolysis of an acidulated solution of the chloride of potassium. But it is not necessary that oxygen should be liberated by the agency of the voltaic battery in order that it should acquire this increase of activity. If hydrated protoxide of nickel, or protoxide of cobalt, be suspended in a solution of caustic potash, it will undergo no change when subjected to a current of oxygen gas; but if a current of chlorine be substituted for the oxygen, the whole of the metallic oxide will be converted into a brown sesquioxide: this change arises from the action of the chlorine upon the potash, during which chloride of potassium is formed whilst oxygen is set free, and at the moment of its liberation attaches itself to the oxide of nickel or of cobalt; $2KH\mathit{O}+Cl_2+2(\mathit{NiO},H_2\mathit{O})=2KCl+\mathit{Ni_2O_3},3H_2\mathit{O}$. Other substances besides oxygen exhibit this peculiarity, and chemists have long recognized the fact, that bodies, when in this *nascent state*—that is to say when in the act of liberation from other substances—display more energetic attractions than they show when once obtained in the isolated form:—For example cyanogen and chlorine do not enter directly into combination; but if cyanogen at the instant that it is set free from another compound, be presented to chlorine, the two bodies combine; so that if moist cyanide of mercury be decomposed by means of chlorine, chloride of cyanogen may be obtained: the chlorine removes the mercury step by step, and the cyanogen at the moment of its liberation enters into combination with another portion of chlorine. In a similar manner sulphur, when set free from an alkaline persulphide in the midst of a solution of hydrochloric acid, combines with hydrogen, and forms persulphide of hydrogen, $K_2\mathit{S}_5+2HCl=H_2\mathit{S}_5+2KCl$, the chlorine taking the potassium, whilst the sulphur and the hydrogen, both in the nascent state, unite to form a new compound, although their chemical attraction is so slight that this compound separates spontaneously into sulphuretted hydrogen and free sulphur. The process of double decomposition is par-

ticularly applicable in cases where the mutual attraction of the bodies which it is desired to obtain in combination is comparatively feeble. It is not impossible that this superior chemical activity of bodies in the nascent state may arise from the fact that their particles are individually electrified at the moment of their separation from a previous state of combination; and that in this condition they may exert upon the particles of dissimilar contiguous matter, a force of induction which may be the agent that determines their chemical combination: if by a process of *double* decomposition the particles of both compounds were oppositely electrified, combination might be expected to be proportionately facilitated:—For instance, if a solution of sulphide of potassium and one of chloride of copper be mixed, they will decompose each other, the sulphur being negative, will tend to combine with the positive copper, and the positive potassium will unite with the negative chlorine. If the brackets in No. 1 represent the mode in which the molecules are arranged on the instant of mixture previous to decomposition, those in No. 2 will illustrate the arrangement of the molecules after mutual decomposition has been effected:—

$$(1)\ \begin{array}{cccc} + & - & + & - \\ K_2 & S & Cu & Cl_2 \\ Cl_2 & Cu & S & K_2 \\ - & + & - & + \end{array} \ \text{become}\ \left\{\begin{array}{cccc} + & - & + & - \\ K_2 & S & Cu & Cl_2 \\ Cl_2 & Cu & S & K_2 \\ - & + & - & + \end{array}\right\}\ (2)$$

(291) *Theory of the Electrical Origin of Chemical Attraction.*—It has already been remarked (245, 257) that whenever two dissimilar substances, electrically insulated, are brought into contact, and are separated from each other, disturbances of their electrical equilibrium is produced; one of the bodies becoming negatively electrified whilst the other indicates a corresponding charge of positive electricity. It is a well ascertained fact, that certain substances, by friction, acquire one kind of electricity more readily than the other; thus, for example, sulphur, when rubbed upon flannel or fur, becomes negatively electric, whilst glass, on the other hand, most readily assumes the positive state. What has been proved to occur when masses of matter are brought into contact was supposed by Davy (*Phil. Trans.*, 1807) to happen also when the molecules of two dissimilar substances are brought within the sphere of mutual activity; he assumed 'that chemical and electrical attractions depend upon the same cause, acting in one case on particles, in the other on masses of matter' (*Phil. Trans.*, 1826, p. 389); and all the phenomena of chemical attraction have been referred to the exertion of mutual electrical attraction between the atoms of each substance in the compound. When, for example, chlorine and potassium are united, it is supposed that each atom of chlorine, by contact with an atom of potassium, becomes negatively electrified, whilst the potassium becomes positively excited; a certain portion of the

positive electricity from the chlorine uniting with a corresponding amount of negative electricity which is liberated from the potassium, thus producing the light and heat which attends the combination of these two bodies (Berzelius). Supposing each atom of both kinds of matter to be associated with equal quantities of both electricities, and that the two different electricities be represented by the signs + and —, we may represent the potassium and chlorine by symbols; (— K +) indicating an atom of potassium, and (— Cl +) an atom of chlorine. As soon as the two bodies are brought into contact, it is supposed that the chlorine loses a certain amount of positive electricity, whilst the potassium loses an equal quantity of negative electricity, the change being symbolized thus (+KCl—) and (+—). When the chloride of potassium is decomposed electrolytically, a quantity of positive electricity is transferred from the positive wire of the battery to the chlorine, and compensates for that which it has lost; and when this amount of electricity has been restored, the chlorine no longer has any tendency to remain in combination with the potassium, and hence it is set free upon the positive plate, whilst a simultaneous transfer of negative electricity to the potassium occurs from the negative plate and the alkaline metal is therefore liberated upon the negative side of the arrangement. The electricity which is set free by the battery is supplied by the action of the sulphion upon the zinc, in the cells of which the battery consists.

The remarkable law discovered by Faraday, that the same current of electricity when transmitted successively through various electrolytes, decomposes each in the proportion of their respective chemical equivalents (282, 4) adds greatly to the probability of the supposition that electrical and chemical phenomena are due to different manifestations of the same agent. So strong was Daniell's conviction upon this point, that he applied the term *current affinity* to the voltaic current; since by means of the proper application of conductors, or channels for the force, the chemical attraction of a portion of zinc and sulphuric acid at one point could be transferred to a distant spot, and could there be made to effect an equivalent amount of chemical decomposition upon a different compound. The chemical equivalent of any substance upon the electro-chemical theory, is that quantity of each body which is associated with an amount of electricity equal to that associated with a given weight of some substance, such as hydrogen, which is selected as the standard of comparison; the proportion of electricity which is associated with a given weight of any substance being inversely as its combining proportion. Assuming the specific electricity of hydrogen to be represented by the arbitrary number 1000, the following is given by Daniell (*Introd. to Chem. Phil.* 2nd Ed. p. 687) as an approximative table of the *specific electricity* (or quantity of electricity associated with *equal weights*) of a few of the more important elements and compounds:—

Cathions	Equivalent.	Specific Electricity.	Anions.	Equivalent.	Specific Electricity.
Hydrogen	1.0	1000	Oxygen	8·0	125
Potassium	39·2	25	Chlorine	35·5	27
Sodium	23·3	43	Iodine	126·0	8
Zinc	32·5	31	Bromine	78·3	12
Copper	31·6	31	Fluorine	18·7	55
Ammonia	17·0	58	Cyanogen	26·0	38
Potash	47·2	21	Sulphuric Acid	40·0	25
Soda	31·3	32	Nitric Acid	54·0	18
Lime	28·5	35	Chloric Acid	75·5	13

Ingenious, however, as is the electrical theory of chemical attraction, it must be admitted that it is far from being free from objection and difficulty when it is attempted to apply it to all cases of chemical action. It has been already stated that a very large number of bodies exist which are not susceptible of electrolysis.* Indeed, the chief classes of electrolytes are: 1, binary compounds of the non-metallic elements with the metals, such as the oxides, chlorides, iodides, bromides, and fluorides; 2, compounds of bodies like cyanogen with the metals, such as the cyanides and the sulphocyanides; and 3, compounds of the metals with the radicles of the oxyacids, such as the nitrates, sulphates, borates, carbonates, acetates, tartrates, &c. Now, so long as a compound consists of two elements only, if it be decomposed at all, there is no difficulty in anticipating the result of the voltaic action;—the electro-negative element will appear at the zincode, and the electro-positive element at the platinode; yet there are binary compounds which are not electrolysable, such, for instance, as pure water, and chloride of sulphur. If their particles be united by electric opposition, why should they not yield to the current? In the case of more complex bodies, such, for example, as nitrate of silver, or borate of lead, it is not possible, *à priori*, to say how the compound would yield under the electric influence. It is quite clear in the case of salt, that the power which holds together the two ions of the salt in the form of two *iso-electric* groups (or groups of equal electric energy), must be of a different order from that which holds the elements of its component ions in combination. The tie which binds together nitrate of silver as Ag,NO_3, must be of an order different from that which unites the elements of *nitrion* (NO_3) together. Sulphate of sodium, again, as an electrolyte is separated into Na_2 and SO_4. But neither nitrion nor sulphion can exist in the separate form; how can they become associated under electric influence? Again, (SO_3) sulphuric anhydride, is not an electrolyte when fused: the same thing may be said of fused boracic anhydride; and examples of this kind might be multiplied almost

* A very numerous series of Grove's battery, amounting to 900, and in some instances even to 950 pairs, produced in the experiments of Lapochin and Tichanowitsch no effect on absolute alcohol, ether, valeric acid, oil of turpentine, bisulphide of carbon, and fused boracic anhydride; fousel-oil was scarcely acted on.

without limit. Why, if chemical attraction be due to the exertion of electric action, should certain bodies be readily decomposable by the voltaic current, and why should others of less complex composition resist it entirely? At present, no hint appears to have been given which offers any clue to the solution of these questions.

Practical Applications of Electrolytic Action.

(292) *Electrotype*, *Voltatype*, or *Galvano-Plastics.*—Shortly after Daniell had invented his constant battery, he observed that when copper was deposited upon a plate of platinum, it furnished a coherent sheet in which the lines and irregularities on the surface of the platinum were faithfully reproduced upon the deposited copper; but he made no practical application of the observation. In the year 1839, Jacobi, of St. Petersburg, announced that he had discovered a method of making exact copies of a metallic surface in copper by means of the voltaic battery, and shortly afterwards Messrs. Spencer and Jordan, who had each independently arrived at a similar result, published the methods which they had employed for the attainment of this object. The processes thus disclosed were so simple and easy of execution, that they were immediately repeated with success; and in the following year Mr. Elkington in England, and M. Ruolz in France, began to apply the voltaic battery on an extensive scale to the arts of plating and gilding. Since this period the voltaic battery has been most extensively employed as a means of depositing not only copper, gold, and silver from their solutions, but zinc, tin, and lead, and occasionally platinum and nickel: many other metals have also, for particular purposes, been reduced from their salts by its means.

For the deposition of metallic copper, a solution of the sulphate of this metal is employed, but the mode of using it varies with the object in view. Suppose that it be desired to obtain a copy of an engraved copper plate: a wire or slip of copper having been soldered to the plate for the purpose of facilitating its connexion with the battery, the back of the plate is covered with a resinous varnish, by which means this surface is electrically insulated from the solution, and it is thus protected from any deposit of reduced metal. The plate thus prepared is connected with the negative electrode of a voltaic battery, consisting of 3 or 4 of Smee's or Daniell's cells, and immersed vertically in a bath consisting of a saturated solution of sulphate of copper. A sheet of copper, equal in size to the one to be copied, is suspended parallel to the latter in the liquid, and connected with the positive electrode of the battery; an immediate decomposition of the solution ensues; metallic copper is deposited upon the entire surface of the negative plate, in the form of a coherent, continuous sheet, and a nearly corresponding amount of copper is dissolved from the positive plate, so that the liquid remains constantly charged with a quantity of sulphate of copper, approximatively equal to that originally employed. At the commencement of the operation, care must be taken to ascertain that the deposit occurs uniformly over the whole surface of the negative plate, for if any portion of it be soiled by grease or resinous matter, the copper will not be thrown down upon those parts: when once the deposition has commenced uniformly, it goes on without difficulty. If the plates be suspended vertically, the solution should be frequently agitated, for unless this precaution be taken, the liquid around the negative plate becomes impoverished, whilst that around the positive plate becomes unduly saturated with the copper salt (287); currents are then produced in the liquid, owing to its unequal density, and they occasion the formation of vertical grooves and striæ upon the back of the sheet of deposited metal. This inconvenience is sometimes obviated by supporting the two plates in the bath in a horizontal position, the negative plate being undermost; the positive plate must in this case be enveloped in flannel, in order to prevent the small particles of metal, which are constantly being detached from it, from falling upon the lower plate, and interfering with the regularity of the deposition.

The deposit varies in hardness and coherence according to the number of cells employed in the battery, the relative size of the plates of the battery and those of the depositing cell, and the temperature and degree of concentration of the solution. The more slowly the action takes place, if the solution be concentrated, the harder and more crystalline is the deposit. By modifying the power of the battery, and the strength of the solution, in the manner which experience soon indicates, copper may be obtained of any desired degree of toughness.

When the deposit has acquired the necessary thickness, it must be detached at its edges from the original plate, and can then be stripped off without difficulty. The thin film of oxide, or of other adhering impurity, derived from the exposure even of a freshly deposited copper plate to the air for a few hours, is sufficient to prevent too intimate an adhesion between the plate and the deposit. In the electrotype thus obtained, the lines which are cut away upon the surface of the original plate are represented in relief in the copy, and if a fac-simile of the engraving be desired, a new deposit must be formed upon the copy thus procured; in this second transfer, an exact duplicate of the original engraving will be presented. Many large and valuable copper plates, amongst which are some of those engraved for the Art Union, have been thus multiplied with success. So faithfully does the deposit reproduce all irregularities upon the surface of the matrix on which it is deposited, that by its means copies of daguerreotype plates have been obtained, in which the original design is accurately transferred to the deposit of copper, without destroying the original impression.

(293) *Preparation of Moulds for Electrotyping.*—In copying medals or other works of art, it is frequently necessary to employ casts of the objects, instead of the original objects themselves,

which might be liable to injury by immersion in the metallic solution. These casts may be made in fusible metal, or in stearine, in plaster, or gutta percha. Gore (*Pharm. Journal*, July, 1855) recommends a mixture of 2 parts of gutta percha and 1 part of marine glue; the materials are to be cut up, and the glue melted at a gentle heat and incorporated with the gutta percha. The paste is to be applied while soft, with a pressure gradually increasing, to the surface of the medal, or other object which it is desired to copy. In certain cases an impression of the object to be copied is obtained in sheet lead by the application of strong pressure. In every instance before proceeding to effect the metallic deposition, the back of the mould, if made of metal, or of a conductor of electricity, must be coated with a resinous varnish, or with some non-conducting matter. When moulds of plaster of Paris are employed, they must be rendered impervious to moisture by immersion in melted wax or tallow; after which the surface to be copied is endued with the power of conducting electricity, by applying finely-powdered black-lead, of good quality, to the surface by means of a brush; taking care that every portion of the surface to be copied is completely coated by it. The cast is then connected with the negative wire of the battery by means of a strip of sheet lead, or a copper wire, which is in electric contact with some portion of the black-lead surface. Impressions of seals in sealing-wax, stamps in relief upon pasteboard or paper, and the engraved blocks used for wood-cuts, after they have been thus rendered conductors upon the surface, may be electrotyped with facility. Even glass may be rendered a conductor by the use of one of the methods of depositing silver upon its surface. Leaves, flowers, fruits, and insects have also been coated with copper, or with silver, by the electrotype process. A mode of producing a conducting surface upon these articles, due to Capt. Ibbetson, consists in immersing them in a weak solution of phosphorus, either in bisulphide of carbon or in ether, allowing the solvent to evaporate from the surface, and then plunging the objects into a solution of nitrate of silver; the phosphorus left upon the surface reduces a very thin film of silver upon the superficial portions of the objects, sufficient to enable them to receive the deposit from the battery, if they be properly connected with the negative wire, and submitted in a metallic bath to the action of the electric current. Steel plates cannot be copied by immersing them in a bath of sulphate of copper, because the steel and the sulphate act chemically on each other, and thus the engraving would be destroyed. This difficulty has been overcome by electrotyping them first in silver, which can be deposited upon the steel without injury, and upon this silver matrix a copper fac-simile of the original plate can afterwards be obtained.

For the electrotyping of small objects, such as coins or medals, it is not necessary to use a separate voltaic battery, since the depositing cell itself may, in the following manner, be converted into a voltaic couple of sufficient power to decompose the sulphate of copper:—Let a glass cylinder, such as the chimney of an argand gas-burner, be closed below by a plug of plaster of Paris, and be supported in a vessel containing a solution of sulphate of copper, in which the mould or the medal to be copied is supported by a metallic wire; let the inner tube be filled with sulphuric acid diluted with 10 or 12 times its bulk of water, and let an amalgamated zinc rod be placed in its axis. If this zinc rod be connected with the wire proceeding from the mould of the medal to be electrotyped, copper will be deposited upon the surface of the mould. The apparatus in fact constitutes a cell of Daniell's battery, with a trifling modification in its form. The solution of copper should be maintained uniformly saturated with sulphate of copper, by suspending crystals of the salt in the upper part of the liquid.

(294) *Electro-zincing.*—Zinc may be deposited from its sulphate on the surface of iron, by processes similar to those used for sulphate of copper. The operation requires but a feeble current, and admits of being performed upon a very large scale: the iron links of the Hungerford suspension bridge, which were passed into the abutments on the side of the river, were successfully submitted to this operation; each of those links is 24 feet in length, and of proportionate width.

It is not possible, however, to obtain coherent plates of all the metals with the same facility as is the case with copper and zinc. Many of the metals are thrown down from their solutions in a crystalline form, whether the deposition be effected rapidly or slowly. Silver is separated thus from its nitrate, and lead exhibits a similar deportment when the acetate or the nitrate of this metal is electrolysed. Gold and platinum do not give coherent plates when solutions of the chlorides of these metals are submitted to voltaic deposition. Lead may be deposited upon iron from a solution of oxide of lead in potash; and a solution of oxide of tin in potash may be used to obtain coherent plates of tin by electrolysis. In like manner ammoniacal solutions of the salts of cobalt and nickel may be employed to furnish electrotype plates of these metals. In some cases, however, when a simple salt fails to give a satisfactory result, the effect may be obtained by the employment of certain double salts of the same metal with potassium or with sodium: thus the double cyanide of gold and potassium is largely employed for gilding, and the corresponding salt of silver is extensively used in electro-silvering. In gilding, silvering, and zincing, one great desideratum is to obtain a firm adherence between the newly deposited metal and the object to be gilt or plated; the surface of the metallic object is therefore first rendered *chemically* clean, a result which is carefully avoided in the process of electrotyping. In the latter case it is usual to expose the object, if freshly polished, to the atmosphere for 24 hours before placing it in the depositing cell, in order to prevent permanent adhesion.

(295). *Electro-Plating*—The metals upon which an adherent coating of silver is most readily deposited are brass, copper, bronze, and German silver; but it may also be effected on steel. The articles to be plated are cleansed from adhering greasy matters either by boiling them in a weak alkaline solution, and then washing; or they are heated to low redness in a muffle: in either case they are next dipped into diluted nitric acid for the purpose of removing any adhering film of oxide. They are then brushed with a hard brush and some sand; and having been rinsed from adhering impurities, and separately attached to a clean copper wire, they are again dipped for an instant into nitric acid, washed, and immersed whilst still wet in the silvering bath. Let fig. 228 represent a plan of this bath, and C Z the voltaic battery; the copper wires attached to the articles to be plated are twisted round the rods P P P, which are connected with the negative wire of the battery, whilst the positive wire is connected with a series of silver plates, Z Z Z, which are also immersed in the silvering liquid. This solution is commonly prepared by dissolving cyanide of silver in a solution either of cyanide or of ferro-cyanide of potassium. Solutions containing hyposulphite or sulphite of silver are occasionally employed. In order to prepare the silvering bath, a solution of nitrate of silver may be precipitated by the addition of cyanide of potassium so long as it produces a precipitate: this precipitate, after having been washed by decantation, is dissolved in a solution of cyanide of potassium.

Fig. 228.

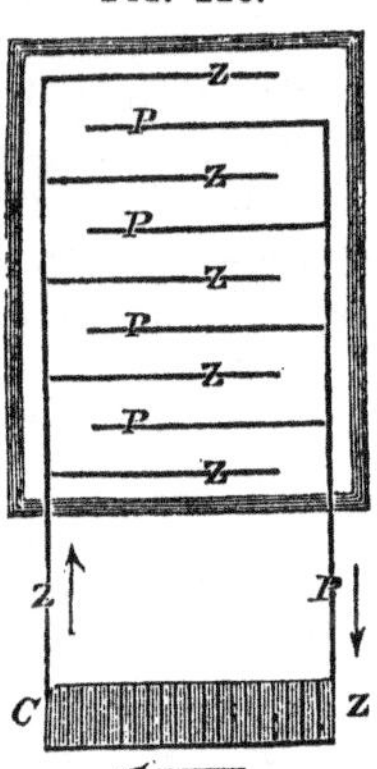

An excess of cyanide of potassium is requisite; at least 3 parts of cyanide of potassium being employed for 1 part of cyanide of silver.* A solution which contains $\frac{1}{50}$ of its weight of silver is found to be of a convenient strength for ordinary operations. When cyanide of potassium is used in the bath as a solvent, the solution gradually becomes alkaline from the formation of carbonate of potassium, which accumulates in the liquid and interferes with the regularity of the decomposition: but if cyanide of calcium be substituted for the cyanide of potassium, this inconvenience is obviated, since carbonate of calcium is formed, and owing to its insolubility, it sinks to the bottom of the bath as fast as it is produced. The articles when plated have a dead white or chalky surface, but they may be burnished by pressure if desired, and they then assume the brilliant lustre of polished silver. It is remarkable that the addition of a very small proportion of bisulphide of carbon to the bath causes the deposited silver to assume the lustre of the polished metal.† The amount

* If ferrocyanide of potassium be used as a solvent of the cyanide of silver, 10 parts of this salt are required for the solution of 1 part of cyanide of silver.

† In order to effect this object, 6 ounces of bisulphide of carbon are directed to be agitated with 1 gallon of the plating liquid, and set aside for 24 hours. Two ounces of the liquid thus obtained, are to be added over night to 20 gallons of the ordinary plating liquid; the bath is ready for use next morning. This addition of the solution of the

of silver which is deposited can be regulated very accurately by weighing the articles before immersion, and weighing them again afterwards. A deposit of from $1\frac{1}{4}$ ounce to $1\frac{1}{2}$ ounce of silver to a square foot of the plated surface answers well in practice; the sheet of silver under these circumstances being of about the thickness of ordinary writing paper. The solution must be frequently stirred in order to preserve the liquid of uniform density and composition throughout.

The batteries used at Birmingham for gilding and silvering are in general simply plates of amalgamated zinc opposed to plates of copper in diluted sulphuric acid: the plates are so arranged that they can be readily raised or lowered in order to expose a smaller or larger surface to the action of the acid. The superficial area, and number of the plates used, are made to vary according to the size and nature of the objects to be operated upon. The workman judges from experience as to the number of pairs to be employed; it seldom happens that more than two or three pairs of plates are needed. In Paris, Bunsen's carbon and zinc batteries are also employed with success in these operations.

(296) *Electro-Gilding and Platinizing.*—It is possible to gild most of the ordinary metals by voltaic action. Articles which consist of brass, bronze, copper, or German silver are first annealed, then *pickled*, as the operation of immersing them into the mixture of diluted nitric and sulphuric acids is termed, after which they are scrubbed and "dipped" in strong nitric acid, and then rinsed in water, as is practised in preparing them for plating. Silver articles are cleansed in a similar manner, but they do not require to be "dipped." Iron and steel may be gilt by cleansing them from grease, first with potash, and then by dipping in nitric acid, and scouring the surface with burnt clay finely sifted, in order to remove the black stains produced by the liberation of carbon. A more powerful current is required for gilding upon iron than upon the metals previously mentioned.

The gilding bath most usually employed consists of cyanide of gold dissolved in cyanide of potassium. It may be prepared by dissolving gold in aqua regia, and adding cyanide of potassium to the diluted liquid so long as it produces a precipitate; a brisk effervescence accompanies the action, and a yellow deposit of protocyanide of gold (AuCy) is formed: the clear liquid is decanted, and the precipitate is redissolved in a solution containing between 7 and 8 parts of the cyanide of potassium to 1 part of gold: the solution is then diluted until 100 parts of the liquid contain 1 part of gold.

M. Ruolz has shown that various other gilding baths may be used instead of the double cyanide of gold and potassium: for example, he finds that the cyanide of gold may be employed when brought into solution by the ferrocyanide, or by the ferri-

bisulphide requires to be renewed daily, to make up for the loss of the bisulphide of carbon by evaporation. Much care is required in the use of such a solution, for it is liable to changes which are produced by very slight modifications in the mode of working.

cyanide of potassium; he has also used with success the double sulphite of gold and sodium, the solution of the double chloride or iodide of gold and sodium with an excess of soda, and even the sulphide of gold dissolved in a solution of protosulphide of potassium.

As yet the deposition of platinum by voltaic action has not been practised to any considerable extent, but it is said that a solution of the double chloride of platinum and potassium in caustic potash may be applied to this purpose with tolerable success.

(297) *Resemblances between the Electricity of the Machine and that of the Voltaic Battery.*—Notwithstanding the extremely brief duration of the discharge from the electrical machine, it produces, while it lasts, phenomena similar to those of the voltaic current, which, indeed, may be regarded as a succession of discharges repeated so frequently as to become continuous. By repeating the discharge from the electrical machine many times through the same liquid conductor, Faraday was enabled to obtain true electrolytic decomposition. The following simple experiment may be adduced as an illustration of this fact:—Upon a plate of glass place a small piece of turmeric-paper, moistened with a solution of iodide of potassium which has been mixed with a little starch; upon one end of this piece of paper allow the point of a fine platinum wire to rest, the other end of the wire being in communication with the prime conductor of the machine; on the other extremity of the paper place a similar wire in communication with the earth: it will be found on setting the machine in action that, after the lapse of one or two minutes, a small blue spot will appear round the point of the wire connected with the prime conductor, owing to the liberation of iodine; while round the wire which communicates with the earth a brown spot will be formed, from the action of the alkali which is set free. If the wires, instead of being connected through the medium of iodide of potassium be made to dip into a drop of a solution of sulphate of copper, metallic copper will be deposited on the wire connected with the earth, and oxygen and sulphuric acid will appear on the other wire. If a piece of litmus or turmeric-paper, moistened with a solution of sulphate of sodium, be supported on a thread of glass between two wires, one of which proceeds from the prime conductor, whilst the other is in communication with the earth, the saline solution in the paper will be decomposed by the electricity, even although the paper does not touch either of the wires: the litmus-paper on the side towards the prime conductor will gradually be reddened, whilst the turmeric-paper will be turned brown at the extremity which is furthest from the prime conductor.

The quantity of electricity which is required to produce chemical decomposition is very great. The fact is strikingly illustrated by a comparison which was made by Faraday between the amount of electricity which is developed from the machine by friction and that which is furnished by the chemical action of the battery. The experiment was performed in the following manner:—A wire of platinum and another wire of zinc, each $\frac{1}{18}$ of an inch in diameter, were immersed $\frac{5}{16}$ of an inch apart, to a depth of $\frac{5}{8}$ of an inch in an extremely dilute acid liquid, prepared by adding a single drop of oil of vitriol to four ounces of water. The current obtained from this combination, at a temperature of 60° F., was transmitted through the coil of a galvanometer consisting of 18 feet of copper wire $\frac{1}{18}$ of an inch thick. It produced in about three seconds as great a deviation of the needle as was obtained by the electricity furnished by thirty turns of a powerful plate-machine in excellent action. This quantity, if concentrated within a space of time constituting only a minute fraction of a second, by discharging it in a single flash from a Leyden battery, exposing 3500 square inches of coated surface, would have been sufficient to kill a small animal, such as a cat or a rat; but the chemical action upon the zinc by which it was produced was so trifling as to be quite inappreciable; and it is estimated by Faraday that not less than 800,000 discharges, each equal in quantity to this, would be required for the decomposition of a single grain of water! Extraordinary as this estimate appears, it has been amply confirmed by later experiments of Becquerel upon this subject; and from the experiments of Weber, it may be calculated that, if the whole of the positive electricity required to decompose a grain of water were accumulated upon a cloud 1000 metres (3281 feet) above the surface of the earth, the attractive force exerted between the cloud and the portion of earth beneath it would be equal to 1497 tons!

(298) *Deluc's Dry Pile.*—The relation between the electricity of the voltaic battery and that of the ordinary electrical machine admits of being traced in an interesting manner by intermediate steps. Deluc, soon after the discovery of the voltaic pile, contrived what he termed the *dry pile.* It may be constructed in the following manner:—Take a number of sheets of paper, one surface of which has been coated with gold or silver leaf, and paste upon the coated surface a sheet of zinc foil; when sufficiently dry, place several of these sheets of paper one over another, the zinc faces all being arranged in one direction; then cut out, with a punch, a number of circular disks, and arrange them in a glass tube, the diameter of which is rather greater than that of the circular disks of paper, to the number of 2000 or upwards, taking care that all the zinc surfaces are in one direction, and all the silvered or gilt surfaces in the opposite direction. A pile analogous to Volta's will thus be obtained; and if these disks be pressed together and connected at each end with a metallic wire, such a pile will cause divergence of the leaves of the gold-leaf electroscope when one extremity of it is made to touch the cap of the instrument, whilst the other end is connected with the earth, either through the human body or by means of any other conductor. If the pile be reversed, and then presented to the still diverging electroscope, the leaves will first collapse, and will then immediately open with the opposite kind of electricity. Indeed, if the wires attached to the two extremities of the pile be

bent round and made each to terminate in a small metallic disk, the two disks being placed at a distance of about an inch and a half from each other, care being taken to maintain their insulation, an insulated slip of gold leaf suspended midway between the two disks will oscillate backwards and forwards between them, if an impulse be first given to it towards either side:—suppose it to approach the positive plate, it acquires a positive charge; it is then repelled from the positive plate, but it is attracted by the negative plate, when it gives up its positive charge and becomes negatively electrified, in which state it is again attracted by the positive plate; this alternate movement of the gold leaf will continue uninterruptedly for months or even years.* With a dry pile, which contained 20,000 pairs, or disks, of zinc and silver paper, sparks have been obtained, and a Leyden battery has been charged sufficiently to produce shocks. It is worthy of remark, that these actions are produced in Deluc's column only when the paper contains that amount of moisture which is found in it under ordinary circumstances, and which is considerable, although it usually passes unnoticed. If the paper be artificially dried, the pile loses its activity, but again recovers its energy as the paper reabsorbs moisture from the air. Provided that the two extremities of the pile be insulated from each other, it will retain its activity unimpaired for years; but if the ends be permanently connected by means of a good conductor, the zinc becomes gradually oxidized, and the electrical effects disappear.

Zamboni obtains a more effective instrument by substituting finely-powdered peroxide of manganese for the gold or silver leaf. One surface of the paper is coated with zinc or tin-foil, and the coating of peroxide may be given to the other surface either by rubbing it on in a dry state, or by applying it in admixture with water to which a little honey has been added. The paper disks are arranged in a column, and are terminated at either extremity by a metallic plate. These metallic plates are made to compress the paper disks by means of ligatures of silk which pass from end to end of the pile and bind the disks firmly together; whilst effectual insulation is provided for by giving the pile a non-conducting coat of sulphur, which is easily applied by a momentary immersion of the whole instrument in a bath of melted sulphur.

(299) *Water Battery.*—It has been already stated (259) that even with a single pair of zinc and copper plates excited by diluted acid, polarization and electric tension may be proved to precede the voltaic current, though the experiment is one of considerable delicacy. These effects of tension are strikingly exhibited in the case of Deluc's pile; but they may be shown in a manner still more decided by employing a numerous series of

* Bohnenberger has contrived an extremely sensitive electroscope, which depends upon a modification of this experiment. Midway between the two insulated terminating disks of Deluc's pile, he suspends a single strip of gold leaf by a metallic wire from an insulated plate of metal; this gold leaf, however, is not near enough to either disk to touch it. If a body with the feeblest electrical charge is made to touch the insulated plate, the gold leaf becomes electric, and is attracted towards the oppositely electrified pole of the pile.

alternations of zinc and copper, each of which need expose only a very small surface, and may be excited simply with distilled water. Such an arrangement or *water battery*, consisting of a thousand couples, produces, if insulated, and connected at each of its extremities with a gold-leaf electroscope, considerable divergence of the leaves of each instrument. Such a battery will communicate a charge to a Leyden battery: this charge, though it rises only to a small extent, may be renewed and discharged for an indefinite number of times in very rapid succession. The wire which is connected with the last zinc plate of this battery is negative, whilst that which is attached to the copper is positive.

Gassiot (*Phil. Trans.*, 1844, p. 39) has given an account of a very powerful and carefully constructed water battery, from which he obtains results of great interest. This battery was composed of 3520 pairs of copper and zinc plates, arranged in separate glass vessels, covered with a coating of lac varnish; the glass cells were supported on slips of glass thickly coated on both sides with shell-lac, and these glass plates were insulated on varnished oaken boards, each board being further insulated by resting on thick plates of glass similarly varnished. All these precautions were found by experience to be necessary in order to preserve the insulation. When the conducting wires of this battery were brought within $\frac{1}{50}$ of an inch of each other, sparks were obtained, and when the wires were made to terminate in brass disks which were brought very near each other, a rapid succession of sparks was maintained, which on one occasion continued without interruption for five weeks. A permanent deflection of the galvanometer was obtained when this instrument was included in the circuit whilst the sparks were passing; under similar circumstances, paper moistened with iodide of potassium and included in the circuit, speedily gave indications of the chemical decomposition of the iodide. The chemical effects produced by the water battery are, however, always feeble, but they are similar in kind and in direction to those which are obtained when acids are employed as the exciting liquid in the cells; and the principal effect that would be obtained if diluted acid were substituted for water in such a combination would be an increase in the quantity of electricity, by increasing the consumption of zinc and the chemical action in each cell in a given time. The intensity of the charge would be increased by the change of the exciting liquid, in proportion as the electro-motive force in each cell was augmented when compared with the resistance offered by the liquid employed in charging the battery. Neither in the water battery nor in any other form of battery is the intensity, as measured by its power of overcoming resistance to conduction, increased by increasing the size of the plates.

It thus appears, 1. That by voltaic arrangements electricity may be obtained, exactly similar to that developed by the common machine, in its effects of tension and induction towards surrounding objects, in the polar character of its action, and in the opposite nature of the electricities accumulated at the extremities of the apparatus. 2. That the quantity of electricity obtained by voltaic action is almost immeasurably greater than that procured by friction; but that unless its intensity be exalted by using a very numerous series, it does not pass so readily through non-conductors in the form of sparks, as the electricity of the common machine. 3. That, on the other hand, by allowing the electricity of the machine to discharge itself gradually through very small masses of imperfect liquid conductors which are susceptible of electrolysis, true electrolytic action may be produced.

The identity of the two forces under these different degrees of intensity no longer admits of question: in the voltaic action the quantity is great, but the intensity is feeble; whilst in the electricity of the machine the reverse is the case, the intensity is very high, whilst the quantity is extremely small.

§ IV. Electro-Magnetism.

(300) *Law of Electro-Magnetic Action--Tangent Galvanometer.*—The influence of an electric current upon a freely suspended magnetic needle has been already pointed out (253), but it will be needful to examine the nature of the connexion between magnetism and electricity somewhat more closely. Mere electricity of tension, or electricity in a state of rest, has no influence upon a magnetized bar. It is only when the electricity is in motion that this magnetic action is excited. It has already been explained (253) that the direction in which a magnetic needle is deflected depends upon the direction of the current; and it has been stated that when the needle points north and south, and a wire is placed parallel to the needle, if the current flow from south to north above the needle, the north end of the needle will move westward. The power which the wire exerts upon the needle is inversely as the distance of the wire from such needle.

Fig. 229.

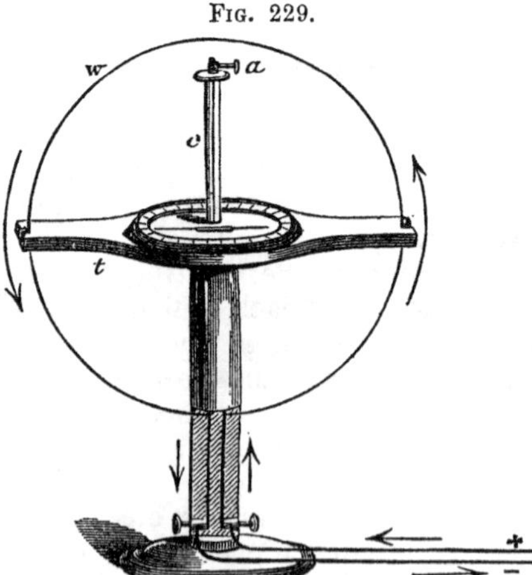

(301) For measuring the force of the current, galvanometers of various forms have been employed. When the power is extremely feeble, the astatic galvanometer (fig. 200,) is well adapted to the purpose, but in this form the value of the angular deviation requires to be experimentally determined for each instrument. When the current has a greater degree of power than can be conveniently estimated by the astatic combination, the *tangent galvanometer* is frequently employed. This instrument is simple, both in construction and in principle. The conductor, *w*, fig. 229, which is used for conveying the current round the

needle, consists of a single coil of thick copper wire, bent into a circle of about one foot in diameter. It is supported vertically in a small table, *t;* the extremities of the wire, which are connected with the battery, are covered with silk, and pass vertically downwards, side by side, close to each other, for some inches; they are thus situated in the same plane as the coil, and in the direction of a prolongation of its radius. The object of this arrangement is to prevent this portion of the wires from exerting any influence on the needle. Within the circle, *w*, a magnetic needle about an inch long is suspended by fibres of unspun silk, *c*, over a copper plate graduated to degrees. In order to enable the movements of the needle to admit of more accurate measurement, its apparent length is increased by fastening a piece of fine copper wire to each end. This arrangement is protected from currents of air by means of a glass shade. The point of suspension of the needle is made to coincide accurately with the centre of the circle formed by the conducting wire: at *a* is a screw for raising or lowering the needle. When the instrument is placed exactly in the magnetic meridian, the needle, under the influence of the directive action of the earth's magnetism, assumes a position parallel to the diameter of the circle. On transmitting the current through the wire, the needle receives an impulse which, if it were free from the inductive action of the earth, would place it exactly at right angles to the coil: owing, however, to the influence of the earth, the needle is unable ever really to assume this position; but it takes one which represents the resultant of the two forces, and as the action of the earth may be assumed to be uniform, the measurement of the angle enables the force of the current which produces the deviation to be calculated. It may be demonstrated that the force of the current is proportioned to the tangent of the angle of deviation. This instrument cannot be relied on for angular deviations which much exceed 70°, owing to the rapidly diminishing angular deviation produced by equal increments in the force of the current when the deflection has reached this extent; but for all currents which produce a deviation of smaller amount, it affords a convenient measure. Other forms of galvanometer have been contrived, which it will not be necessary to describe in this work.

(302) *Influence of a Conducting Wire in exciting Magnetism.*—The action of the conducting wire upon the magnetic needle is not interfered with by interposing a sheet of glass or other insulator of electricity, and the magnetic influence is equally transmitted, although a sheet of copper, of lead, or of any other non-magnetic metallic conductor of electricity be introduced between the needle and the wire. The electric current, however, produces no divergence of the leaves of an electroscope which is brought into its vicinity. Not only does a wire which is conveying electricity affect a needle which has been already magnetized, but the conducting wire itself, so long as it is transmitting the electric current, displays magnetic properties. If a thin wire of copper, or of any other non-magnetic metal, be employed to com-

plete the voltaic circuit, such a wire will, for the time, attract iron filings; and the filings will be arranged in a layer of uniform thickness around the whole circumference of the wire, and along its whole length. The moment that the connexion with the battery is broken, the magnetism ceases, and the filings fall off; but the attractive power may be again instantly renewed on completing the circuit. The iron filings in this case become magnets, the poles of which are arranged alternately north and south around the wire. This arrangement may be better understood by reference to fig. 230, in which if W be supposed to represent a section of the wire which is transmitting a current from + to —, the north end of each fragment of iron would be arranged as represented by the points, *n*, *n*, of the arrows. If short wires of soft iron be placed in the direction of the arrows around the wire, they become temporary magnets, the north and south poles of which are indicated by the letters *n* and *s*. If pieces of steel be substituted for soft iron, they become permanently magnetic; all those which are above the wire, if the current be passing in the direction shown in the figure, will have their north ends to the left, whilst in all those below, the north ends will be to the right.

Fig. 230.

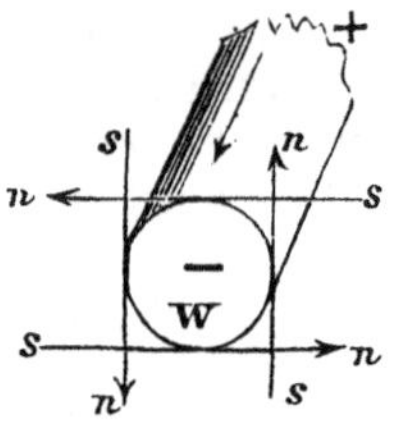

(303) *Formation of Electro-Magnets.*—We see, then, that every part of the wire along which a current is passing is magnetic. By coiling the conducting wire into a ring, a larger number of particles is brought to act upon a piece of soft iron which is passed through the axis of the ring at right angles to the plane in which it lies; and by coiling up the wire into a spiral form, without allowing the spires to touch each other, and supporting them upon a glass tube, the action of a very considerable length of wire may be concentrated in a very effective manner upon the same piece of soft iron, placed as at *c*, *d*, fig. 231. Very powerful temporary magnets may thus be obtained. If the wire be covered with cotton, or, still better, with silk, to insulate the coils from each other, the effects may be greatly augmented by winding a second series of coils upon the first, and a third upon the second, and so on, till six or seven layers of wire are coiled around the bar which is to be magnetized. A row of coils which follows the direction of a left-handed screw would neutralize the effect produced by the right-handed spiral, unless the current were reversed in its direction as it passes through such a coil, as a glance at fig. 232 will show, where A represents a right-handed spiral, B, a left-handed spiral: in the straight portions of the wire, the current, as indicated by the arrows, flows

Fig. 231.

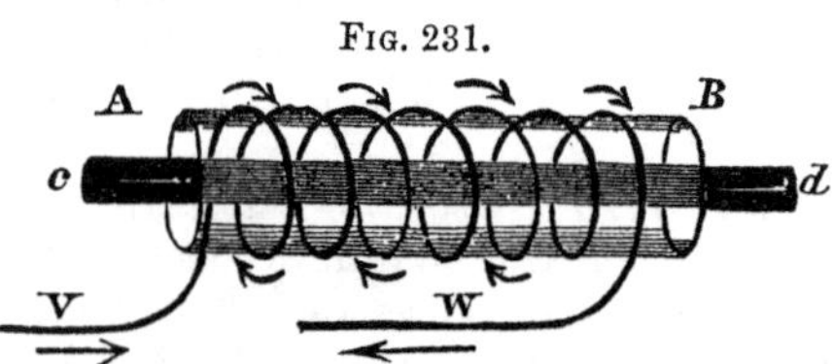

in the same direction in both; but it is reversed in the spirals. Such a spiral coil of wire is usually termed a *helix*. In preparing an electro-magnetic coil it is not necessary, however, that the wire be coiled in one direction only, if the wire be continuous; for instance, if the coils follow the direction of the thread of a right-handed screw in the first layer, as in A B, fig. 231, the wire in winding it backwards from B to A will be formed into a left-handed spiral, but this is of no consequence, because the direction of the current is also reversed in this layer, being now from B to A, so that the effect of the reversed twist of the wire is neutralized.

FIG. 232.

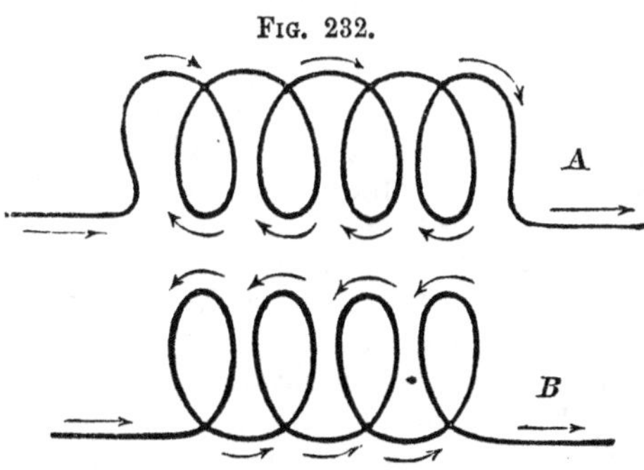

A helix through which an electric current is passing is powerfully magnetic; the two magnetic forces accumulating at its opposite extremities. If the helix be supported with its axis in a vertical position, and a bar of soft iron be partially introduced within it, as soon as an electric current of sufficient power is transmitted through the coils, the bar will start up, and will raise itself in mid-air nearly equidistant between the two extremities of the coil, the iron, by induction, becoming for the time a powerful magnet the poles of the iron bar are of course exactly the reverse of those of the helix by which its magnetism is produced.

The most powerful electro-magnets, however, are those in which the iron is bent into the form of a horse-shoe, and around which an insulating conducting wire is coiled in several layers, with due attention to the direction in which the coils are arranged. In this way magnets have been constructed which are able to sustain a weight exceeding that of a ton. The magnetism developed in the soft iron, under the influence of the voltaic current, attains its maximum in a few moments. It ceases as quickly, when the contact of the wires with the battery is broken; and, by reversing the direction of the current, the magnetic polarity of the bar is instantly reversed.

(304) *Molecular Movements during the Magnetization of Bars.*—The production of magnetism in a bar of iron, and the cessation of magnetism, are both attended with molecular motion, which pervades the whole mass of iron. Joule has shown that the bar, on becoming magnetic, acquires a slight increase in length, and suddenly contracts to its former dimensions when the magnetism ceases, the elongation of the bar being proportional to the square of the intensity of the magnetism developed within it. It has been observed by Guillemin, that if an iron bar be supported at one end so as to bend by its own weight, it becomes straightened to a greater or less extent when magnetized. Wer-

theim has also observed that the co-efficient of the elasticity of both iron and steel is diminished by magnetization. Each time that the bar either becomes magnetic or loses its magnetism, a distinct sound is emitted, the note being similar to that elicited by striking one end of the bar so as to produce vibrations in a longitudinal direction. The molecular movements, if repeated in quick succession by rapidly making and breaking contact between the ends of the helix and the wires of the battery, so as repeatedly and quickly to magnetize and demagnetize the bar, produce an elevation of temperature, which, as Grove has shown, is quite independent of the heat produced in the conducting wire by the current. In connexion with these molecular movements, it may be noted that Wiedemann finds when a current is transmitted along the axis of a magnet, the magnet suffers a slight degree of twisting.

(305). *Laws of Electro-Magnetism.*—According to the researches of Lenz and Jacobi, it appears that if the battery current be maintained of a uniform strength—1. That the magnetism which is induced in any given bar is directly proportioned to the number of coils which act upon the bar: it is a matter of indifference whether the coils be uniformly distributed over the whole length of the bar, or whether they be accumulated towards its two extremities. 2. That the diameter of the coils which surround the bar does not influence the result, provided that the current be in all cases of uniform strength; for though the inductive influence decreases as the distance of the magnet from the wire, the induction produced by the increased length of the wire in the circumference of the coil is augmented in precisely the same proportion. 3. That the thickness of the wire composing the coil does not influence its effect upon the bar. 4. That the energy of the magnetism is, *cæteris paribus*, proportioned to the strength of the current, being directly as the electro-motive force and inversely as the resistances of the circuit.* 5. That the *retentive* power of the magnet, like the attractive power in electricity, increases as the square of the intensity of the magnetism. 6. That the intensity of the magnetism induced upon a solid bar by a given current is proportioned to the surface which the bar exposes; or in cylindrical bars it is as the square of the weight.† Bundles of isolated wires expose a larger surface than a solid bar, and hence they are susceptible of a higher amount of magnetism than a solid bar of equal weight. 7. That the employment of long bars has no other advantage over the use of short

* This increase of power, it must be observed, only occurs up to a certain point, as there appears to be a limit to the amount of magnetic force which can be developed in iron, although the amount of electric action may be indefinitely increased.

† Dub, however, confirms the observations of Müller, which give a different result, viz., that the intensity of the magnetism in cylindrical bars is, for equal currents in coils of equal number, proportioned to the square root of the diameter of the bar; the magnetism developed in a bar 4 inches thick being twice as powerful as that produced in a bar of 1 inch in thickness; so that the *retentive* power is directly proportioned to the diameter of the bars.

bars than that of removing to a greater distance the counteracting influence of the two magnetic poles upon each other.

The practical question in preparing an electro-magnet resolves itself into the determination of the thickness and length of the wires which are required to produce the *maximum* effect. It is obvious, that for a battery of a given power, the longer the wire which is employed, the greater is the resistance introduced, so that the number of convolutions practically has a limit beyond which nothing is gained by increasing them, and this limit is attained when the increased resistance introduced by the increasing length of the wire balances the gain produced by the influence of the additional coils upon the bar; the greater the diameter of the coil, the longer, of course, will be the wire required to form it, and the greater will be the resistance of such a coil in proportion to its magnetizing power. Experience shows, that in order to attain the most economical combination in the battery in proportion to the quantity of materials consumed, when magnetic power is required, the same rule must be followed as when chemical resistance has to be overcome—viz., that that combination is the most effective in which the resistance of the wires and of the coils which are exterior to the battery is equal to the resistance of the liquids and other materials used in the construction of the battery itself, or when in Ohm's Formula ($\frac{nE}{nR+r}=A$) the value of A most nearly approaches 0·5; in which case $r=nR$.

(306) *Ampère's Theory of Electro-Magnetism.*—It will be necessary to examine somewhat further the properties of a spiral wire which is conveying a current, in order that the reader may be enabled to understand the theory of Ampère, by which he accounts for the mutual action of magnets and electric currents. If a simple helix, which for lightness may be made of thin wire, be freely suspended, it will, whilst conveying the current, place itself in the magnetic meridian; that is to say, it will point north and south, and will be attracted and repelled by a magnet which is presented to it, just as an ordinary bar magnet would be. Fig. 233 shows a method of suspending the helix, or *electro-dynamic cylinder*, *n s*, so as to exhibit these effects; the wire, *a*, terminates in a small hook, which dips into a cup containing mercury, and this is connected with one of the wires from a small voltaic battery; the other end, *b*, of the coil dips into a second mercury cup, which is in communication with the other wire of the battery: the magnetism corresponding with that of the north end of the needle accumulates at one extremity of the coil, whilst the opposite magnetism accumulates at the other extremity: this effect neces-

Fig. 233.

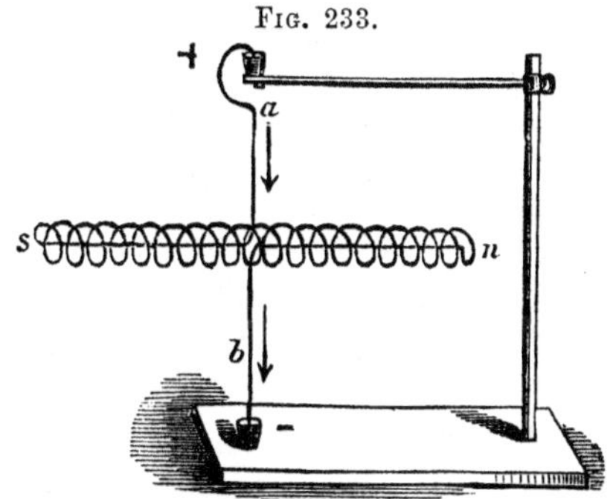

sarily follows from the influence of each coil upon its neighbours, since the north side of every coil is in one direction, whilst the south side is in the opposite. Ampère, who first pointed out the remarkable analogy between an ordinary magnet and the helix when conveying an electric current, has deduced from it a theory of the connexion between magnetism and electricity which has satisfied, hitherto, the rigorous requirements of mathematical analysis, and has also explained all the phenomena of electro-magnetism that have as yet been discovered. Ampère assumes that all bodies which exhibit magnetic polarity, derive this polarity from currents of electricity which are perpetually circulating around the particles of which the magnetic bodies are composed. Around each particle an electric current is supposed continually to circulate; the direction of these currents is supposed to be uniform, each current circulating in a plane at right angles to the axis of the magnetic power. In fig. 234, the currents are shown as at *a*, *b*, *c*, circulating in a uniform direction around the particles of a bar magnet, of which the south pole, s, is nearest the observer. The resultant effect of these united and concordant small currents would be equivalent to that produced by a single current winding in a spiral direction uniformly around the bar which would occupy the axis of such a spiral. In an ordinary magnetic needle, which is pointing north and south, currents would ascend on the western side and descend on the eastern. No definite proof of the existence of these currents can be given, nor can a reason for the persistence of such currents in permanent magnets be assigned; but granting that such currents do exist, all the mutual actions between wires which convey currents and permanent magnets follow as a matter of necessity.

Fig. 234.

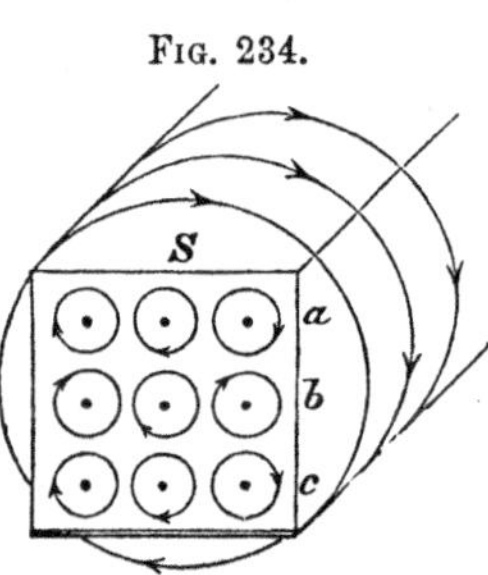

(307) *Mutual Influence of Wires which are conveying Currents.*—We proceed to point out one or two of these consequences. When two wires are freely suspended near each other, and electrical currents are transmitted through them, the wires will be mutually repulsive if the currents pass in opposite directions, but they will attract each other if the currents be in the same direction. Fig. 235 will explain the reason. When the currents are in opposite directions (No. 1), the magnetism on one side of the wires is exactly similar to that in the contiguous side of the second wire, as indicated by

Fig. 235.

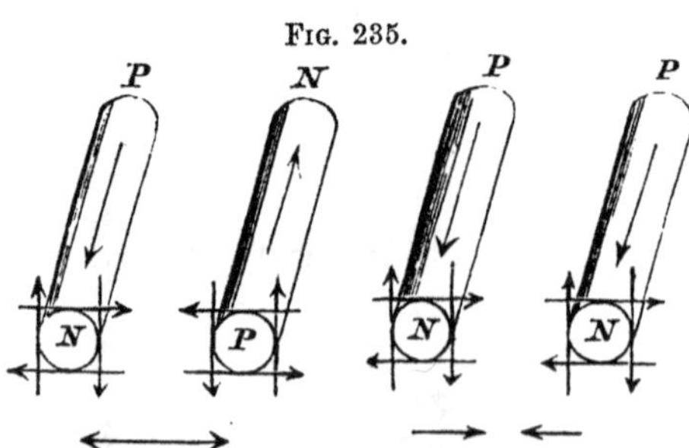

the arrows arranged around P and N. The two north poles and the two south poles consequently repel each other: whereas when the current is passing through the two wires in the same direction, as shown in No. 2, the effects are exactly reversed; attraction follows, and if the wires be freely suspended, as in Snow Harris's arrangement, represented in fig. 236, they will place themselves parallel to each other. Three concentric troughs containing mercury are arranged on a small stand; the current passes from one of the wires of the battery to the central trough, returns by the inner loop of wire to the second trough, and by the outer loop is transmitted to the exterior trough, which is in communication with the other wire from the battery. This attraction between currents which are passing in the same direction may be rendered evident in the contiguous coils of a helix: from this cause, a helix formed of a slender harpsichord wire shortens itself when the current is transmitted, but recovers its former dimensions when the current is intermitted.

FIG. 236.

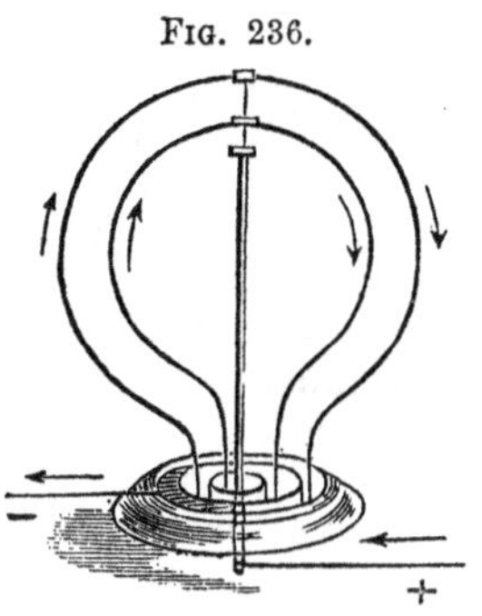

Now if it be granted that in every bar magnet electrical currents are perpetually circulating around the particles of which it is composed, in a direction at right angles to a line joining the magnetic poles, we have in the foregoing experiments an explanation of the tendency of a magnet to place itself across a wire which is conveying an electric current, since, by such a movement, the currents in the magnet and in the wire assume a direction parallel to each other. Let P Q (fig. 237), represent a wire conveying an electric current in the direction of the arrow; N will indicate the north end of a magnet in which the currents supposed to circulate around its particles would be parallel to the current in the wire P Q.

FIG. 237.

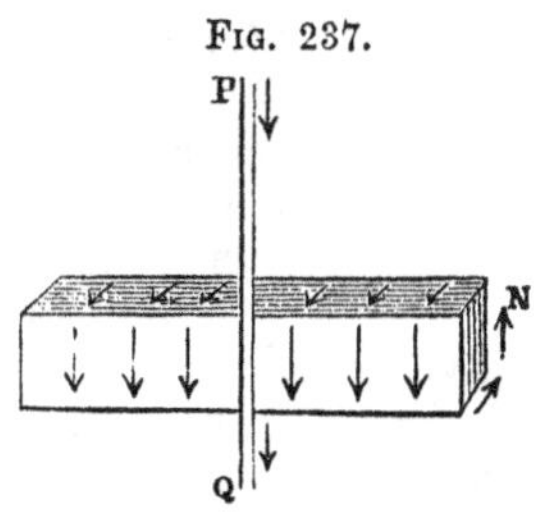

If the magnet be stationary whilst the wire is moveable, the wire will place itself at right angles to the magnet. In fig. 238, a plate of zinc, Z, is represented as connected by a loop of wire with the copper plate C; both are suspended in a tube containing diluted acid, and the little battery is made to float in a vessel of water by the aid of a piece of cork, D. If the north end of

FIG. 238.

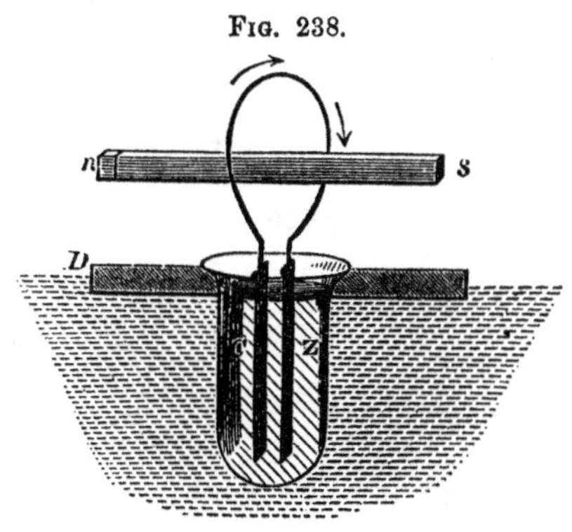

a magnet, *n*, be presented towards the loop in the direction shown in the cut, the wire will be attracted, and will place itself midway between the two extremities of the magnet; but if the south end be presented, the wire will be repelled; the little floating combination will turn half round so as to reverse its direction, and then will be attracted.

Motion is also produced in a wire which conveys a current, if it be suspended perpendicularly between the two poles of a horseshoe magnet placed upon its side, the lower extremity of the wire dipping into a trough of mercury connected with one wire of the battery, whilst it rests by a hook at its upper end upon a metallic arm which is in communication with the other wire of the battery; according to the direction in which the current is passing, the suspended wire will be either attracted or repelled, by the simultaneous action of the two poles of the magnet on the opposite magnetism of the two sides of the wire; the lower end will be thrown out of the trough of mercury; this movement will break the connexion with the battery, and the wire will then cease to be acted upon by the magnet until it falls back again into the mercury; the battery contact is by this means renewed, and the same series of motions is repeated. A spur wheel or star, if substituted for the wire, may in this manner be kept in continual revolution; for as one radius is thrown out, another enters the mercury, and thus renews the connexion with the battery, till it in its turn makes way for another.

(308) *Electro-Magnetic Rotations.*—The movements just described are not the only ones which the magnet and the wire produce on each other. If the action of the electric current be limited to a single pole of the magnet, a continuous rotation of the pole round the connecting wire may be obtained; or if the magnet be fixed whilst the wire is moveable, the wire will revolve around the magnet.

Faraday, by whom these rotations were first investigated, was led to their discovery by observing the manner in which a voltaic current acts upon a magnetic needle which is moved in its vicinity. If the conducting wire be placed perpendicularly, and a needle poised horizontally at its centre be made gradually to approach the wire on one side, each pole of the needle is first attracted, and on continuing the movement across the wire, is then repelled by the wire; on the other side of the wire the needle is repelled where it was previously attracted. The points indicated in fig. 239 by the letters A A, represent the positions of the wire when it produced attraction; R R, those in which it occasioned repulsion: at the points S and N midway between A and R, the needle is neither attracted nor repelled. From these results Faraday concluded that each pole has a tendency to revolve round the wire, and therefore that the wire had a similar tendency to revolve round the poles; the revolution of the north

Fig. 239.

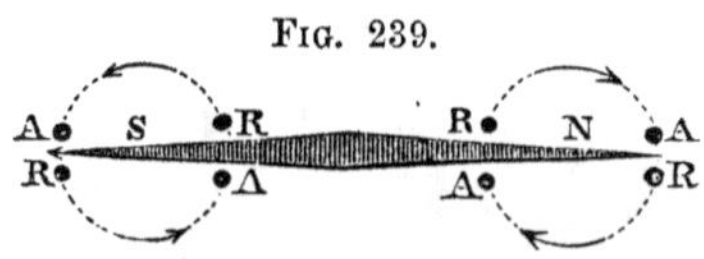

end of the needle, it was expected, would be in a direction the reverse of that assumed by the south end. Experiment completely verified these expectations. The facts admit of being shown in a variety of forms.

No. 1, fig. 240, shows an arrangement by which the magnet may be made to revolve around the fixed wire, *a b*; *f f* are the north ends of two bar magnets, which are united below, and terminate in a pivot, *g*; this pivot works upon a hard steel plate in the board, A B: *c d* is a wooden ring which contains mercury, and is in metallic communication with the cup, *e*. At the centre of each of the magnets is a small brass hook which dips into the mercury of the trough, *c d*, for conveying the current transmitted through the wire, *a b*, which is supported by the arm C. As soon as the connexion of the cups *a* and *e* is made with the battery, the magnet begins to rotate around the wire, *a b*, and continues to do so as long as the current passes; if the direction of the current be reversed, the direction of the rotation is reversed likewise. No. 2 is a similar arrangement for showing the rotation of the wire, *g h*, around the north end of the magnet, *a b*; the current enters at the cup, *f*, divides itself, and passes down *g* and *h* into the ring, *c d*, which contains mercury, and is supported above the board, C D, by the stand, A B; the circuit is completed by means of the cup *e*: reversal of the current reverses the direction of the rotation. If the current descend in the wire around the north end of the magnet, the direction of the rotation is the same as that of the hands of a watch lying with the face upwards. The current may be transmitted through the upper half of the magnet itself, and if delicately poised, the bar may thus be made to rotate rapidly upon its own axis. These rotations may also be exhibited by liquid and by gaseous conductors; if the wires from a powerful voltaic battery be made to dip into mercury, the mercury over the point where the wires terminate will rotate rapidly if a magnet be held above or below the spot. The flame of the voltaic arc revolves with equal regularity and distinctness under magnetic influence; thus by making a powerful horse-shoe magnet a part of the circuit, and transmitting the current through the magnet itself, the voltaic arc of flame which may be drawn from one of its poles will rotate in the opposite direction to the flame which may be

Fig. 240.

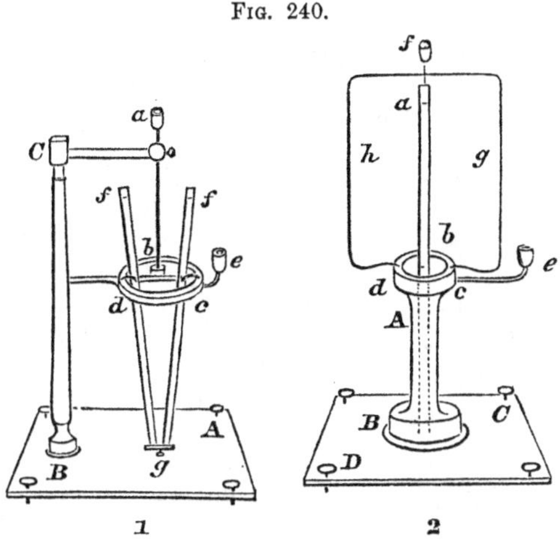

drawn from the other pole. This magnetic rotation of the electric discharge is also well exhibited when the induced current of Ruhmkorff's coil is transmitted through an exhausted globe immediately over the pole of an electro-magnet, the direction of the rotation being reversed with each reversal of the magnetism. —(De La Rive, *Electricity*, Walker's Translation, Vol. ii. p. 308.)

A beautiful proof of the magnetic condition of the liquid part of the circuit so long as the current is passing, is exhibited by the rotation of the battery itself, in obedience to the action of a magnet; the experiment may be made as follows:—Let a double cylinder of copper, shown in section at c, fig. 241, of about two inches in diameter and three inches high, be formed into a cell capable of containing liquid, and be supported by a point attached to a connecting strip of copper, over one end of a bar magnet; let a cylinder of zinc, z, be supported on a second point in metallic communication with the copper: as soon as a little diluted acid is poured into the cell, the zinc will begin to revolve around the magnet in one direction, while the copper rotates in the opposite; the current is ascending in the copper, whilst in the zinc it is descending around the same magnetic pole: round the north end of the magnet, the cylinder of zinc will move in the same direction as the hands of a watch which is lying with its face upwards.

Fig. 241.

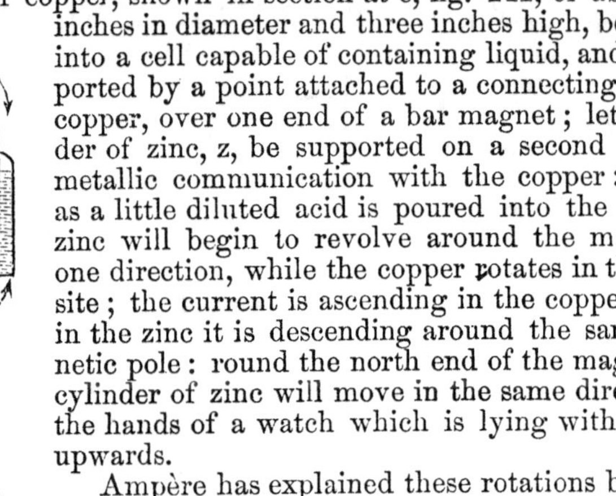

Ampère has explained these rotations by means of the theory to which allusion has already been made; but it will not be needful to pursue this part of the subject further.

(309) *Electric Telegraph.*—The most important and remarkable of the uses which have been made of electricity, consists in its application to telegraphic purposes; an application which has not only brought distant towns upon the same island or continent within the means of instantaneous communication with each other, but which has spanned the seas, and placed an insular metropolis like London within momentary reach of the distant capitals of the continent.

It would be impossible in a work like the present, to give even a sketch of the numberless modifications and improvements in the apparatus which have been suggested or practised for carrying out telegraphic communications by means of electricity, since the year 1837, which is memorable as the period at which Cooke and Wheatstone took out their first patent for electric telegraphing, and proved to the world the possibility of transmitting and receiving signals produced by electricity, with facility and with certainty through insulating wires of great length. On the present occasion, an outline of the essential parts of the telegraphic system which is generally adopted in this country is all that can be attempted.

The electric telegraph may be regarded as consisting of three parts—viz.: 1. The *Battery*, or source of electric power. 2. The *line*, or the means of transmitting the signals. 3. The *telegraphic indicator*, or instrument for exhibiting the signals.

1. *The Battery.*—The apparatus for producing the signals is simply a voltaic battery, any form of which may be used; but the one commonly employed consists of a series of alternate pairs of copper and amalgamated zinc plates arranged in wooden troughs, sub-divided into compartments, similar to those used with Smee's battery (fig. 213). These compartments, after the plates have been introduced, are filled with sand, which is then moistened with diluted sulphuric acid. In this form of instrument the risk of leakage is diminished and the amount of evaporation is lessened: the charge requires renewing once in ten days or a fortnight, according to the frequency with which the telegraph is used. Another form of battery which has been found to be effective for a long period, consists of plates of amalgamated zinc, and gas coke, excited by solid sulphate of mercury moistened with water; they are arranged in compartments, similar to those used for the moistened sand.

2. *The Line.*—The conducting wire was formerly made of copper, but is now generally made of iron wire about one-third of an inch thick, coated with zinc, to protect it from oxidation. For the purpose of insulation this wire is supported upon wooden posts, which are firmly sunk into the earth, and which are kept dry at the upper extremity by means of a cap or case of wood, of fourteen or sixteen inches long, between the sides of which and the post is an interval of air. To the sides of this cap short tubes of porcelain, or supports of glass, are attached, and through these insulating tubes the wire passes. Suppose that a message is to be transmitted from London to Manchester; a continuous insulated conducting wire must extend between the instrument or battery in London and the instrument at Manchester which is to receive the signals, and there must also be a continuous conducting communication to complete the circuit between Manchester and London. This return conductor may consist of a second metallic wire which must be insulated from the earth and from the first wire, though it may be suspended from the same posts side by side with the first. The earlier telegraphic lines were all made in this way.

It was, however, discovered by Steinheil that the second metallic wire may be dispensed with, and that the earth itself may be employed as the conductor for completing the return communication between the two distant stations. The possibility of doing this arises from the law of conduction in solids—viz., that the conducting power increases in proportion to the area of the section of the conductor. The earth as a conductor of electricity is many thousand times inferior in power to any of the metals, if columns of each metal and of the earth of equal diameter be compared. But it is possible to multiply indefinitely the area of the conducting portion of the earth between the two stations, and thus a line of communication may be obtained which actually offers a smaller amount of resistance than the metallic part of the circuit. In practice all that is found necessary, in order to take advantage of this conducting power of the earth, and to substitute it for the return wire of the telegraph, consists in leading a wire from the telegraphic apparatus at one end, into the earth, the wire being attached to a plate of copper which exposes several square feet of surface, and this copper plate is buried in the ground, as represented at P (figs. 242, 243, 244). By increasing the size of this plate, any extent of surface of contact with the earth may be obtained, and thus the intrinsic inferiority of the earth to the metals as regards its conducting power is more than compensated for.

The general plan of this arrangement will be understood from fig. 242, in which M and I represent two telegraphic instruments,

FIG. 242.

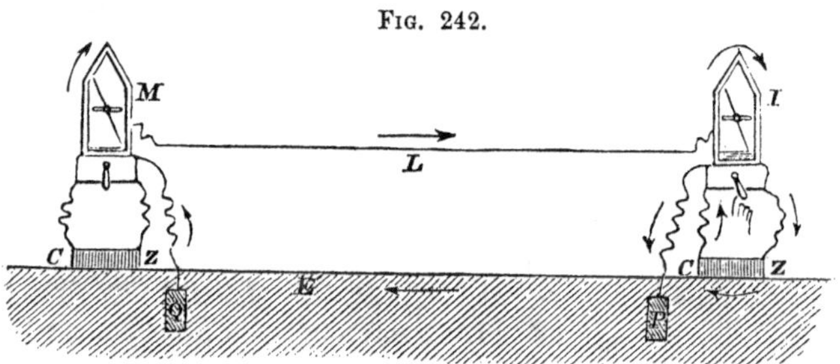

one stationed, we will suppose, in Manchester, the other in London. L is the metallic line or wire of communication which connects the stations; E is the earth; and P, Q, copper plates attached to wires, one of which proceeds from each instrument. Suppose, for example, a message to be in the act of transmission from I, the instrument in London, to M, the instrument in Manchester; if C Z represent the battery at the London station, the current will take the course indicated by the arrows; it will pass from C to a wire connected with the earth plate, P, thence it will pass through the 200 miles of earth between the two cities; at Q it will be taken up again, and be transmitted by the wire to the instrument, M, thence it will be conveyed along the metallic wire, L, and back again to London, where it will pass through the instrument, I, and so return to the end, Z, of the battery.

When it is impossible to insulate the conducting wire by supporting it in the air on posts, the whole length of the wire requires to be covered with an insulating material. Caoutchouc and gutta-percha are found to be well adapted to this purpose. In this case it is usual to substitute copper wires for the iron ones, as owing to the superior conducting power of copper, a wire of much smaller diameter can be employed without adding to the resistance, and a saving of space and of insulating material is thus effected. The wires, after having been covered with a coating of gutta-percha about $\frac{1}{8}$ of an inch thick, may be inclosed either singly, or several of them side by side, in iron tubing, to protect them from mechanical injury; they are then placed under ground, in the same manner as pipes for the conveyance of gas or water. In the sub-marine telegraphs, copper wires coated with gutta-percha are carefully arranged round a central rope of tarred hemp into a compound rope, which contains several strands of conducting wire; the whole is protected by enclosing it in a flexible metallic covering, formed by carefully twisting several iron wires around the compound conducting rope already described; the exterior is often further protected by an outer covering of tarred hemp or other analogous material. The cable having been previously coiled up in the hold of a vessel, and one of its extremities having been properly secured upon the shore, it is carefully lowered into the sea; from its weight, the electric rope at once sinks to the bottom as it is gradually paid out over the ship's side. When the opposite shore is safely gained, the extremities of the conducting wire are connected on either side with other wires which are in communication with the telegraphic apparatus, and the signals can be at once transmitted.

In cases in which the wires are insulated with gutta-percha, and are then encased in iron tubes, or sunk beneath a body of water, it has been observed that if the wire be connected with the battery, the signal is not instantaneously transmitted to the opposite extremity; and that if the battery contact be broken, there is not an instantaneous cessation of electric action at the distant point.

Faraday (*Phil. Mag.*, March, 1854) has shown that this retardation is produced by the action of the current upon the gutta-percha insulator. The insulated wire, in fact, forms a Leyden jar; the gutta-percha is the dielectric; the wire within forms the inner coating, and the iron tube, or water of the ocean which surrounds it, forms the exterior coating. The time lost at first is that which is expended in giving to the gutta-percha its charge; and the current which is observed to continue for a short time after the wire has been disconnected with the battery, is produced by the gradual discharge of the electricity which had been communicated by lateral induction to the gutta-percha: the gutta-percha in this case becomes polarized, just in the same manner as the glass of an ordinary Leyden jar. When the wires are suspended in air, no retardation of this kind is observed; and no after current is perceived. The gutta-percha in such a case cannot assume the polarized condition, owing to the absence of any conducting communication with its external surface, by which the induced electricity could be carried off.

Supposing that the line of communication has been established, we have now to consider:—

3. *The Instrument for Exhibiting the Signals.*—The indicator, or instrument by which the signals are exhibited, is essentially a galvanometer, in which the astatic needles are suspended vertically, instead of being placed in a horizontal direction. A

side view of the coil is shown at G, fig. 243. One of the needles is shown vertically suspended within it; the other needle, *n s*, is represented in front of the dial-plate, F F, of the instrument. The needles are slightly heavier at their lower extremities than at their upper ones, in order that when disturbed from the vertical line, they may again resume it when the disturbing force ceases to act. The motions of the needle to the right or to the left are limited by a little ivory stud, which projects on either side from the face of the dial: loss of time, which would otherwise be occasioned by the unnecessary length of the oscillations of the needle, is thus prevented. L and P are the wires which communicate with the distant station; C Z is the battery; H is the handle by which the instrument is worked. Fig. 244 is intended to illustrate the principle upon which such an instrument is made to exhibit the signals; the details of its construction have been slightly modified in the diagrams, in order that the course of the electric current may be

Fig. 243.

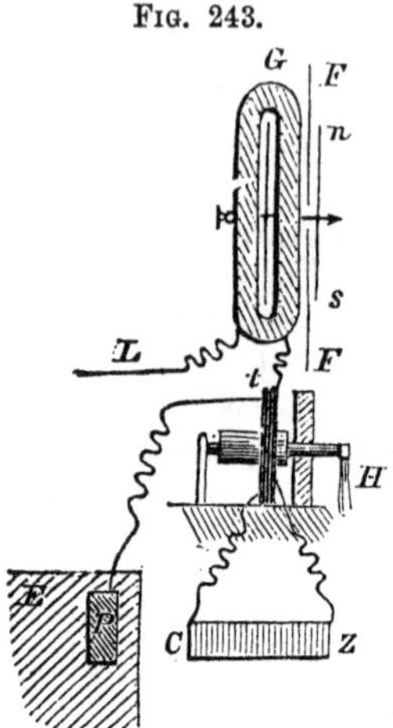

Fig. 244.

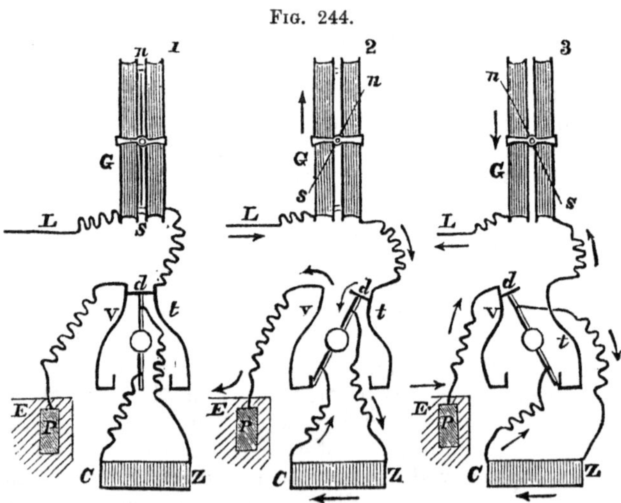

more clearly traced. No. 1 represents a back view of the essential parts of the instrument, when at rest and in a position to receive a message from the distant extremity. In this position, supposing the current to originate from the distant battery, and to enter the galvanometer G by the wire L, it will pass through the coil, will make its exit by the wire upon the right hand, which is attached to the metallic spring *t*; thence it will pass along the brass crosspiece, *d*, into the metallic spring, V, and complete the circuit through the wire attached to the plate P and the earth E, by which it is returned to the distant station. The battery shown at C Z is inactive during the whole of this stage: the wires which proceed from its two extremities are attached to insulated pieces of brass at either end of the vertical piece which is connected with *d*. No current therefore can in this position be transmitted from this battery, since the wire proceeding from C is completely insulated. But suppose it be desired to transmit a signal from this instrument to the distant station:—by means of the handle H (fig. 243), the piece to which *d* is attached can be pressed against one of the springs at *t* (fig. 244, 2), whilst its lower extremity by the same movement is pressed against the other spring V; the current now passes from the battery in the direction shown by the arrows. From C it proceeds to V, thence, through the wire attached to P, into the earth; then, through the distant station, where the instrument is arranged for receiving the signals, as in No. 1, and it then produces a deflection of its needle. Thence the current returns by L to the galvanometer coil G, and then deflects the needle, returns through the wire attached to the spring *t*, and by the metallic piece *d* completes the circuit through the wire attached to Z.

It is obvious that by reversing the movement given to the handle H, the direction of the current and the motion of the needles in the coil will be reversed both in the near and in the distant instrument, as shown at No. 3. As soon as the operator has finished making his signals, the springs, V and *t*, restore the crosspiece *d*, to the position shown in No. 1, and thus the instrument at once adjusts itself for receiving the signals from the distant station; the battery at C Z being thrown out of action and the conducting communication with the line being restored through the crosspiece, *d*, by the self-acting power of the instrument itself.

By this arrangement a corresponding motion of the needle is always produced at the same instant at both stations, so that the giver and the receiver of the message each perceive the signal. Since the needle admits of being moved either to the right or to the left, it is clear that by combining together on a definite plan a certain number of these movements, any letter or word may be transmitted; thus two movements of the upper end of the needle to the right may show the letter *A*; three movements in the same direction the letter *B*; four might indicate *C*; one to the right and one to the left *D*; and so on.

By employing two or more needles in each instrument, a greater number and variety of signals can be transmitted in the same time, but each needle requires a separate conducting wire, though the number of batteries need not be increased.

§ V. MAGNETO-ELECTRICITY.

(310) *Volta-Electric Induction.*—The term *volta-electric induction* was given by Faraday to the production of secondary cur-

rents, or currents in closed wires obtained by inductive action, from wires conveying currents in the vicinity of such closed circuits. The circumstances under which these currents are formed will be best understood by a description of an experiment. If a wire through which a voltaic current is passing be placed parallel to a second wire, the two extremities of which are connected with the ends of a sensitive galvanometer, no perceptible effect is produced in the second wire so long as the current passes without interruption through the first wire; but if the current through the first wire (or *primary current* as it may for the sake of distinction be termed) be suddenly stopped by interrupting the connexion with the battery, a *secondary current* of momentary duration is produced in the second wire, and this current is *direct*, that is to say, it is in the same direction as that in the battery wire. On again completing the communication between the first wire and the battery, a momentary current or wave of electricity is again transmitted through the second wire, but it is now *inverse*, or in the opposite direction to the primary current.

These effects may be much increased, if instead of employing simple wires, the wires be coiled into the form of two concentric helices; the wire which is to convey the primary current, or primary coil, being placed in the axis of the coil for the secondary current, and the ends of the secondary coil being connected as before with the extremities of the galvanometer. Under these circumstances the needle will receive a powerful impulse at the moment the primary coil is connected with the battery, but after a few oscillations the needle will return to its original position, notwithstanding that the current through the primary coil is maintained; the instant, however, that the primary coil is separated from its contact with the battery, a powerful momentary impulse, from a current through the secondary coil in a direction the reverse of the former, will be produced upon the galvanometer needle.

Similar effects are exhibited by causing the primary coil, whilst it is transmitting the battery current, suddenly to approach towards, or to recede from, the secondary coil which is in connexion with the galvanometer. During the approach of the coil, the secondary current is in the opposite direction to the primary one, but during the withdrawal of the coil the secondary current is in the same direction as the primary current. If a small helix be substituted for the galvanometer in the secondary coil, a steel needle may be magnetized by the induction of these instantaneous currents, and the intensity of the magnetism thus induced is proportional to the intensity of the secondary current. By discharging a Leyden jar through a primary coil properly insulated, a secondary current may be obtained in the other helix, but in this case it is always in the same direction as the current produced on breaking contact with the battery.

(311) *Magneto-Electric Induction.*—Since electricity may be made to elicit magnetism it seems reasonable to expect that the converse operation of obtaining electricity by means of magnetism

should likewise be practicable. After several fruitless attempts to solve this problem, Faraday succeeded in discovering the conditions necessary to ensure the result (*Phil. Trans.*, 1832, p. 125). The following experiment will serve to illustrate these conditions. Let the extremities of a helix of copper wire be connected by means of wires several feet in length with the two ends of a galvanometer, so that the needles shall be beyond the direct influence of the magnetic bars to be employed. Motion of a permanent magnet across the coils of the helix instantly produces a current in the wire; if, for example, a bar magnet be introduced into the axis of the helix, an immediate deflection of the galvanometer needle is produced; but if the magnet be allowed to remain motionless within the helix, the needle after a few oscillations returns to its zero; the instant, however, that the magnet is withdrawn, the galvanometer needle is deflected to the same extent as before, but in the opposite direction. When the marked end of a magnetic bar is introduced into a right-handed helix, the current which is produced so passes through the coils as to enter the helix at that extremity at which the magnet enters; so that the current under these circumstances moves in the opposite direction to that of the hands of a watch which is lying with its face upwards.

If a bar of soft iron be placed in the axis of the helix, so long as it remains unmagnetized no current is produced, but if the opposite poles of two bar magnets be presented one to each extremity of the soft iron, so as to render it temporarily magnetic by induction, a momentary current is produced whilst it is acquiring magnetism, and this current corresponds in direction with that which would be occasioned by introducing a bar magnet, the poles of which correspond in direction with those of the temporary magnet.

In like manner when two concentric helices are arranged as in the experiment on volta-electric induction (310), and a bar of soft iron is placed in the axis of the primary coil, a much more powerful secondary current is obtained than when the two coils only are used; since the soft iron in acquiring and in losing magnetism produces a secondary current, which in each case occurs in the same direction as that induced by the primary coil alone. If a bar of copper be substituted for the iron bar or *core* in the primary coil, the current is not stronger than when the two coils alone are employed.

If, as Ampère supposes, a series of electric currents are perpetually circulating around the component particles of a bar magnet, in planes at right angles to the magnetic axis,—the motion of a magnet in the axis of a helix, the opposite extremities of which are in metallic communication with each other so as to form a closed circuit, must necessarily produce a current in such a helix; for the magnet corresponds to a helix through which an electric current is passing; experiment shows that the direction of the currents induced by the magnet is precisely such as would be required by Ampère's theory.

(312) *Ruhmkorff's Induction Coil.*—The secondary currents which are obtained by magnetic induction possess a high degree of intensity; if the circuit be broken at the moment that the current is passing, a brilliant spark will be observed at the point at which the interruption is occasioned.

An effective apparatus for exhibiting these secondary currents has been in use for several years, but it has recently been rendered still more efficient by Ruhmkorff. One of its forms is represented in fig. 245, in which No. 1 shows a vertical section of

FIG. 245.

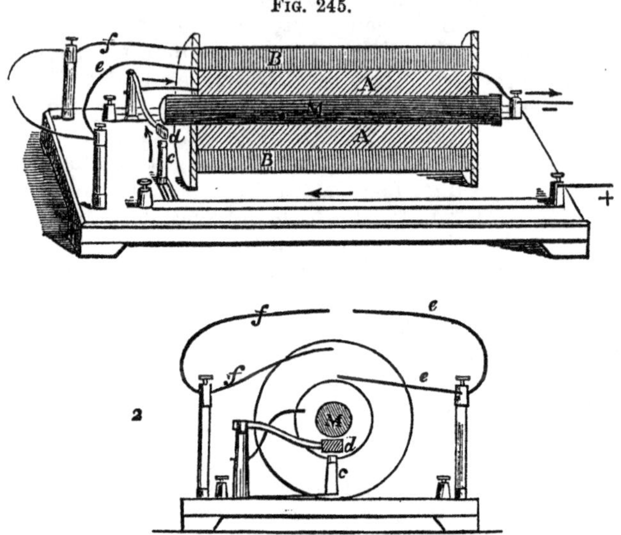

the coil through its long axis, the other parts being shown in perspective. It consists mainly of two concentric helices of copper wire; the primary or inner coil, A A, consisting of a stouter and shorter wire than the secondary coil, B B, which is made of a very long, thin wire, insulated by silk, and each layer of coils is carefully insulated from the adjacent layer: * M is a bundle of soft iron wire placed in the axis of the coils. At + and — are binding-screws for connecting the primary coil with a voltaic battery of three or four elements. This primary coil is not continuous throughout its length, but admits of being broken at *c* and *d*; *d* is a small armature of soft iron, to the under surface of which a plate of platinum is riveted, and the upper surface of *c* is also faced with platinum. So long as *c* and *d* touch each other, the current circulates uninterruptedly through A A: but as soon as the current passes through A A, the iron core M, becomes magnetic and attracts *d*, consequently the contact between *c* and *d* is inter-

* In Ruhmkorff's 10-inch coil the inner or primary wire is 0·08854 inch thick and 132 feet long, 300 turns of wire being formed upon the instrument. The outer or secondary coil is 0·01312 inch thick, and 26,246 feet in length, distributed in 25,000 coils.

rupted; the current immediately ceases to flow through A A, the magnetism in M disappears instantly, the hammer, *d*, falls, contact with *c* and with the battery is immediately renewed, *d* is attracted again, and it immediately falls back upon *c*. Thus the battery itself acts as a means of making and breaking the contact several hundred times in a minute. A powerful current is induced in the secondary coil, B B, by each of these momentary currents in A A. In this instrument the secondary current is always transmitted in one direction only, the induced current on breaking contact being the only one which has sufficient intensity to traverse the coil. No. 2 shows an end view of the coil, and exhibits more distinctly the parts by which the contact is made and broken. The same letters apply in both cases. The shocks are of such intensity as to be very painful and often dangerous, even though experienced only for an instant. A continuous stream of sparks will pass between the insulated ends of the secondary wire, *e f*. A Leyden jar may be charged by the secondary current, and the power of the instrument may be much increased by connecting the *primary* wire with the modification of the Leyden jar, which is commonly called a *condenser:* it consists of a band of brown paper, or, better, of oiled silk, on either side of which a sheet of tinfoil is pasted. 40 or 50 square feet of coated surface are thus prepared and folded between two other bands of brown paper or of silk, and packed in a flat wooden case. The two coatings are connected with the binding-screws attached to *c* and *d* in the primary current. The principle of its action is not clearly understood; it does not increase the quantity of electricity in the secondary current, but it adds greatly to its intensity and augments the striking distance, so that, by its employment, and by increasing the dimensions of the coil, paying scrupulous attention to the insulation of the conducting wires, sparks of 18 or 20 inches in length and of great intensity have been obtained. The intensity of this spark is also greatly increased by increasing the suddenness with which the continuity of the primary wire is broken. It is obvious that by this machine electricity of low tension may be rendered as intense as that from an ordinary plate-machine whilst its quantity is much greater. An induction coil may indeed be substituted for an ordinary electrical machine in most cases, with great advantage, where a continuous discharge of sparks is required.

If the shadow of the spark obtained between the secondary wires of a Ruhmkorff's coil be thrown upon a screen by the intense light of the electric lamp, a cone of vapour will appear to issue from the point of each wire, due to the unequal refraction produced by the current of heated air; but the cone from the negative wire being more powerful apparently beats back the heated stream from the positive wire. These effects are the reverse of those produced in the ordinary voltaic arc, in which the greatest dispersion of matter and the highest temperature is observed to occur at the positive electrode (280). If the discharge of the secondary coil be allowed to occur in an exhausted receiver, the phenomenon of the auroral light is exhibited in a most beautiful manner through an interval of several feet. Gassiot has contrived a very striking modification of this experiment by placing within the receiver of the air-pump a small tumbler or beaker lined with tinfoil about half way up the inside. The receiver should be open at top for the admission of a sliding rod, which passes air-tight through a brass plate, ground to fit the top of the jar; the sliding rod is enclosed in a glass tube open at bottom, and passes down to the inside of the tumbler and touches the metallic lining. On exhausting the receiver whilst the plate of the pump is connected with one terminal of the secondary coil, and the sliding rod with the other terminal, a beautiful and continuous cascade of electric light pours over the edge of the tumbler upon the metallic plate of the pump. The effect is heightened if the tumbler be made of a fluorescent material, such as uranium glass, and rests upon a glass dish washed over with sulphate of quinine, the blue fluorescence of which contrasts well with the yellow of the uranium. If, instead of using the sort of Leyden jar employed in the foregoing experiment, this discharge be taken in an exhausted glass globe between two brass balls, it exhibits a very interesting appearance; the negative ball becomes covered with a quiet glow of light, whilst a pear-shaped luminous discharge takes place from the positive ball; between the two balls is a small interval nearer to the negative than to the positive ball which is not luminous: when the exhaustion of the receiver is very perfect, the luminous portion is observed to be traversed by a series of dark bands or arches concentric with the positive ball; the presence of a little vapour of phosphorus renders these dark bands much more distinct. (Grove.)

The occurrence of these bands is as yet unexplained; but the attempts to trace them to their cause have led to numerous interesting investigations by Grove, who first observed them, by Robinson, and by others, but particularly by Gassiot, who has varied the experiment in numberless ways (*Phil. Trans.*, 1858, 1859). Gassiot's principal method of procedure has been to seal wires of platinum and of other materials of various sizes and forms, into glass vessels or tubes. These tubes and vessels were subsequently exhausted more or less completely. Various gaseous bodies were then introduced, and were afterwards more or less completely removed by the air-pump: effects of great variety and beauty were thus obtained. The general appearances may be thus described:—If a long wide glass tube (fig. 246) containing sticks of caustic potash, at P, be filled with well-dried carbonic acid gas, and afterwards exhausted by the air-pump, the residual carbonic acid will be gradually absorbed by the caustic potash at P. The effects observed on connecting the wires +, −, with the secondary wires of the Ruhmkorff's coil, vary with the perfection of the vacuum. If the vacuum be merely that which can be obtained by an ordinary air-pump, no stratification is perceptible; a diffuse lambent light fills the tube: if the rarefaction be carried a step further, narrow striæ, like ruled lines, about $\frac{1}{20}$th inch in thickness traverse the tube transverse to the line of the

FIG. 246.

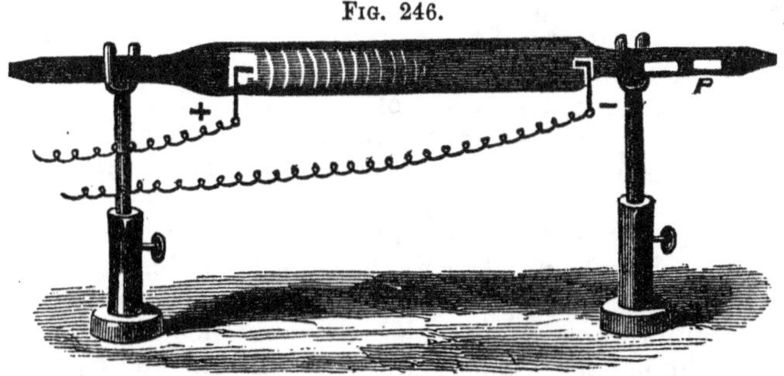

discharge, as shown in fig. 247, No. 1. A step further in the rarefaction increases the breadth of the bands as seen in fig. 246; next the segments of light assume a cup-shaped or conical form, fig. 247, No. 2; and by carrying the rarefaction still further, a series

FIG. 247.

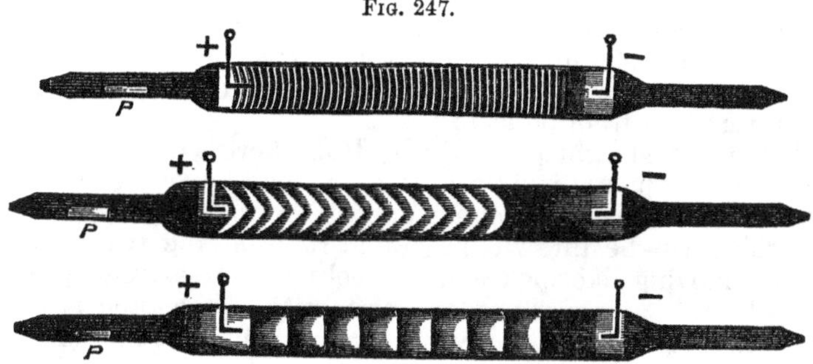

of luminous cylinders, of an inch or so in depth, with narrow dark lines between them, are seen, fig. 247, No. 3. Finally, when the vacuum approaches perfection, there is neither discharge, light, nor conduction. Hence it would appear that the presence of material particles is absolutely necessary to the transfer of the electric current.

When the stratification is most distinctly visible, a dark space will always be observed near the negative pole, which, if of platinum, is seen to be covered with a bluish glow of light, within which, the wire, by an optical illusion, has the appearance of being red hot. Portions of the negative electrode are gradually thrown off in the form of fine metallic particles as the experiment is continued, and the wire rises considerably in temperature. The appearance of the stratification varies greatly with the modifications in form given to the wires. If the negative wire be enclosed with a capillary glass tube which is open, and projects beyond the wire for an eighth of an inch, or a little more, all the stratification disappears, and a jet of light escapes from the open end of the capillary tube, passing down the exhausted vessel.

These stratified bands and luminous discharges are powerfully affected by the magnet; if the negative wire be undermost in one of these exhausted tubes suspended vertically, and it be completely covered with a stratum of mercury, it will be found on causing one end of a magnet to approach the termination of the luminous bands in the direction of the axis of the tube, that the stratification will become modified, and will present an appearance resembling that which might be occasioned by stretching a spiral spring, supposing it were luminous; indeed, by suitable means, the discharge may, as De La Rive has shown, be made to rotate around the magnetic pole. Plücker has shown that the light from the negative pole is also specially affected by the magnetic force, the lines of light becoming parallel to the magnetic curves; and Gassiot has found, that by arranging a tube so as to cross the lines of magnetic force which emanate from the poles of a powerful electro-magnet, he can instantly arrest the luminous discharge by magnetizing the electro-magnet; but on breaking the connexion of the magnet with the battery, the discharge is immediately renewed.

The phenomena above described have recently attracted a large share of the attention of electricians from their intimate connexion with the mode in which the electric force is propagated and transmitted from point to point.

The stratified light produced by Ruhmkorff's coil is, from the nature of the apparatus, intermittent, as may be very simply and beautifully shown by attaching one of the vacuum tubes to an axle which can be thrown into rapid rotation, the two arms of the tube moving like spokes of a wheel upon the extremity of the axle. In this arrangement, one extremity of the tube is maintained in unbroken contact with one extremity of the induction coil, while the other extremity is in like manner connected with the other end of the induction coil. As the rotation proceeds, if the experiment be made in a darkened room, the tube will be visible momentarily, several times during each rotation, and will produce the appearance of a star of light, each arm of the star exhibiting distinct stratified bands, and appearing to be stationary, owing to the briefness of the time for which it is visible.

It was supposed that these phenomena of stratification were connected with undulations produced by the rapidly succeeding currents of the induction coil. Gassiot, however, has shown that this is not the cause, by producing the stratified appearance from the discharge of a Leyden jar when somewhat prolonged by transmitting it through a portion of wet string; Quet and Seguin, by charging the jar feebly, have obtained similar effects without the use of the wet string. Gassiot also obtained them directly from the water battery of 3500 cells (299), as well as from a series of 400 carefully insulated small pairs of Grove's construction, and connecting each terminal of the battery with one of the insulated wires of the exhausted tube. A beautifully distinct stratified discharge was produced, which was not arrested by the introduction of a voltameter into the circuit. The quantity of electricity thus transmitted is so small that the amount of water decomposed is barely perceptible. This is, therefore, not the true voltaic arc. On causing the terminals of the Grove's battery in the exhausted tube gradually to approach each other till within about an inch and a half, the true voltaic arc was suddenly established, and an immense rise of temperature instantly occurred; but the interesting point of the experiment was that the arc itself was distinctly seen to be stratified.

The passage of the electric spark through compound gases or vapours is attended with a partial separation of their components in the line of the discharge. But the experiments of Perrot (*Ann. de Chimie*, III. lxi. 161) appear to have proved that the spark from Ruhmkorff's coil produces in addition a true electrolytic decomposition of the compound vapour. In the case of steam, for example, oxygen appears in larger quantity at the positive wire, and hydrogen in excess is collected at the negative; but a much larger quantity of the two gases is evolved than is due to true electrolysis. Long sparks, if transmitting equal amounts of electricity in equal times, were found to be more effectual in producing decomposition than small ones. In synthetic experiments on the combination of oxygen and nitrogen to produce nitric acid, it was found that long sparks also furnish a larger quantity of acid than short ones. If the length of the spark be increased in any given circuit, the gain increases only up to a certain point, the resistance offered by the length of the interposed stratum of air beyond this point diminishes the amount of electricity which circulates, to an extent which more than counterbalances the gain obtained by increasing the length of the spark.

The energy of the secondary induced current in effecting the combination or the decomposition of gases and vapours is much greater than that of the ordinary cylinder or plate electrical machine. The interposition of a condenser into the induced circuit augments the intensity of the chemical action of the spark; but it decreases the number of sparks in a given time, so that if the spark possess sufficient intensity to pass, no gain in the amount of the body decomposed is effected by the use of the condenser.*

(313) *Inductive Action of Currents—Henry's Coils.*—When the connexion between the plates of a battery is made by means of a single, long straight wire, a brilliant spark is seen at the moment that the contact with the battery is broken; but when the connexion is made by means of a short wire, and contact is broken, only a very small spark is produced. When a long wire is employed, the same length of wire, if coiled into a helix, gives a

* Full details of the numerous researches made by Quet and others with Ruhmkorff's coil will be found in Du Moncel's *Notice sur l'Appareil d'Induction Electrique de Ruhmkorff*, 4th edit.

much brighter spark than when it is used merely as a straight conductor. The brilliant spark which is observed when the long wire is used, is produced by the inductive action of the battery upon the electricity of the wire itself. The bright spark obtained from the battery wire on breaking contact arises from a current which is transmitted through the wire in the same direction as that from the battery itself. This inductive action may be entirely diverted, if a second helix, the ends of which are in metallic communication with each other, be placed either within the primary coil or exterior of it.

If the conducting wire be coiled into a helix within which an iron core is placed, the current on breaking contact acquires sufficient intensity to communicate a powerful shock, when the ends of the wire are grasped by the hand at the moment that the wire is disconnected with the battery, although the battery itself may be quite inadequate to produce any shock when its extremities are connected by a short wire. A striking experiment of this kind is related by Prof. Jos. Henry (*Phil. Mag.* 1840, vol. xvi. p. 205). A very small compound battery was formed of six pieces of copper bell-wire each about an inch and a half long, and six pieces of zinc of the same size; the current which this arrangement produced was transmitted through a spool of copper wire covered with cotton: this wire was 5 miles in length, and $\frac{1}{16}$ of an inch in diameter, and it was wound upon a small axis of iron. The shock, on breaking the connexion with the little battery, was distinctly felt simultaneously by twenty-six persons who had formed a circle by joined hands, and who completed the circuit between the two ends of the wire. The shock which was felt on making contact with the battery was barely perceptible. A current is produced on making contact, but it is feeble, and in a direction the reverse of that emanating from that battery. Even a thermo-electric battery (317), if the current which it yields be transmitted through the coil, will furnish sparks on breaking contact.

Henry, in the paper above referred to, has made some interesting observations upon the action of the battery current in inducing secondary currents. He employed for transmitting the primary current a flat coil or ribbon of sheet copper about 93 feet long and $1\frac{1}{2}$ inch wide. This ribbon was sometimes coiled in the manner shown at *a*, fig. 248, sometimes in the form of a ring as shown at *b*. This coil was combined under various circumstances with other similar coils, each about 60 feet long, or with helices of fine copper wire of various lengths. The form of ribbon is a very advantageous one, as it offers a large sectional area in the conductor, and thus diminishes the resistance, whilst the different layers of the coil are approximated to each other with the smallest possible intervals between them. When coiled as at *b*, and a helix was placed within the ring so formed, each time that the current from the battery through the ribbon was interrupted, a secondary current of considerable intensity was obtained in the helix: the helix could be supported upon a plate of glass which rested upon the flat coil, and still the inductive action was obtained; but if a metallic plate were interposed between the coil and the helix, no secondary current was obtained in the helix, because it was transferred to the interposed conducting plate.

By arranging a series of coils in the manner represented in fig. 248, Henry succeeded in obtaining a succession of induced

FIG. 248.

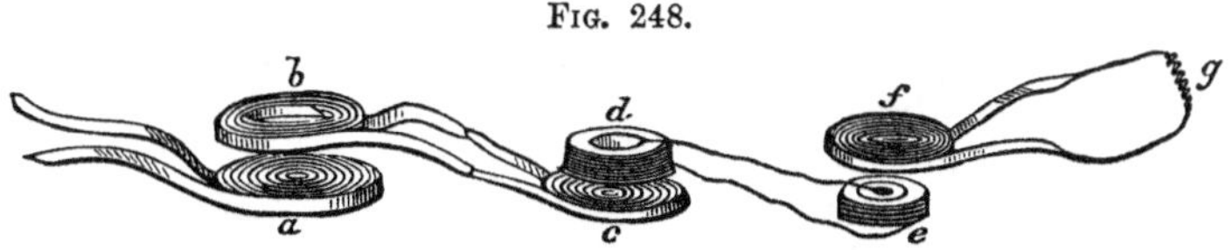

currents by their mutual action. If *a* represent the coil in connexion with the battery, *b* and *c* are arranged to form a continuous coil, through which, by induction, a momentary current is produced each time that the connexion of the coil *a* with the battery is broken; the current in *b c* then being direct, or in the same direction as in *a*. Now if two wire helices be connected together and placed as at *d* and *e*, the induced current in *c* will produce a second induced current, or *current of the third order*, in *d e*; but this current will be in the opposite direction to that in *b c*. If *f* be a ribbon coil placed above *e*, with its ends united by a small helix at *g*, a third current, or *current of the fourth order*, will be obtained, but it will be in the opposite direction to that in *d e*. Thus if the currents be compared together, they will be in the direction following:—

a	primary current (on breaking)	
b, *c*,	secondary current . . .	direct
d, *e*,	current of the third order .	inverse
f, *g*,	current of the fourth order	direct.

By acting upon the principle just explained, and carefully insulating the coils, currents even of the seventh order have been obtained, the successive currents being alternately direct and inverse.

Similar currents of equal amount, but of lower tension, are obtained each time that the primary circuit is completed, but the direction of the currents in this case is reversed; thus on completing the primary circuit the currents would be as follows:—

a	primary current (on making)	direct
b, *c*,	secondary	inverse
d, *e*,	tertiary	direct
f, *g*,	quaternary	inverse; and so on.

These effects are produced by a series of complicated actions, which admit of being summed up as follows:—The primary current has the power of producing two induced secondary currents in opposite directions one on making, the other on breaking contact; these currents admit of being separated from each other. They are equal in amount, but the current on breaking contact has the highest tension, and will traverse the greater distance in the form of a spark. *Each* secondary current in *b c* may give rise to *two* opposite tertiary currents in *d e*, but these currents are separated by an interval of time too small to be appreciated, because the secondary current itself is instantaneous. These two tertiary currents are equal in quantity, but differ in tension; the tertiary current produced by the cessation of the secondary being the stronger. Again, each of these momentary tertiary currents is in its turn capable of developing in *f g* two opposite quaternary currents, equal in amount but differing in tension. At each interruption of the primary current, therefore, we have one instantaneous secondary current in *b c*, two tertiary in *d e*, and four quaternary ones in *f g*. If all these currents were equal in tension as well as equal in quantity, they would neutralize each other; but since their tension is not equal, a series of phenomena are produced, owing to the alternate predominance of the tension of the currents moving in one direction in one circuit, and in the opposite direction in the succeeding circuit.

Henry has shown that induced currents of several successive orders may also be obtained by the momentary passage of electricity occasioned by the discharge of the Leyden jar.

These induced currents not only give powerful shocks, but they magnetize steel bars and produce chemical decomposition. The latter may be shown by interposing acidulated water or a solution of iodide of potassium between platinum wires which are in connexion with the ends of the coil. It is easy to obtain either currents of high intensity such as those required to produce shocks, or currents of large quantity such as would be required for magnetizing steel or for igniting platinum wire, by varying the diameter and length of the conductor. When a long thin wire was employed, as by uniting the two helices as at *d* and *e*, a current of great intensity, producing powerful shocks, was obtained; but this same current could be made to induce in the flat coil *f* a current of greater quantity, but of less intensity.

Owing to these variations in quantity and intensity, the investigation of the laws of such induced currents is complicated and difficult. Abria (*Ann. de Chimie*, III. i. 385, and iii. 5) has published some careful researches upon them, but additional experiments are still needed.

(314) *Arago's Rotations.*—A remarkable exemplification of the facility with which secondary currents are induced by magnetic influence, and of the mutual action of such induced currents, is exhibited by the following experiments of Arago. If a magnet be suspended freely by its centre in a horizontal direction, parallel to a circular disk of copper which can be made to rotate horizontally beneath the magnet, it will be found, if the centre of suspension for the magnet be directly over the axis of the rotating disk, that when the disk is made to revolve with a certain degree of velocity the magnet begins to rotate also in the same direction as the disk; and the more closely the disk and the magnet are approximated, the more rapid is the rotation, whilst at the same

time a repulsive action is exerted upon the magnet in a direction perpendicular to the plane of the disk. This rotation occurs as freely when a sheet of paper or of glass is interposed between the magnet and the metallic disk, as when air only intervenes. Disks of other metals by their rotation also produce this effect upon the magnet, but none of them show it so readily as copper; the facility with which the effect is produced being directly as the power of the rotating disk to conduct electric currents. If a narrow strip be cut out of the metallic disk, extending from its circumference to the centre, no motion will be produced in the magnet when the disk is made to revolve; but if the cut edges of the divided disk be connected by soldering a piece of wire across the division, the rotation may be effected as readily as when the disk was entire. From causes similar to those which produce the foregoing results, it is found that if a magnetic needle or a bar magnet be set vibrating parallel to the surface of a disk of copper, it will come to rest much more speedily than if vibrating over paper or glass.

These effects were first satisfactorily explained by Faraday; he found that whenever a piece of conducting matter is made to pass either before a single pole or between the opposite poles of a magnet so as to cut the magnetic curves at right angles, electrical currents are produced across the metal, transverse to the direction of motion. For example, let the copper disk c, fig. 249, be made to revolve, in the direction of the arrows on the cir-

Fig. 249.

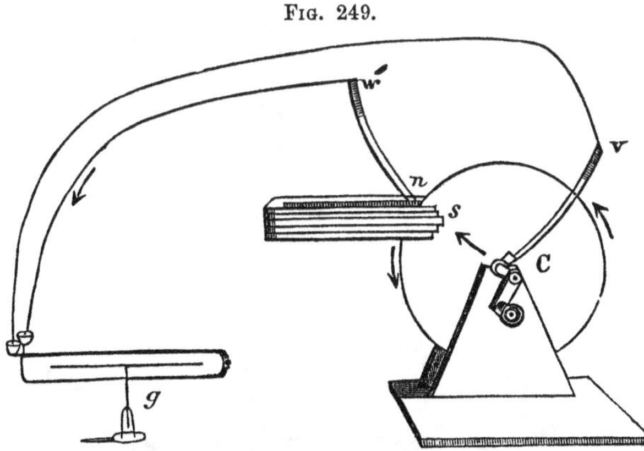

cumference, between the poles, *n s*, of a horse-shoe magnet, and let a wire, *w*, which is connected with one end of the galvanometer, *g*, be pressed against the centre of the disk, whilst the other wire *w'* from the galvanometer rests against the edge of the disk between the magnetic poles. Under these circumstances, a current will be found to flow from the centre towards the circumference of the disk, c, and then through the wires, as shown by the arrows. If the disk be made to revolve in the opposite direction, the current will flow from the circumference towards the centre of the disk. Currents may also be obtained from any of the forms of the apparatus which exhibit the rotation of magnets round a conducting wire, or of the wire round the magnet, if a galvanometer be substituted for the battery, and if the magnet or the wire be made to revolve by hand.

Now let us suppose that in Arago's experiment we are looking down upon the revolving disk, *c*, fig. 250; when the disk revolves beneath the magnet, it cuts the magnetic curves at right angles; currents are produced underneath the north pole, from the centre of the plate towards the circumference, *a*, beyond the pole: these currents occur in the opposite direction—viz., from the circumference to the centre, underneath the south pole, and thus traverse the diameter of the plate parallel to the magnet, returning by the more distant parts of the plate, as shown by the dotted arrows. Such currents necessarily exert a repulsive action upon the magnet in a direction which coincides with that in which motion is observed, and no currents are obtained until either the magnet or the plate is set in motion.

Fig. 250.

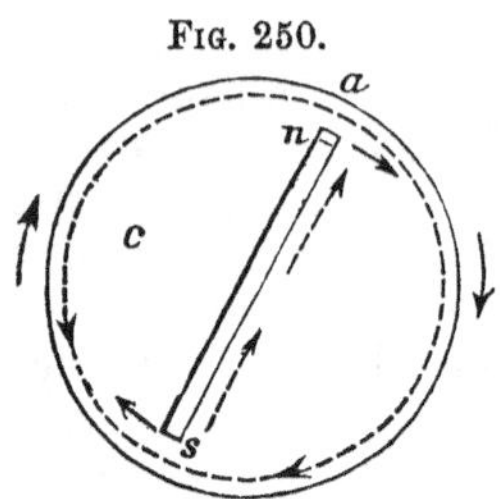

(315) *Magneto-Electric Machines.*—Various machines have been contrived for the production of magneto-electric currents.

Fig. 251.

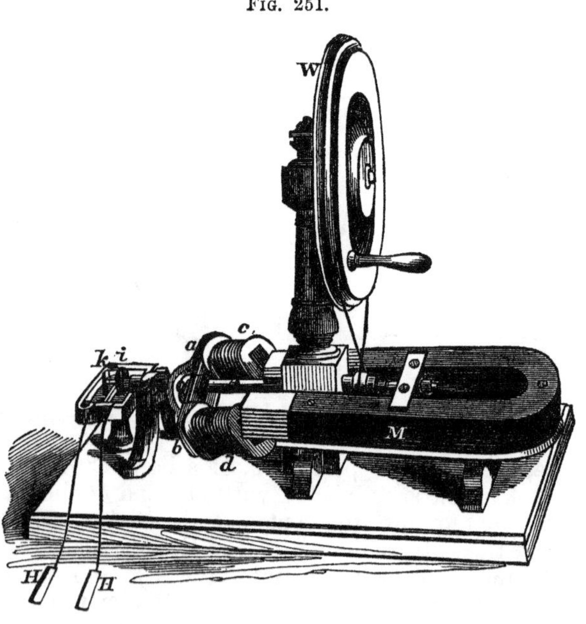

The most convenient of these is Saxton's Magneto-Electric Machine. It is represented in fig. 251, in perspective; fig. 252

shows a section of the coils and armature on a larger scale. It consists of a powerful horse-shoe magnet, M, placed horizontally upon one of its sides: in front of its ends or poles, and as close to them as is possible without producing actual contact, an armature of soft iron, *a b*, is made to revolve upon a horizontal axis, A, which admits of being turned by means of a strap passing over a multiplying wheel, W. This armature consists of two straight pieces of iron, about two inches in length, which, by means of a crosspiece of iron, X, are connected together parallel to each other, at such a distance that they shall be opposite the middle of each pole of the horse-shoe magnet. Around each limb, *c*, *d*, of the armature, a long fine copper wire, covered with silk to insulate the coils from each other, is wound in several successive layers. The corresponding ends of each of these helices are connected together; one pair, *e f*, is soldered to the spindle, *s*, on which the armature rotates, and through it is connected with a circular copper disk, *i*, the edge of which dips into a cup of mercury, *m*, whilst the other pair of wires, *g*, *h*, is connected with a stout piece of copper which passes through the axis of the spindle, *s*, from which it is electrically insulated, and terminates in a slip of copper, *k*, placed nearly at right angles to the crosspiece, X, which connects the two limbs of the soft iron armature. Beneath the slip of copper, *k*, is a second mercury cup, *l*, which can be made to communicate with the cup, *m*, either by a wire, or by some other conductor of the current. The arms of the slip, *k*, alternately dip into the mercury, and rise above it, and the points of contact are so arranged that the circuit (which, when *l* and *m* are properly connected, is complete so long as *k* is beneath the

FIG. 252.

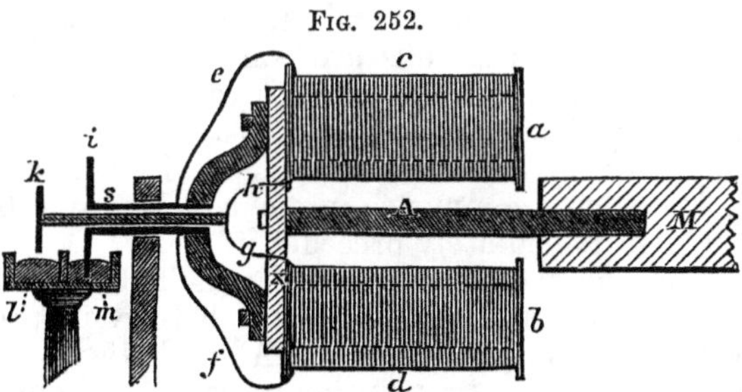

mercury) shall be broken at the time that the armature loses its magnetism. Under these circumstances a bright spark is obtained each time that the slip *k* quits the mercury. Four currents are therefore produced in the wire surrounding the armature during each complete revolution, two successive currents being in one direction, and the two others being in the opposite direction. Suppose, for example, that the limb, *c*, of the armature is opposite the marked pole of the steel magnet; if now it be made to recede from this pole a current will be produced in a given direction, through the coil which surrounds this limb, and on the approach of the same limb towards the unmarked end of the magnet, a second current will be produced in the same direction through the coil; a third current will be produced, but in a reversed direction, as the limb *c* leaves the unmarked end of the magnet, whilst a fourth current will be produced on the approach of the limb *c* to the marked pole of the magnet, and will coincide with the reversed direction of the third current. If the connexion between the mercury cups, *l* and *m*, be effected by grasping with the hands two copper cylinders, H H, each of which by means of a wire is in connexion separately with one of the cups, a succession of powerful shocks will be experienced. Acidulated water and many saline solutions may be decomposed if these currents be transmitted through them; but in order to produce polar decomposition, it is necessary to suppress or turn up one of the points of the slip *k*, and thus to lose half the power of the machine; otherwise the currents at each half revolution are in opposite directions.

In the construction of these magneto-electric machines, great care must be taken that the insulation of the coils is very perfect. Different effects are obtained from such a machine by varying the length and the diameter of the wire which is wound around the armature. When currents of high intensity are required, such as those needed for giving shocks, or for the decomposition of electrolytes, a great length of thin wire is preferable; but a much smaller length of thicker wire will give the largest sparks, and will ignite the greatest length of fine platinum wire.*

Wheatstone and others have contrived magneto-electric machines, by which a continuous electric current in a uniform direction may be kept up for any length of time. These batteries are in fact, combinations of several simple machines, similar in principle to Saxton's; the coils are connected together so as to form a continuous circuit. The armatures are so arranged that each shall in turn become magnetic, just before the preceding armature has entirely lost its magnetism. By this contrivance, the current is made to commence in one coil before it has ceased in the coil which immediately precedes it.

Magneto-electric machines are now used in Birmingham on a large scale, as a substitute for the voltaic battery in processes of electro-silvering and electro-gilding. A single Saxton's machine will, if kept in continuous revolution, precipitate from 90 to 120 ounces of silver per week from its solutions: and machines have been constructed by which 2½ ounces of silver per hour have been deposited upon articles properly prepared for this mode of plating.

Mr. Holmes has succeeded, by the use of a powerful magneto-electric machine, in producing a light of great steadiness and intensity between two points of gas coke: this light can be main-

* A machine upon this principle has been contrived by Wheatstone for exploding charges of gunpowder, when provided with Abel's magnet fuse, which seems to leave little to be desired in simplicity, certainty, and facility of application. (*Report to Secretary of War*, Wheatstone and Abel, Nov., 1860.)

tained without interruption so long as the magnets are kept in rotation, and the charcoal continues unconsumed.

The machine consists of 48 pairs of compound bar magnets, arranged in 6 parallel planes, so as to form a large compound wheel, between which the armatures, 160 in number, are arranged in 5 sets, the total amount of wire being about half a mile in length. The wires are insulated by cotton, and the contacts are so arranged as to maintain a continuous current in the same direction, varying from a maximum to exactly half the amount of the maximum, in rapid succession. The steel bars weigh about 1 ton, and the wheel is made, by the aid of a small steam engine, to revolve with a rapidity varying from 150 to 250 times per minute. This light was for several months in successful operation at the South Foreland Lighthouse, and subsequently at Dungeness, the actual expense of fuel in working the engine being about equal to that of the oil formerly used, while the light is far more brilliant.

§ VI. Thermo-Electricity.

(316) The phenomena due to the development of electricity by heat are arranged under the head of *thermo-electricity*,—a term which serves to recal to mind the manner in which the force originates in these cases. The present section contains a summary of the more important facts which have been ascertained on this subject.

As any obstruction to the passage of the electric current in a conductor occasions the development of heat, so any obstruction to the equal propagation of heat in a conducting circuit produces a current of electricity. This important result was first obtained by Seebeck, in the year 1822.

If the extremities of the wire of a sensitive galvanometer be united by means of a straight piece of platinum wire, this wire may be heated at any point at a distance from its connexions with the galvanometer wire, without producing a current through the circuit; but if the platinum wire be twisted into a loop, its molecular tension at this point is slightly altered, and if heat be applied to the wire close to the loop and to the right of it, a current will flow through the apparatus from right to left, owing to the inequality of the conducting power, and the disturbance of regularity in the transmission of the force from the hotter to the colder portions. These effects are still more readily produced by dividing the wire into two portions, and coiling each extremity into a flat spiral. If one of these spirals be heated to redness, and be brought into contact with the cold spiral, deflection of the needle immediately follows, in a direction which indicates the flow of a current from the hotter to the colder portion. Metals such as bismuth or antimony, in which a crystalline structure is strongly developed, but which possess an inferior power of conducting electricity, display these thermo-electric phenomena in a more perfect degree. If one half of a ring or rectangular frame composed of either of these metals be heated, and the other half be kept cool, a current sufficient to deflect a magnetic needle suspended within the frame or ring, will be produced. Metals which are better conductors, such as copper or silver, although they also show the phenomena, exhibit it much less distinctly.

Prof. W. Thomson has shown that if portions of a metallic wire be stretched by weights, and be connected with other portions of the same wire not so stretched, on applying heat to their junctions, a current is produced from the stretched to the unstretched wire through the heated point.

If the rectangle be composed of two dissimilar metals, as when a bar of antimony, A A, fig. 253, is soldered to a bar of bismuth, B B, the application of heat, such as the flame of a spirit-lamp, to one of the junctions will cause deflection of the suspended needle, *n s*. A bar of bismuth when soldered to a copper wire, will readily deflect the needle of a galvanometer of moderate sensibility, if even the warmth of the hand only be applied to one of the junctions. The earlier researches upon this subject appeared to show that so long as the resistance in the circuit continue unchanged, the amount of force in circulation is exactly proportioned to the difference in temperature of the two junctions. Becquerel, relying upon the accuracy of this datum, has applied a thermo-electric pair of metals to the measurement of temperature. Amongst other experiments, he endeavoured to ascertain the temperature of flames; the metals which he employed were thin wires of platinum and palladium; the junction of the wires was introduced into different parts of the flame which, as might be supposed, were found to vary considerably in temperature. The proportionality of the current to the temperature, however, only holds good with those non-crystalline metals which do not oxidize when powerfully heated: and even these are liable to irregularity, so that the determination of temperatures by this means must not be relied on without special verifications, which, at high temperatures, can scarcely be effected with accuracy. For small differences of temperature, however, the thermo-electric pair or pile (317) surpasses in sensitiveness all other thermometric means at present in use.

Fig. 253.

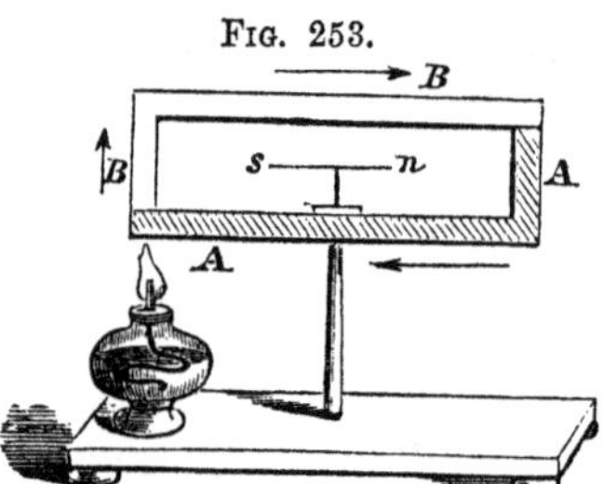

If one of the junctions of a thermo-electric pair be maintained steadily at a low temperature, such as 32°, whilst the temperature of the other junction is gradually raised, it happens with some combinations, that the current increases in intensity up to a certain point, then declines, and is reversed; in the case of zinc and silver, the rise continues up to 248° F.; then the current declines, becomes null, and ultimately is reversed, as the temperature continues to rise. Most probably this is due to the peculiar effect which heat has upon the crystalline structure of zinc. Iron and antimony exhibit the same effect, but to a less marked extent; and Thomson has extended the observation to a number of other metals. So important is the crystalline structure in these arrangements, that the thermo-electric power of bismuth is very materially reduced by the addition of a small per-centage of tin, which impairs its tendency to crystallize.*

It may indeed be stated that when two dissimilar metals are connected in any way so as to produce a closed circuit, an electric current is established each time that any difference in temperature is produced between the two points of contact; and the current is maintained so long as the difference of temperature continues.

The metals may be arranged in the following thermo-electric order:—

Bismuth	Copper and Silver
Platinum	Zinc
Lead	Iron
Tin	Antimony.

When heated together, the current proceeds from those which stand last on the list towards those which precede them. It is to be remarked that the thermo-electric order of the metals is entirely different from their voltaic order.† According to the experiments of Wheatstone and Pouillet, who have arrived at the same result by very different methods, the electro-motive force of a pair of bismuth and copper, when one junction is maintained at 212° and the other at 32° F., is $\frac{1}{95}$ of that exerted between a pair of copper and zinc plates arranged in voltaic relation, as in Daniell's battery.

Thermo-electric circuits may also be formed with inferior conductors. Nobili brought the point of a heated one of porcelain clay into contact with a cold cylinder of the same material, each connected with the galvanometer by cotton soaked in a conducting liquid: the current passed from the cone to the cylinder.

(317) *Thermo-Multiplier.*—By connecting together successive pairs of two different metals, and heating the alternate joints, whilst the other junctions are kept cool, a thermo-electric battery

* An important connexion between the direction of the planes of cleavage and the direction of the thermo-electric current in crystalline metals was shown to exist by Svanberg. In bismuth and in antimony, for example, there is one particular plane of cleavage endowed with greater brilliancy than the rest. Bars of these metals, when placed with this plane of cleavage perpendicularly to the direction of the current, are more highly negative than when placed in any other position; whilst, if a second plane of cleavage, somewhat less brilliant than the former, be placed across the line of current, the bar is more highly positive, thermo-electrically, than in any other position.

† Matthiessen has published (*Phil. Trans.*, 1858) the results of a careful series of experiments upon the thermo-electric order and energy of various bodies, for temperatures usually ranging between about 40° and 100° F. If the electro-motive force of the thermo-electric current excited between silver and copper be taken as equal to 1 (the current passing from the silver to the copper at the heated junction), the force of the current between silver and each metal in succession heated to the same point, will be represented by the numbers given in the following table. Where the positive sign is prefixed the current is from the silver to the other metal at the heated junction; when

may be constructed. The size of the elements which are employed contributes nothing to the effect, except so far as by increasing the area of the conducting section, the conducting power of the circuit is increased. Such a battery will decompose a solution of iodide of potassium, and Botto states that with a pile consisting of 100 pairs of platinum and iron wire, each 1 inch long and $\frac{1}{100}$ of an inch in diameter, he succeeded in decomposing even diluted sulphuric acid. A thermo-electric current from a single pair is sufficient to convulse the limbs of a frog. The principle of the arrangement by which a *thermo-multiplier* or thermo-electric battery may be constructed, is shown in fig. 254; to one series of junctions, a high temperature, to the other a low temperature may be applied; the shaded bars, A, represent bars of antimony, those in outline, B, indicate bars of bismuth. The intensity of such a current, however, is comparatively feeble, and the resistance which it experiences in traversing even metallic conductors of considerable diameter, such as the metallic bars themselves which are used in the construction of the battery, seriously reduces its power. A very cheap and effective thermo-electric pile may be made of wires of iron and German silver. Nobili and Melloni applied a thermo-electric battery, consisting of 36 pairs of small bars of bismuth and antimony, to thermometric purposes. Such a battery was employed by Melloni, in his

Fig. 254.

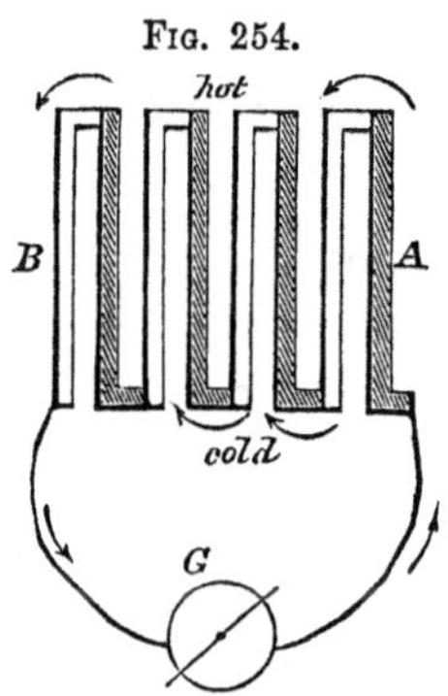

the negative sign is prefixed, the current is from the other metal at the heated point towards the silver. The substances marked with an asterisk are supposed to have been chemically pure:—

Thermo-Electric Order of Metals, &c.

	+		−
Bismuth, commercial, pressed wire	35·81		
*Bismuth, pressed wire	32·91	Gas coke, hard	0·057
*Bismuth, cast	24·96	*Zinc, pressed wire	0·208
Crystallized bismuth, axial	24·59	*Copper voltaic	0·244
Crystal of bismuth, equatorial	17·17	*Cadmium	0·332
Cobalt	8·97	Antimony, pressed wire	1·897
Potassium	5·49	Strontium	2·028
Nickel	5·02	Lithium	3·768
Palladium	3·56	*Arsenic	3·828
Sodium	3·094	Calcium	4·260
*Mercury	2·524	Iron, piano wire	5·218
Aluminum	1·283	Antimony, axial	6·965
Magnesium	1·175	Antimony, equatorial	9·435
*Lead, pressed wire	1·029	*Red phosphorus	9·600
*Tin, pressed wire	1·000	*Antimony, cast	9·871
Copper wire	1·000	Alloy, 12 bismuth, 1 tin, cast	13·67
Platinum	0·723	Alloy, 2 antimony, 1 zinc, cast	22·70
Iridium	0·163		
*Antimony, pressed wire	0·036	*Tellurium	179·8
*Silver	0·	*Selenium	290·0

investigations on radiant heat, to the exclusion of almost every other thermoscopic means. When the alternate junctions of the bars at each end of the pile were covered with lampblack, a coating was obtained which absorbed the radiations proceeding from a surface the temperature of which was much below that of the human body; even the amount of radiant heat emitted by insects could be estimated by connecting this battery with a galvanometer of extreme sensitiveness.*

The conducting power of red phosphorus and of selenium is so slight that neither of them can be used for the construction of thermo-electric piles: that of tellurium is also small, but it is sufficient to admit of its use, and its electro-motive power, when opposed thermo-electrically to bismuth, is so great, that a pile consisting of 8 pairs of these elements, where the alternate junctions are heated to 212°, whilst the others are cooled to 32°, will decompose a solution of sulphate of copper; and Matthiessen estimates the electro-motive force of 100 pairs of such a pile as equal to that of 4 cells of Daniell's arrangement.

(318) In connexion with these thermo-electric effects, a curious observation was made by Peltier (*Ann. de Chimie*, II. lvi. 379, and lxxxi. 301):—when a weak current of electricity was transmitted through a compound bar of bismuth and antimony, from the antimony to the bismuth, as in No. 1, fig. 255, a thermometer, placed at the point of junction, was observed in one experiment to rise 80° F., but when the current was reversed, as in No. 2, the temperature fell 6°·5 F. In some later experiments, Peltier succeeded even in freezing water placed in a cavity drilled at the point of junction of the two metals, when the bar was cooled to 32° by immersion in snow. When feeble currents of equal intensity are transmitted through a compound metallic bar, whatever metals be employed, there is a difference in the temperature at the points of junction, according to the direction in which the current is passing; the amount of the difference of temperature varying with the metals which are used. The rise of temperature occurs almost uniformly when the current passes through the two metals in the same direction as that in which the thermo-electric current would be produced by elevation of temperature.† For example, there is a rise of temperature when the current passes from iron to zinc, from iron to platinum, from iron to copper, from zinc to

FIG. 255.

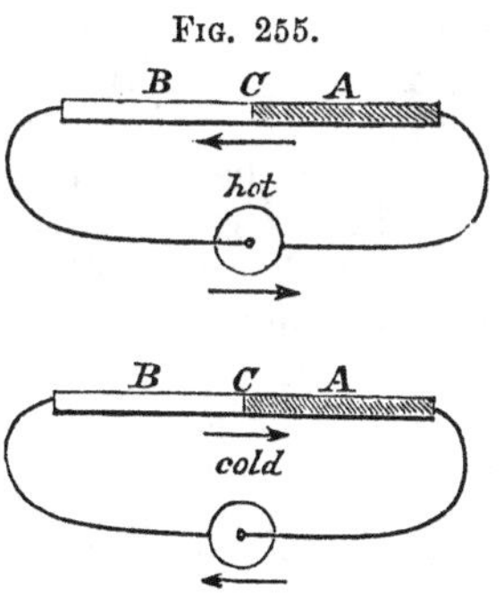

* Melloni used a galvanometer formed of copper wire $\frac{1}{50}$ of an inch in diameter, about 8 yards long, and arranged around the astatic needles in 40 convolutions. Much of the sensitiveness of the instrument depends upon the exact equality of the magnetization of the two needles: the compound needle should require from 55 to 60 seconds in order to complete an oscillation.

† An exception is presented in the case of lead and copper, and tin and copper, in which the current is towards the copper from the heated metal.

copper, from copper to bismuth, and from antimony to copper; but when the current is reversed between the same pairs, there is either a much smaller elevation, or in some cases even an actual depression of temperature. This subject has been discussed at great length by Clausius and by Thomson, in their researches on the mechanical theory of heat.

§ VII. Animal Electricity.

(319) Some fish, particularly the torpedo, and the electrical eel (*Gymnotus electricus*) have the remarkable power of giving electrical shocks at pleasure, by means of an apparatus specially adapted to the purpose.

The torpedo, which is a species of ray, is a flat fish, tolerably abundant in the Mediterranean; it is provided with two electrical organs situated one on each side of the spine near the head, occupying the whole thickness of the fish; these organs are supplied with large thick nerves; and it has been found that on cutting these nerves all voluntary electric power ceases: but according to Matteucci, the irritation of that end of the cut nerve which is attached to the organ in a lively torpedo occasions the electric discharge, and even irritation of detached portions of the organ produces contraction in the limb of a frog recently killed, if the crural nerve of the frog be allowed to rest upon the organ of the torpedo. The structure of the electrical organs is gelatinous, and the material is divided by membranous septa into 400 or 500 columns, which have some resemblance to grains of rice in appearance; these columns run from the dorsal to the ventral surface of the fish, and are about the thickness of a goose-quill; the dorsal surface is positive, the ventral negative. The electricity is most strongly developed just at the points where the nerves enter the organ; a powerful shock is received on simultaneously touching the back and the belly of the fish at any part, but the shock obtained is strongest immediately over the two organs. A weaker shock is experienced on touching different parts even of the same surface, since the electric charge differs in intensity at different points of the same surface. Frequent discharges exhaust the animal quickly: the frequency of the discharge is under the control of the animal, but not its direction. The electric discharges of the torpedo are partly dissipated when the fish is immersed in water by the conducting power of this liquid, and Matteucci estimated that in air the shock given by the animal is four times as powerful as when it is in water.

(320) In the gymnotus, which is a fresh-water fish, tolerably abundant in the marshes of Surinam, and in the tributaries to the Orinoco there are four electrical organs, a large and a small one on each side running from the head to the tail of the animal. These organs, like those of the torpedo, are supplied with large nerves, and have a membranous structure, the septa running in a more or less longitudinal direction from the head towards the tail. The longer the column that produces the shock, the greater is the

force of the electric discharge: the anterior portions of this animal are positive to the posterior, so that the strongest shocks are obtained by touching the fish simultaneously near the head and near the tail; but shocks more or less intense may be obtained from any part of the body, if the hands be separated for a short distance in the direction of the head and tail of the animal; scarcely any shock is felt if the hands be placed one on each side of the fish at the same distances from the head or the tail. So great is the electric energy of the animal, that the specimen which was exhibited in the Adelaide Gallery, 40 inches in length, was calculated by Faraday, at each medium discharge, to emit as great a force as the highest discharge of a Leyden battery of fifteen jars, exposing 3500 square inches of coated surface. Shocks differing in intensity with the position of the observer and his distance from the fish, were felt in all parts of the tub which contained it; this tub was 46 inches in diameter. The shocks from the gymnotus have power sufficient to kill or to stun fish: the same discharge produces a more powerful effect upon a large fish than it does upon a small one, since the larger animal exposes a larger conducting surface to the water through the mass of which the electricity is passing, and consequently it receives a more violent shock. On one occasion when a live fish was put into a tub, the animal was seen by Faraday to coil itself into the form of a semicircle, the fish lying across the diameter: this position was the one most favorable to the full effect of the electrical discharge; an instant afterwards the fish floated motionless upon its side, deprived of life by the shock it had received, and was then speedily devoured by the gymnotus.

The shock of both the torpedo and the gymnotus gives rise to momentary currents sufficient to deflect the galvanometer, to magnetize a needle, and to decompose iodide of potassium: from both species sparks have also been obtained between two insulated gold leaves properly connected with the fish.

(321) *The Muscular Current in Living Animals.*—The researches of Matteucci have shown that in the living animal an electrical current is perpetually circulating between the internal portion of a muscle and its external surface; this current is due probably to the chemical actions which are produced by the vital changes which are continually occurring in the organic tissue. The *muscular current*, as it has been termed, ceases to manifest itself in warm-blooded animals in a very few minutes after the life of the entire animal has terminated; but in cold-blooded animals, and especially in the frog, it continues for a much longer period. Vital contractility also continues in these animals for a longer period than in the higher orders of the vertebrata, and hence the frog has been extensively employed in researches of this description.

The following is one of the forms of experiment, devised by Matteucci, to show the existence of the muscular current:—Five or six frogs are killed by dividing the spinal column just below the head; the lower limbs are removed, and the integuments stripped off them; the thighs are next separated from the legs at the knee-joint, and are cut across transversely. The lower halves of these prepared thighs are then placed upon a varnished board, and so arranged that the knee-joint of one limb shall be in contact with the transverse section of the next, and thus a muscular pile is formed consisting of ten or twelve elements; the terminal pieces of this pile are each made to dip into a separate small cavity in the board, in which a little distilled water is placed. If the wires of a sensitive galvanometer be attached to a pair of platinum plates, and these plates be plunged simultaneously one into each cavity in connexion with the muscular pile, a deviation of the galvanometer needle will be observed in a direction which indicates the existence of a current passing from the centre or cut transverse surface of the muscle towards its exterior.

Dubois Reymond, by the use of still more sensitive instruments, has shown that even the smallest shreds of muscular tissue exhibit proof of the existence of such a current, and the conclusion which he draws from his experiments is the following:—Any point of the natural or artificial *longitudinal* section of a muscle is positive in relation to any point of the natural or artificial *transverse* section.

Interesting as this subject is in a chemical point of view, in connexion with the changes which take place in the circulating fluids, it would be irrelevant to our present purpose to pursue it further. The question belongs more properly to the physiologist than to the chemist; and the reader who desires fuller information upon this branch of inquiry is referred to the various papers of Matteucci in the *Annales de Chimie*, and the *Philosophical Transactions*, and to the work of Dubois Reymond, or to the more recent systematic treatises on physiology.

§ VIII. Magnetic Polarization of Light—Diamagnetism.

(322) *Influence of Magnetism on Polarized Light transmitted through Uncrystallized Transparent Bodies.*—Allusion has been already made (127) to a peculiar kind of polarization to which light is subject, when transmitted through certain transparent media, which are under the influence of magnets of high power. Some transparent bodies are better fitted than others to exhibit this phenomenon. Some years ago Faraday prepared a peculiar kind of glass for optical purposes; it consisted of a mixture of silicate and borate of lead, and was much denser than ordinary flint glass: this glass is particularly well adapted to display the effects of magnetic polarization. Let a piece of this glass which has been properly annealed be cut into the form of a rectangular bar or prism, terminated by flat parallel faces, and let it be placed between the poles of a powerful electro-magnet not in action, the axis of the prism being parallel to a line which joins the two poles—in fact in the direction of the keeper of a horse-shoe magnet. A ray of polarized light may be transmitted along the axis of the glass bar, and if examined by an analysing plate in the usual manner (120) the light will disappear when the plane of

reflection from the analysing plate is at right angles to the plane of polarization. If, now, whilst the polarized ray is at the point of maximum obscuration, the soft iron be magnetized by the action of the battery, the light will instantly reappear, and if white light be used, the reflected ray will be coloured. The moment that the connexion with the battery is broken, the light will disappear; but it will again become visible each time that the iron is rendered magnetic. If the north end of the magnet be towards the observer, the rotation of the plane of polarization is to the right, as represented in fig. 256, No. 1; but if the direction of the magnetism be reversed, so that the south end is nearest the observer, the rotation is to the left, as in No. 2.

FIG. 256.

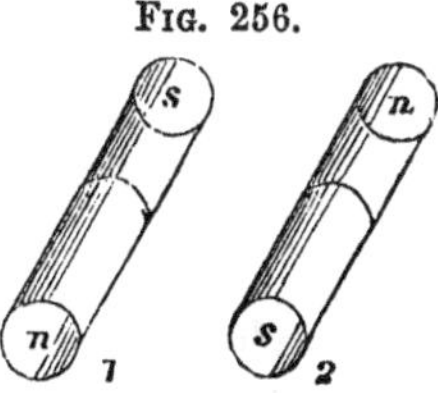

Different bodies, when placed between the poles of an electro-magnet, possess this property of causing the ray to rotate in different degrees, but all singly refracting solids and liquids manifest it: in magnetized gases, and *in vacuo*, no such effects have been discovered. The extent of the rotation is, *cæteris paribus*, directly as the intensity of the magnetism, and as the length of the medium traversed by the ray. By placing the transparent bodies in the axis of a coil of wire conveying an electric current, the same effects are produced, but in a lower degree: the more numerous the coils of the helix, and the longer the column of the transparent body which is traversed by the ray, the greater is the extent of the rotation. When an electric current passes round a ray of polarized light, in a plane perpendicular to the direction of the ray, it causes rotation of the ray in the same direction as that in which the current is passing. The interposition of bodies which are not susceptible of magnetism, between the coils of the helix and the transparent body placed in its axis, does not sensibly affect the polarizing action, but the interposition of a hollow iron core between the helix and the transparent body in its axis, in some cases greatly heightens the effect, in others it neutralizes it, the rotatory influence varying with the thickness of the core.

Matteucci found that by elevating the temperature of a bar of heavy glass to about 600°, the rotatory power was increased by about one-third, when compared with the effect of the same bar at ordinary temperatures. Bertin (*Ann. de Chimie*, III. xxvii. 31) gives the following rotatory power for columns of equal length of various bodies at ordinary temperatures, assuming that of heavy glass as equal to 1:—

Heavy glass	1·00
Perchloride of tin	0·77
Bisulphide of carbon	0·74
Terchloride of phosphorus	0·51
Water	0·25
Alcohol (sp. gr. 0·850)	0·18
Ether	0·15

The salts of calcium, of zinc, and of magnesium, as well as many other saline substances, increase the rotatory power of water, when added to it, the effect being proportioned to the strength of the solution. Verdet has determined by careful measurement (*Ann. de Chimie*, III. lii. 129) the extent to which this rotatory power is possessed by various bodies in solution; and the same observer has shown that the addition of a salt of iron to water diminishes the rotatory power of the liquid; an aqueous solution of perchloride of iron, containing 40 per cent. of the salt, gives a *negative* rotation, which is five or six times as powerful as the positive rotation possessed by water. Salts of chromium, titanium, cerium, uranium, and lanthanum produce a similar effect; whilst the salts of nickel and cobalt, which are also magnetic, produce a *positive* effect, and increase the ordinary rotatory power. Ferrocyanide of potassium, although it contains iron, exerts a positive rotatory effect.

Bodies, such as oil of turpentine, which naturally produce coloured circular polarization (126) have the power exalted, annihilated, or reversed, according to the direction and intensity of the electric current which is transmitted through the coil. The polarization produced by magnetism differs from the ordinary coloured circular polarization shown by oil of turpentine in this remarkable particular—viz., that the magnetic rotation is always in the same direction as that of the current which circulates around the coil.

Fig. 257.

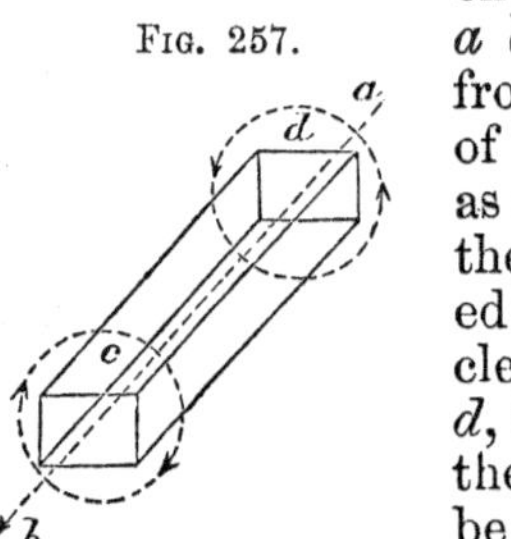

Let *c d*, fig. 257, represent a vessel filled with oil of turpentine endowed with right-handed rotation, and let *a b* be a polarized ray. If the ray proceed from *a* to the observer at *b*, the rotation will of course appear to be right-handed to him, as shown by the circle, *c*; and if from *b* to *a*, the rotation will still appear to be right-handed to the observer at *a*, as shown by the circle, *d*. If now a current be passed round *c d*, in the direction of the circular arrow at *c*, the rotation to the observer at *b* will appear to be increased; while to an observer at *a* it will appear to be neutralized or reversed.

(323) *Magnetism of Bodies in general.*—It was formerly imagined since iron was susceptible of magnetism in a high degree, nickel in an inferior degree, and cobalt in a degree still less, that all other substances might also be magnetic, although to an extent so minute as to elude the ordinary means of observation. Moreover, as experiment had proved that a reduction of temperature exalts the magnetic power of iron and of nickel, it seemed not unreasonable to anticipate that by extreme depression of temperature a point might be attained at which every species of matter would show itself obedient to the magnet. Experiments made upon this subject at very low temperatures have not, however, justified these expectations. The employment of magnets of un-

usual power has, on the other hand, revealed the existence of a susceptibility to this force in cases where under ordinary circumstances it had not been observed. (Faraday, *Phil. Trans.* 1846.)

Before adverting to these experiments, it will be advisable to define clearly the different parts of the space between the two poles where the magnetic action is manifested. Let us suppose that we are looking down upon the poles, N, S (fig. 258), of a powerful horse-shoe magnet; the space between them has been termed by Faraday *the magnetic field;* the line, A X, will give the direction of its *axis;* the line, E Q, which is in the same horizontal plane, but at right angles to A X, will form the *equator* of the magnetic field. A bar of iron suspended by its centre above such a magnet, will take a horizontal direction parallel to the axis, A X, and is said to point *axially.* By using electro-magnets of enormous power (303) many bodies not usually reputed to be magnetic will take the axial position like a bar of iron. For example, if an elongated fragment of hæmatite, or red oxide of iron, which is indifferent to a common magnet, be suspended horizontally at its centre by a few fibres of silk between the poles of such an electro-magnet, it will point axially; even a sheet of writing-paper rolled up so as to form a short cylinder will, usually, owing to the small quantity of iron or of cobalt that it contains, assume a similar direction.

Fig. 258.

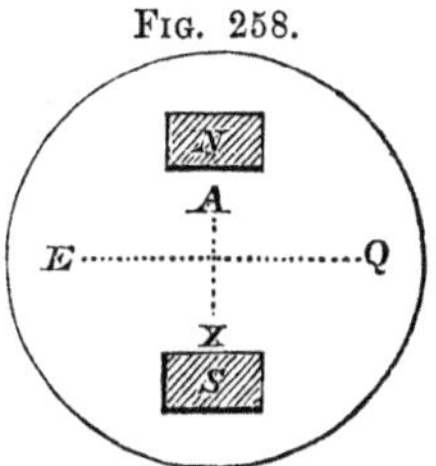

Faraday has found as a general rule that the salts of the magnetic metals are themselves magnetic, provided that these metals enter into the *base* of the salts. For instance, crystals of green sulphate of iron placed in a thin glass tube, which is not magnetic, will cause the tube to point axially. Such salts preserve their magnetic properties even when dissolved in water: if the solution be placed in a glass tube of the form shown in fig. 259, the tube, when suspended by a loop of copper wire and a few fibres of raw silk, will take an axial position between the poles of the magnet. Solutions of sulphate of nickel and of sulphate of cobalt act in a manner similar to the solutions of the salts of iron. The pure salts of chromium and of manganese have in like manner proved to be magnetic, and hence these metals themselves are inferred to be so, although, from the high temperature required to reduce them to the metallic condition, it is almost impossible to obtain them in such a state of chemical purity as would enable the fact to be verified by experiments upon the metals themselves in an uncombined state.

Fig. 259.

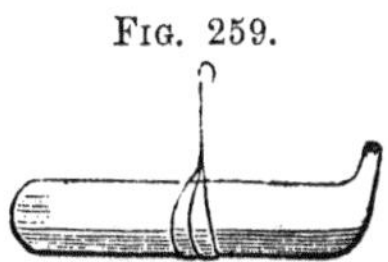

(324) *Diamagnetism.*—All the magnetic bodies mentioned above are attracted indifferently by either magnetic pole; and, if of elongated form, they place themselves with their longest diameter in the axial direction when suspended by their centre

between two contrary magnetic poles. It is, however, far from being true that all substances are magnetic. Bodies exist which, when brought near to a magnetic pole, are repelled instead of being attracted: such substances have been termed *diamagnetics*. If a straw (s, fig. 260) be suspended horizontally by a silk fibre, and from one extremity of the straw a small piece of phosphorus, P, be supported in a ring of fine copper wire, repulsion of the phosphorus will be produced indifferently by either pole. In such an experiment it will be found convenient to place a soft iron armature, bevelled off to a blunt point, upon the pole of the magnet, in order to concentrate the power, because the repulsive force is very feeble when compared with the attractive power developed in iron. If a stick of phosphorus be suspended between the two poles of the electro-magnet, it takes the *equatorial* position, assuming a direction at right angles to that of a bar of iron, the phosphorus being repelled by each pole to the greatest distance possible. Phosphorus, it will be observed, is a non-conductor of electricity; but some of the metals, of which bismuth and antimony are the most remarkable, exhibit this repulsive action in a still higher degree. Substances of an organic nature, such as slices of wood, apple, potato, or flesh, likewise show this diamagnetic power, though not strongly. In fact, all bodies which are not magnetic, exhibit diamagnetic properties. Owing to the feeble amount of these repulsive actions, it is necessary to screen the objects under experiment from the influence of currents of air, by surrounding them with a glass case, as represented in fig. 261, in which *b* represents a bar of bismuth, or other diamagnetic body, delicately suspended by a few fibres of unspun silk, *c*. The bismuth bar is shown in the equatorial position between the two poles of the electro-magnet, which project through apertures made for their reception in the table.

Fig. 260.

S

P

Fig. 261.

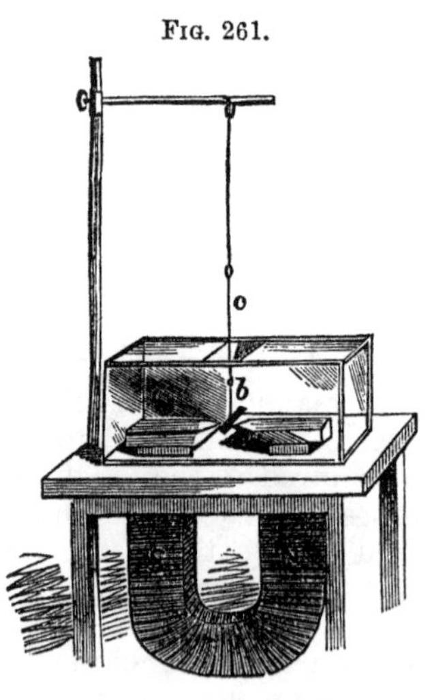

(325) *Diamagnetism of Gases.*—The earlier experiments upon the gases, owing to the very small amount of ponderable matter to be acted upon, gave results which seemed to prove that they were indifferent to the influence of the magnet; but subsequent researches have shown that even the different gases and vapours are susceptible of the diamagnetic influ-

ence in a degree which varies with the nature of the gas. (Faraday, *Phil. Mag.* 1847, xxxi. p. 401.)

The gases upon which experiments were made by Faraday appear to stand in the following order, beginning with those which are least diamagnetic :—atmospheric air, nitric oxide, nitrogen, carbonic acid, nitrous oxide, carbonic oxide, hydrogen, coal gas, olefiant gas, hydrochloric acid, ammonia, and chlorine.

Elevation of temperature exalts the diamagnetic condition,—a stream of hot oxygen appearing to be diamagnetic in an atmosphere of cold oxygen. A similar result was obtained with all such gases as were compared with each other at high and at low temperatures. On the other hand, depression of temperature lowers the diamagnetic force, so that a current of cooled gas when allowed to flow into a warmer atmosphere of the same kind, takes an axial position in the magnetic field. If a stream of one gas be allowed to escape into an atmosphere of a second gas more diamagnetic than itself, the less diamagnetic gas takes the axial position; when atmospheric air, for instance, is made to flow into coal gas, the air takes the axial or magnetic position between the poles; though air itself would take the equatorial position in oxygen gas. The diamagnetism of gases was first indicated in an experiment by Bancalari: he found that the flame of burning bodies was influenced by the action of a powerful electro-magnet. This effect is beautifully exhibited by simply placing the flame of a taper, or of any combustible substance, between the poles of the magnet, when in action; the flame appears to be repelled towards either side by the poles, and if the magnet be sufficiently powerful, the flame divides into two streams which pass off horizontally, one on either side, in the equatorial direction. If the taper be extinguished, whilst the wick still continues to glow, the ascending column of smoke when placed between the poles of the magnet exhibits these motions equally well.

The following simple contrivance was employed by Faraday to show the position assumed by the different gases. A bent tube conveyed the gas for experiment in a very slow but continuous stream into the centre of the magnetic field; generally a piece of paper, moistened with a solution of ammonia, was placed in the bent tube. Supposing the gas to be lighter than air, three wide glass tubes, open at each end, and three or four inches long, were suspended with their lower apertures in the equatorial line, as represented in fig. 262, with the middle tube just above the bent tube for the delivery of the gas. In each tube a piece of paper moistened with hydrochloric acid was suspended. The whole was screened from currents of air by plates of glass. So long as the iron was not magnetized, the gas flowed readily up the axis of the middle tube; but on bringing the electro-magnet into action,

Fig. 262.

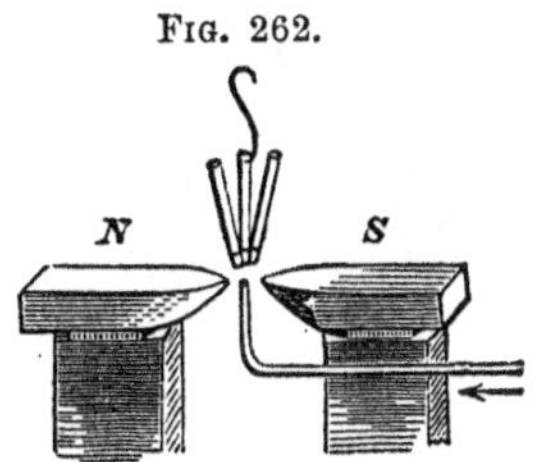

the gas, instead of passing directly up the central tube, was, when more diamagnetic than air, diverted into each of the side tubes; and the currents were rendered visible by the white fumes produced when the ammonia carried by the gas came into contact with the vapours of the acid contained in the tube. If the gas under experiment were heavier than atmospheric air, the position of all the tubes was inverted, and, in place of ascending currents, descending currents were obtained. The action of the magnet upon the different gases was also shown by blowing soap bubbles, filled with each gas for trial, upon the end of a capillary tube, and bringing the suspended bubble near to the pole of the magnet; on completing the circuit the bubble was attracted or repelled according as the gas was magnetic or diamagnetic.

By suspending a feebly magnetic glass tube, attached to the thread of a delicate torsion balance, between the magnetic poles successively in oxygen and *in vacuo*, E. Becquerel (*Ann. de Chimie*, III. xxviii. 324) found that the tube was less strongly attracted in oxygen than in the exhausted receiver, and by varying the experiment in different ways he succeeded in proving that oxygen is a decidedly magnetic body; he has calculated that a cubic metre of oxygen, which at 32° F. and 29·92 inches Bar. weighs 22015 grains, if it were condensed till it had a specific gravity equal to that of iron, would act upon a magnetic needle, with a force equal to that of a little cube of iron weighing $8\frac{1}{3}$ grains; or that the magnetism of oxygen is to that of metallic iron as 1 : 2647. He computes that the magnetic effect of the oxygen in the air is equal to that of a shell of metallic iron $\frac{1}{250}$ of an inch in thickness surrounding the globe of the earth.

The fact of the magnetism of oxygen was first suggested by Faraday (*Phil. Mag.*, 1847) and was amply proved by him (*Phil. Trans.*, 1851, p. 23), independently of Becquerel. He has further ascertained that, like iron, it loses its magnetism when strongly heated, but recovers it when the temperature falls. In this diminution in magnetic intensity as the temperature rises, he considers, probably lies the explanation of the diurnal variations of the needle, the cause of which has so much perplexed magnetic observers: the explanation is, however, not regarded as adequate by some eminent magneticians.

(326) The following table contains a list of various substances, arranged in the order of their magnetic* and diamagnetic powers, as approximately determined by Faraday:—

* Faraday regards all substances as magnetic, and designates those substances generally termed magnetic, as *para*magnetic, in contradistinction to those which are diamagnetic.

Magnetic.	*Diamagnetic.*
Iron	Bismuth
Nickel	Phosphorus
Cobalt	Antimony
Manganese	Zinc
Chromium	Silico-borate of lead
Cerium	Tin
Titanium	Cadmium
Palladium	Sodium
Crown glass	Flint glass
Platinum	Mercury
Osmium	Lead
Oxygen	Silver
	Copper
	Water
	Gold
	Alcohol
	Ether
	Arsenic
	Uranium
	Rhodium
	Iridium
	Tungsten

Nitrogen.

It is worthy of particular remark that the same substance may appear to be either magnetic or diamagnetic according to the nature of the medium in which it is placed. If a glass rod be suspended horizontally in a vessel of water which is a strongly diamagnetic body, it will point axially, like a rod of iron; whereas the same rod, if suspended in a solution of sulphate of iron which is magnetic, will point in the equatorial direction. In like manner a tube containing a solution of sulphate of iron will in pure water seem to be magnetic, while in a still stronger solution of the sulphate it will act as a diamagnetic substance; just as a soap bubble filled with carbonic acid, which is heavier than air, will fall to the ground, while if filled with hydrogen, which is much lighter than the atmosphere, it will ascend.

Air, in consequence of its containing oxygen in an uncombined condition, is a magnetic substance.

(327) *The same Elements in combination may be Magnetic or Diamagnetic according to the nature of the Compound.*—One of the most interesting peculiarities of diamagnetism is exhibited in the circumstance that the same body may assume the magnetic or the diamagnetic state according to the nature of the compound which it forms. A metal may, for example, occur as the basis or electro-positive constituent of a compound, or it may enter into the composition of those substances which form the acid or electro-negative constituent of the compound. A good illustration of the difference thus produced occurs in the case of iron. Iron

acts as a base in the crystals of green vitriol ($FeSO_4 + 7H_2O$) of which the metal forms about a fifth by weight, and it gives to them a decidedly magnetic power; but in the yellow ferrocyanide of potassium ($K_4FeCy_6 + 3H_2O$), which also contains iron, to the extent of more than an eighth of its weight, the crystals are diamagnetic. The iron in this case occurs in the electro-negative constituent of the salt, and not as a base.* In the same way, acid chromate of potassium (K_2CrO_4, CrO_3), where the chromium forms part of the acid, is diamagnetic, while the sulphate of chromium ($Cr_2 3SO_4$), where the metal acts as a base, is decidedly magnetic. Some of the compounds of cobalt exhibit analogous differences.

(328) *Influence of Structure on Diamagnetism.*—In prosecuting this subject, Tyndall and Knoblauch (*Phil. Mag.*, 1850, vol. xxxvi. p. 178, and xxxvii. p. 1) have been led to the conclusion that a substance may appear to be either magnetic or diamagnetic according to the arrangement of its component particles. It must not, however, be supposed that there is not a real distinction between the two classes of substances; but that, under certain circumstances, a truly magnetic body may appear to be diamagnetic and a body truly diamagnetic may appear to be magnetic. The following experiment may be cited in order to explain this point. A small flat circular disk was prepared with a paste of wheaten flour; and in this disk a number of short pieces of iron wire were placed, all parallel to each other, and all passing from one surface of the disk to the other, perpendicularly to its two faces. This disk was suspended from a fibre of silk, by its edge, in a vertical direction, between the poles of an electro-magnet; but though it was undoubtedly magnetic, the plate placed itself with its faces parallel to the equator of the magnetic field. Each of the short pieces of wire, however, had assumed the axial position, although the disk as a whole arranged itself in a diamagnetic position.

When a similar disk was prepared in which threads of bismuth were substituted for the iron wire, the disk placed itself in the magnetic direction with its faces parallel to the axis of the magnetic field. The bismuth, however, is unquestionably diamagnetic, and each of the pieces of this metal which the plate contains assumes the diamagnetic direction.

The conclusion which Tyndall and Knoblauch draw from these experiments is, that if in a magnetic or in a diamagnetic mass, there be one particular direction in which the particles which compose it are more closely approximated to each other than in any other direction, the line which corresponds to this direction of greatest density will be the one in which the magnetic or diamagnetic action is most strongly marked. One of the experiments made in support of this view is the following:—

* It is, however, remarkable that the red ferricyanide of potassium is, according to Plücker's observation, distinctly, though feebly, magnetic. Faraday enumerates it among the diamagnetic class.

Powdered bismuth was formed by means of gum-water into a mass sufficiently coherent to be worked into a small cylindrical bar about an inch long and a quarter of an inch thick. When this cylinder was suspended by its centre in a horizontal direction between the poles of the electro-magnet, it pointed equatorially as an ordinary bar of bismuth would have done; but when this same cylinder was compressed laterally, so as to form a flat plate, it assumed a direction with its face parallel to the axial position, though its length in some cases was ten times as great as its thickness.

Again, carbonate of iron is a magnetic body: if reduced to fine powder and formed into a cylinder similar to that made with the bismuth, it will point axially, or like a magnet, between the poles; but if compressed into a plate, this plate will set with its faces parallel to the equatorial direction. Here, in each case, those parts in which the particles of the bismuth, or the salt of iron, are by compression brought the nearest to each other, are those in which the diamagnetic or the magnetic action predominates. It is by an application of this principle that Tyndall and Knoblauch account for the fact discovered by Plücker, that in all crystalline bodies belonging to those systems which exercise a doubly refractive influence on light, the optic axis assumes a definite direction under the influence of the electro-magnet. Assuming that the optic axis of a crystal is the direction in which the particles of the crystal have experienced the greatest degree of condensation, the effects obtained by experiment admit of explanation. The position assumed by the optic axis is not uniformly the same in different specimens of the same substance, though in the same specimen it is always the same. For example: Iceland spar, when pure, is a diamagnetic substance; but, if it contain carbonate of iron, it exhibits magnetic properties. In the course of their researches, Tyndall and Knoblauch took pieces from several specimens of Iceland spar, some of which were magnetic, others diamagnetic. These different samples were cut in the form of disks, or flat circular plates, the surfaces of which were parallel to the optic axis of the crystals. When the disks were suspended horizontally at their centres between the poles of an electro-magnet, so that the optic axis of the crystal was in a horizontal plane, each disk always assumed a determinate direction. When the disk was taken from a magnetic crystal, the optic axis placed itself axially between the poles; when from a diamagnetic crystal, the optic axis assumed the equatorial direction. Thus it appears, that whether the crystal be magnetic or diamagnetic, the action is exhibited in each case most powerfully in the direction of the optic axis, which is assumed to be the line in which the particles are most closely approximated to each other. Faraday has shown that the directive force of the crystal, whether magnetic or diamagnetic, diminishes as the temperature rises.

(329) *Law of Diamagnetic Repulsion.*—It has been ascertained by E. Becquerel and by Tyndall, that the diamagnetic repulsion, as measured by means of the torsion balance, is as the

square of the intensity of the current. The phenomena of diamagnetism may be accounted for, as was remarked by Faraday, on the supposition that electric currents are circulating around the particles of the diamagnetic body in a direction the reverse of those which are supposed to exist in magnetic bodies, though he was unable to satisfy himself, by experiment, of the existence of such polarity; but the experiments of Reich, of Weber,* and

* The principle of Weber's beautiful apparatus, with which Tyndall's decisive experiments were made, will be understood without difficulty. Let H, H' (fig. 263) represent two similar vertical helices of copper wire; *a*, *b*, *c*, *d*, two bars of bismuth or other diamagnetic body attached to cords which pass over the wheels W, W', so that

Fig. 263. Fig. 264.

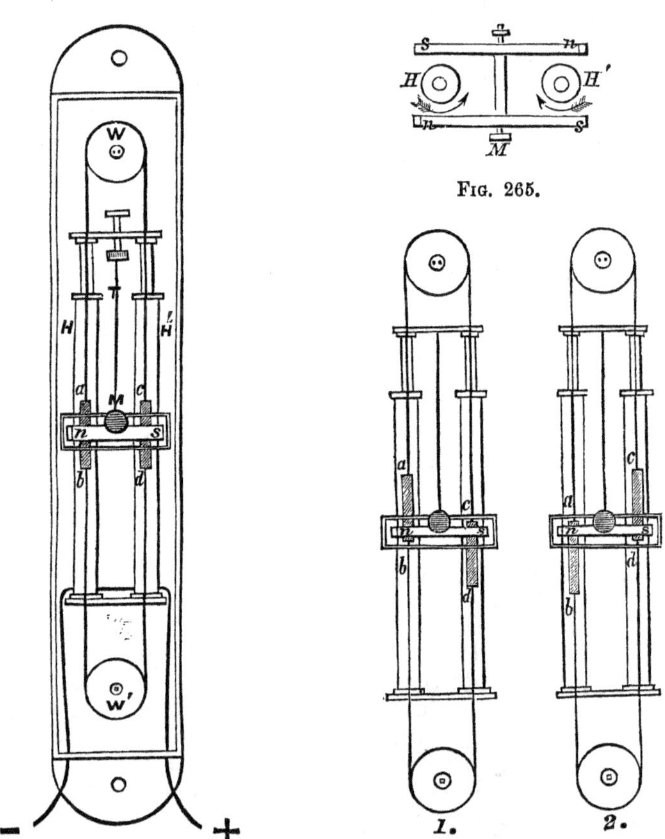

Fig. 265.

they can, by moving one of the wheels, be placed, at pleasure, in either of the positions shown in fig. 265, 1 and 2. *n s* represents one of a pair of bar magnets, arranged astatically, and delicately suspended side by side by a few fibres of unspun silk, T. M is a mirror attached to the centre of the magnet, and by viewing a scale reflected in this mirror through a telescope at a distance of 8 or 10 feet, the smallest deflection of the magnets may be estimated and measured. On transmitting a voltaic current from one or two of Grove's cells through the coils in opposite directions, the bismuth bars within the helices will become diamagnetized; and by carefully raising or lowering the astatic bars *n s*, *s n*, shown in section with the coils H, H', in fig. 264, until they are opposite the middle of of Tyndall (*Phil. Trans.*, 1855, 1856), appear to have proved conclusively that bodies which are under diamagnetic influence, exhibit polar characters. The polarity of these bodies is such that a diamagnetic substance possesses a feeble magnetic polarity, the magnetism of each pole being *similar* to that of the pole of the inducing magnet in its vicinity: whereas in an ordinary magnetic substance the inducing magnetism is *opposite* to that of the magnetic pole by which the magnetism is elicited.

(330) *Definite Quantity of Force; Indestructibility of Force: Mutual Relations of Different Kinds of Force.*—The progress of philosophical inquiries for many years past has been of such a nature as to produce a growing conviction in the minds of the active cultivators of science, that force is equally indestructible with matter; and that, consequently, the amount of force which is in operation in the earth (probably in the solar system), is as definite as that of the material elements through which its existence is made known to us.

That the quantity of force associated with matter is definite, may be illustrated in various ways; one or two examples must suffice. The first which we will select will show the fixity in the proportion of heat which is associated with a given quantity of matter. A pound of charcoal, when burned with a free supply of air, combines with 2⅔ lb. of oxygen, and produces 3⅔ lb. of carbonic acid. The chemical action produced by this combustion is attended with the extrication of a definite quantity of heat: and this amount of heat, if it be applied without loss, is sufficient to convert 12½ lb. of water at 60°, into steam at 212° F.: associated with each pound of charcoal there must therefore be a definite amount of power, which is brought into action when that charcoal is burned. A different but equally definite amount of heat is emitted when a pound of phosphorus, of sulphur, of hydrogen, or of any other combustible is burned with free access of

the coils, a position may be found in which the magnets become indifferent to the action of the current. If, whilst the apparatus is thus arranged, the wheel w be turned to the right, the bismuth bars will be brought into the position, fig. 265, 1, and a deflection of the astatic magnets will be effected. The lower end, *b*, of one bismuth bar, if polar, would be (from the reversed direction of the currents in the helices) in the same condition as the upper end, *c*, of the other bismuth bar, and each will therefore attract one particular end, say the north, of each magnet composing the astatic combination, and would repel the south end; each conspiring to produce a deflection of both magnets in the same direction: but on turning the wheel to the left, so as to bring the bismuth bars into the position shown in 265, 2, the astatic combination will be deflected to an equal extent in the opposite direction.

These effects are most marked with bodies like bismuth and antimony, which have the greatest diamagnetic energy; but they are also distinctly shown even in non-conducting bodies, such as heavy glass, phosphorus, and sulphur.

If solid bismuth give a deviation which is represented by 75 divisions of the scale employed, the following table will represent the action, found by Tyndall, of the other bodies enumerated in it:—

Bismuth	75	Heavy glass	4
Powdered bismuth	37	Phosphorus	4
Antimony	13.5	Distilled water	4
Bisulphide of carbon	5.5	Calc-spar	2
White marble	5	Nitre	1.7

air (199 *et seq*). The quantity of electricity associated with a given quantity of matter is equally definite (282). When a piece of amalgamated zinc is placed in voltaic relation with a plate of platinum in diluted sulphuric acid, for each pound of zinc which is dissolved, a quantity of electricity is liberated, by means of which a pound of metallic copper may be separated from the solution of a sufficient quantity of the sulphate of copper, or $3\frac{2}{5}$ lb. of silver may be reduced from a solution of nitrate of silver.

But it appears further, that there is no such thing as a destruction of force. The cases in which a superficial examination would lead to the conclusion that force is annihilated, show on closer investigation that such a supposition is erroneous. The only mode in which we can judge of the existence of a force is from the effects which it produces, and of these effects that which is most universal is the power either of producing motion, of arresting it, or of altering its direction: whatever possesses this power has been looked upon as a form of force. Motion is consequently regarded as the signal of force. There is no difficulty in showing that gravity, elasticity, cohesion, and adhesion, are all forces in the sense of the above definition. But even the more subtle and complex agents—light, heat, electricity, magnetism, and chemical action, are all capable of originating motion, and may thus fairly be admitted under the definition of force above given.

If we except the case of light, for which, when it has disappeared by absorption, no satisfactory account has yet been given, it will be found that in all cases in which force disappears, it has expended itself either in eliciting or setting into action an equivalent amount of some other force, or else it has temporarily disappeared in producing a definite amount of motion. In this case it is especially to be remarked that the amount of motion which it has thus brought into action, when that motion is destroyed, will again give rise either to an equal amount of the force which originally produced it, or to an equivalent quantity of some other manifestation of force.

For example, the chemical action between charcoal and oxygen terminates as soon as the charcoal is wholly converted into carbonic acid; and a quantity of heat, which is equivalent to that amount of chemical action, remains as the representative of the force thus expended. The heat which has thus been developed is ready to do other work; it may be employed in converting a certain quantity of water into steam, and the steam so obtained can be applied to the production of motion, the amount of which may be measured by determining the number of pounds weight which can be lifted through a given distance by the steam thus produced. Motion may again be made to produce heat, and, as Joule's experiments show, the quantity of heat thus developed is strictly determined by the amount of motion which is applied to its development.

It appears, however, not only that force is definite in its amount, and indestructible in its essence, but that many of the more important varieties of force are intimately related, and are capable in turn of eliciting each other. The forces amongst which such mutual relations have been experimentally proved to exist in the closest manner, are those of light, heat, electricity, magnetism, and chemical attraction. The transfer of any one of these forces from one point to another, or, in other words, the exertion of any one of these forces, is always attended with a collateral manifestation of one or more of the other forms of force. In the action of a voltaic circuit, consisting of a single pair of plates of zinc and platinum, the solution of a certain quantity of zinc, or the *chemical action* between the zinc and the acid, may be made to develop several forces—viz.: 1. *Electricity*, but there is no direct manifestation of this force so long as the circuit is closed. 2. *Chemical action:* if a voltameter, charged with a solution of sulphate of copper, be interposed in the circuit between two electrodes of copper, a certain quantity of copper, corresponding to the zinc which is being dissolved in the battery, will be deposited on one electrode, whilst a corresponding amount of copper will be dissolved from the other electrode. Here is a chemical action, which corresponds in amount to that which is taking place between the zinc and sulphuric acid in the active cell of the battery. 3. *Magnetism:* if the connecting wire be coiled around a piece of soft iron, the iron will become powerfully magnetic for the time during which the current is traversing the conducting wire. 4. *Heat:* if, whilst the voltameter, the electro-magnet, and the galvanometer are still included in the circuit, part of the circuit be composed of a thin wire which traverses the bulb of Harris's air thermometer, an elevation of temperature in the wire proportioned to the amount of electricity in circulation will be obtained, but in proportion to the quantity of heat evolved the chemical action is lessened, and the power of the magnet is reduced; and 5. *Light:* on interrupting the connexion of any part of the circuit, a bright spark is obtained. Chemical attraction, then, while in operation, can throw a current of electricity into circulation, and a current of electricity will develop an equivalent amount of magnetism in a direction at right angles to such current. It also produces in conductors, heat proportioned to the resistance which it experiences, and if the heat be sufficiently intense, it is attended with the emission of light.

The observations of Favre already quoted (280) showing the dependence of the quantity of heat evolved in any given circuit upon the amount of magnetic or mechanical work which it is producing, afford interesting additional proofs of the important proposition that force is never really either generated or destroyed. Man has but the power to elicit it when latent, to transfer its energy to new points, or to change the form of its manifestation so as to obtain an equivalent amount of power under new conditions.

The more closely the investigation is followed in this direction, the more completely is the truth of this principle rendered manifest. Thus Soret (*Comptes Rendus*, xlv. 301) transmitted a continuous electric current through portions of conductors which, like Ampère's wires (fig. 236), are free to obey their mutual impulse of attraction and repulsion; and he found that if the moveable conductors were allowed to approach each other in accordance with the direction of the attraction, a diminution of the intensity of the current is observed during the occurrence of this motion,—a portion of the intensity of the current being expended in the production of motion. If, on the other hand, a compulsory movement in opposition to the attractive force is effected, the intensity of the current is increased during the act of movement.

Again, the same observer found, as might indeed have been anticipated from Faraday's magneto-electric researches (311), that if a battery in connexion with a helix be in conducting communication with a galvanometer, the current through the galvanometer is reduced during the introduction of a soft iron core into the axis of the helix; but it is increased at the moment of withdrawing the iron core. The introduction of a non-magnetic substance, such as a core of copper, produces no sensible effect.

We have already traced briefly the evolution of electricity from chemical action; and Faraday has further shown that the electricity developed by friction in the ordinary electrical machine produces either a corresponding amount of magnetic action on the needle of the galvanometer, or an equivalent amount of chemical decomposition in electrolytes through which it is transmitted (297); whilst in the fusion of metallic wires we have evidence of its heating power, and in the electric spark we see its agency in producing light.

The experiments of Faraday, followed by those of other philosophers, have proved that the motion of a magnet of a given strength, under certain conditions, produces, in a closed metallic conductor, a definite current of electricity, and through the electricity thus set in motion, light, heat, and chemical action may be developed, as is beautifully shown in the magneto-electric machine (315).

On the other hand, heat may be made to develop electricity; and the thermo-multiplier (317) of Nobili and Melloni shows that the current of electricity which is produced is exactly proportioned, *cæteris paribus*, to the amount of heat by which it is excited. The ignition of solid matter shows that heat may elicit light under favourable circumstances. It further appears that heat may excite chemical action; and as it may also give rise to a current of electricity, through that current of electricity it may produce the development of magnetism.

Light may produce important chemical actions, but these actions have only in a few cases been reduced to a form in which they can develop electricity, magnetism, or heat. The definite connexion of light with the other forces, and the quantitative valuation of that relation still remain to be wrought out. Indeed, the subject appears to offer a field for research, difficult, because as yet scarcely trodden, though full of interest and promise.

The reader who desires to pursue the subject of the mutual relations of different kinds of force, is referred to an interesting essay on the subject by Grove, entitled *On the Correlation of the Physical Forces.* For further information on the other subjects which have been treated of in this chapter, in addition to the papers already quoted, the student is referred to the important series of memoirs by Faraday, published during the last thirty years in the *Philosophical Transactions*, which have also been reprinted in a separate form; or to the *Treatises* of Becquerel and De La Rive on *Electricity and Magnetism*, and to Tyndall's work on *Heat considered as a Mode of Motion.*

www.ingramcontent.com/pod-product-compliance
Lightning Source LLC
LaVergne TN
LVHW011221110826
845150LV00006B/1503

* 9 7 8 1 4 2 5 5 1 6 3 7 6 *